Don't Leave It to Chance

Chance

A Guide for Families of Problem Gamblers

Edward J. Federman, Ph.D.
Charles E. Drebing, Ph.D.
Christopher Krebs, M.A.

New Harbinger Publications, Inc.

Publisher's Note

This publication is designed to provide accurate and authoritative information in regard to the subject matter covered. It is sold with the understanding that the publisher is not engaged in rendering psychological, financial, legal, or other professional services. If expert assistance or counseling is needed, the services of a competent professional should be sought.

Distributed in the U.S.A. by Publishers Group West; in Canada by Raincoast Books; in Great Britain by Airlift Book Company, Ltd.; in South Africa by Real Books, Ltd.; in Australia by Boobook; and in New Zealand by Tandem Press.

Cover design by SHELBY DESIGNS & ILLUSTRATES
Cover illustration by artville.com
Edited by Kayla Sussell
Text design by Tracy Marie Powell

Library of Congress Catalog Card Number: 99-75295
ISBN 1-57224-200-0 Paperback

New Harbinger Publications' Web site address: www.newharbinger.com

02   01   00

10   9   8   7   6   5   4   3   2   1

First printing

"An extremely valuable resource for problem gamblers and their families. I especially appreciate the authors' tone of compassion and respect for the reader and their depth of understanding of the problem. The book is extremely thorough and gently holds out specific ways for families to move through the devastation of problem gambling to a place of peace."

—Kathleen M. Scanlan, M.A., Executive Director, Massachusetts Council on Compulsive Gambling

"This book provides . . . wise suggestions on how gamblers and their families can cope with the fallout from reckless gambling. For many, it can provide helpful first steps for getting back on track."

—William R. Eadington, Professor of Economics and Director, Institute for the Study of Gambling and Commercial Gaming, University of Nevada, Reno

"This is an excellent book designed to help interrupt the gambler's downward spiral and to assist the entire family. The authors integrate our current knowledge of gambling problems and dispel the myths surrounding problem gambling. Their useful recommendations and practical information to help the gambler and his/her family are accompanied with personal accounts and clinical histories. This is a must read for all family members where a gambling problem is suspected."

—Jeffrey L. Derevensky, Ph.D., child psychologist and Professor, School and Applied Child Psychology and Associate Professor of Psychiatry at McGill University

"If someone close to you has a problem with gambling, this book is meant for you. It offers readers practical guidance on how to confront the gambler, put damage control and treatment alternatives in place, and restructure your financial affairs. That is a big order, yet this team of experienced professionals provide time-tested, sympathetic, and easy-to-follow paths toward each of these objectives."

—Durand F. Jacobs, Ph.D., A.P.B.B., Clinical Professor of Psychiatry, Loma Linda University Medical School, Loma Linda, California

Dedications

To Mary.
    —Edward J. Federman, Ph.D.

To my father who worked faithfully all his life to support his children's dreams.
    —Charles E. Drebing, Ph.D.

To all my teachers, those who know who they are and those who don't.
    —Christopher Krebs, M.A.

Contents

Acknowledgments

Thanks are due to many people who worked with us to build the Center for Problem Gambling at the Edith Nourse Rogers VA Medical Center in Bedford, Massachusetts. Walter Penk, Ph.D., created an environment that nourished new programs during an era when services were contracting. Godehard Oepen, M.D., Ph.D., turned a bright light on the significance of problem gambling when many were looking the other way. Dewey Jacobs, Ph.D., patiently provided guidance to a fledgling program. Our postdoctoral fellows and predoctoral students—Melinda Salomon, Ph.D., Eric Goodman, M.A., Rico Mello, M.A., Tom Sheeran, Ph.D., Robin Abrams, Ph.D., Lori Azzarra, M.A., Ron Vallee, M.A., and Robert Tepley, Ph.D.—freely contributed clinical and research insights and countless hours of hard work.

We are grateful for the help and support from the Massachusetts Council on Compulsive Gambling. The late Tom Cummings worked tirelessly years before most people recognized problem gambling. Kathy Scanlan, Blase Gambino, Ph.D., Joann Callfer, Dana Forman, and Peggie Milisci have been generous with their time and expert knowledge as have all the staff at the Massachusetts Council. Dr. Howard Shaffer's commitment to a scientific understanding of problem gambling has played a generative role not only for us but for the entire field.

Thanks are also due to Mike Wortzman for his help.

We appreciate the creative input of Matt McKay, Ph.D., and the contributions of Catharine Sutker, Kayla Sussell, Amy Shoup, and Kirk Johnson, as well as the responsiveness of all the staff at New Harbinger.

We also want to thank our patients and their families whom we serve and who are our best teachers.

Chapter 1

Problem Gambling: Myths and Realities

Six hundred billion dollars a year are wagered *legally* in the United States—an amount exceeding one-third the entire federal budget. That's more than $2,000 for every man, woman, and child in the United States. This is the money that is wagered legally; the amount of illegal wagering could easily double that figure.

Even with revenues at this level, the marketplace for gambling shows no signs of satiation. People fill up casinos as quickly as they appear. "If you build it, they will come" accurately describes this phenomenon. (The line from the aptly named movie *Field of Dreams* originally referred to a baseball field.) In countries where gambling is readily available, between 80 and 90 percent of adults gamble at least a few times a year (Dickerson 1984) and for more than 4 percent of adults, gambling causes problems. Despite these high levels, the *myth* prevails that gambling problems are rare as the following case example illustrates.

Myth #1: Gambling Problems Are Rare

Chris had been moody for months. He had been like this once before ten years ago when his company was downsized and he had been under the constant threat of being laid off. That was shortly after Chris and Linda were married and before the birth of their two kids. But Linda knew that this time was different. Nowadays Chris rarely mentioned what was on his mind and he often came home late with only a throwaway comment—he had been "stuck at the office" or had stopped for a couple of beers on the way home. If Linda asked for more information, Chris replied with a scowl.

Because his behavior was so different from anything she had seen before, Linda dismissed the idea that work problems could be the entire explanation. Frightening thoughts came to her mind: perhaps he was ill or having an affair. She needed more information and she got it when she bounced a check. Chris had been taking care of most of their bills and he balanced the checkbook in their joint account, but now Linda examined the account herself. Not only was the account depleted but the mortgage had not been paid in two months. She quickly reviewed their other major assets and saw that virtually all of their savings—more than $20,000—had disappeared.

Linda was dumbfounded. No illness would generate these expenses without a lengthy hospitalization or major surgical procedure and she knew that hadn't occurred. She could barely imagine an affair consuming that much money. Was Chris paying for another apartment? Was he lavishing exotic gifts on a lover?

That night when Chris came home, he saw the checkbook on the kitchen table and he didn't have the courage to meet his wife's steady gaze. Linda sat quietly for a moment thinking about the months of anxiety she had endured, and then she exploded in accusations. Chris thought about trying to blame the whole thing on business losses but he knew that was an unbelievable explanation and that Linda would remain convinced he was having an affair. After years of deception, he finally admitted that he had been gambling and losing heavily.

Chris had always liked to play cards and bet on sports. They used to joke that he had his bookie on speed dial, but his gambling had always been something they could afford. Linda had even gotten a kick out of Chris' betting. He knew so much about sports and Linda had enjoyed Super Bowl parties even more because they had a $100 bet on the outcome. Back in college, Chris had gotten in over his head gambling for a few months but that was nothing like this.

Linda knew that an affair would destroy their marriage and she was relieved to put this fear to rest. But she was furious that their life savings were gone. That night Chris told her the whole story. For years, he had been gambling much more than she had realized. There had always been the office pools and weekly card games. At first, he bet only on the big games—the Super Bowl, the NBA championships, the World Series. Linda knew that much and she also knew that Chris had extended his betting to one football game each of the sixteen Sundays professional football was played. But beyond that, Chris had kept his increasing involvement a secret.

He knew there was always a game happening somewhere—football, basketball, baseball, and there were college as well as professional games. He hadn't liked waiting the weeks between the big games to bet and had started filling in the "slow weeks" with betting on lesser games. After a while, a week was too long and then even three days was more time than he could bear to wait to place a bet. His gambling had increased in this way until he was placing bets daily. For a couple of years, he had stayed at that frequency and was never more than $3,000 down in a year, which he had been able to conceal since he handled all the finances.

But six months ago, he had hit a bad streak and had lost $6,000 in just one month. Then he started chasing—raising his bets and betting even more frequently trying to recoup his losses. It had taken just five more months for him to lose another $40,000. Not only were their life savings of $20,000 gone but he had accumulated another $20,000 debt. Some of it was owed to loan sharks who were harassing him.

There was more. Chris had borrowed money from family members, hers as well as his own. He had told them that they were having a "minor rough spot" and that Linda would be terribly ashamed if she knew about it, so he asked their relatives to keep it secret from her. Chris had borrowed two thousand from each of Linda's two brothers and they hadn't breathed a word of it to her.

Linda couldn't believe this had been going on for years without her knowledge. She had always thought that she and Chris had a completely open, honest relationship and told each other everything. Yet, Chris was even in debt to her brothers! This news left her feeling isolated and ashamed. She knew that some people had gambling problems but she had never known any personally. And besides, they weren't people like Chris. Chris was bright, sociable, and had a family. He knew the odds. For Chris, gambling was supposed to be like an amusement ride; he paid, he got a ride, and he knew where it started and stopped.

The Recognition of Problem Gambling Is Often Delayed

Several aspects of Chris and Linda's situation are common in families with a problem gambler. First, the gambler often keeps his problems secret as long as possible, which requires deception and perhaps outright lies. By the time the problem comes to light, family relationships, finances, and emotional well-being may be damaged and work problems, illegal activities, and external pressures may be present.

Although Linda saw many signs of trouble, she did not consider problem gambling as a possible cause of the difficulties despite the fact that she had an underlying concept of problem gambling that approximated the following definition.

"Problem Gambling is gambling behavior which causes disruption in any major area of life: psychological, physical, social or vocational" (National Council on Problem Gambling 1999 website).

Rather, she overlooked problem gambling as a potential cause for the changes she noticed in Chris because she believed that problem gambling was rare. This idea was reinforced by her belief that people with families and jobs didn't become problem gamblers.

Like Linda, most people—even most mental health professionals—do not yet fully recognize the extent of the problem, although newspapers, television, and radio carry stories about problem gambling. Again, this is understandable since most gamblers and their families keep the problem secret. So, even if you are aware that 4 percent of all American adults have gambling problems (among adolescents and college students the percentage is higher), these statistics don't become fully meaningful until you translate them into your everyday life. Consider what these statistics imply for your personal world. How many people over the age of twelve do you know—counting family, friends, acquaintances, people at work, church, school, other organizations, stores, service stations, and neighbors? If your answer is 200, then on the average eight (or more) of them will have hidden gambling problems; if your answer is 400, then sixteen will have difficulties with gambling, and so on. Now consider how many people you know who have a gambling problem. For many people, a family member whom they have become concerned about is the first—and often the only—person they are *aware* of with a gambling problem.

If this is true for you, it would be natural to think that problem gambling is rare or, at least, that it is rare among people you know. This myth can make it harder for you to identify problem gambling and harder to seek appropriate help from family, friends, and the broader community.

A Brief History of Gambling

Not only is problem gambling widespread today, it has been common throughout recorded history. Accounts of gambling appear in ancient writings. The early Romans adapted the chariot wheel into a forerunner of the roulette wheel. Modern technology has yielded interesting variations (e.g., Internet gambling, telephoning the bookie, pari-mutuel boards) on this theme, but the basic concepts of gambling and its appeal have remained unchanged. Gambling's long-standing appeal has, in turn, yielded some creative developments: the Earl of Sandwich devised a transportable meal so that he could eat at the gaming tables rather than interrupt his play. The sandwich remains his enduring legacy.

Gambling's consistent appeal across time has been obscured because its very popularity has led to periodic prohibitions. There was widespread legalized gambling in the United States through the mid 19th century and "lottomania" was first noted in America around 1812 (more than 170 years before "powerball"). Although the government derived significant revenue from lotteries at that time, an increase in social ills associated with gambling led to its prohibition toward the end of the 19th century. The same pattern appeared in Canada, France, and Britain, as well. In the United States, the first modern state-sponsored lottery reappeared in the 1960s, some 100 years after being prohibited. By 2000, thirty-seven more states had endorsed state-run lotteries. Religions have also adopted different stances toward gambling. Many religious groups raise revenues through gambling; others prohibit it entirely. Often these injunctions, like government-enforced prohibitions, developed in response to widespread excessive or problem gambling.

What are the social ills that periodically lead cultures to prohibit gambling and abandon a ready source of revenue? Like gambling's appeal, its underbelly shows a remarkable consistency over time. Some 1500 years before the birth of Christ, problem gambling was noted in an Indus River tribesman. In the early Middle Ages, problem gambling prevented soldiers from purchasing weapons and also led to "heinous murders, robberies and felonies" (Blaszczynski 1996).

A manuscript published in 1619 notes "Most gamesters begin at small games, and by degrees ... rise to great sums; some have played first all their money, then their rings, coach and horses, ... and then such a farm; and at last perhaps a lordship" (cited in Brenner and Brenner 1990). The difficulties associated with problem gambling—disruption of work and family, depression, suicide, and antisocial behavior—that we see today have been ever present.

Myth #2: Gambling Is Glamorous

Greg's parents had told him stories of the "comps"—the fancy rooms and meals casinos provide "free." From his Uncle Bob, he had heard even spicier stories about what the casinos could provide. At age seventeen he had been playing poker weekly with his friends for two years. Poker *is* a game of skill and over time Greg had been the most consistent winner in his circle of friends. They played for stakes they could all afford; there must be more than a million games a week like that in the United States. He wanted more but wasn't old enough to go to the casinos or to bet legally in any forum other than this poker game.

Greg had a "friend," Johnny, five years his senior who was willing to buy lottery tickets and play Keno (a rapid action gambling game) for him for 5 percent of the sales price and 5 percent of any winnings. Outside Boston, where Greg lived, drawings were held every five minutes, in convenience stores, bars, and so forth. Greg would hang out with Johnny in a convenience store ostensibly reading magazines but directing the numbers choices while Johnny placed the bets and retrieved the winnings. Three parties made a profit on these transactions—Johnny, the convenience store owner, and the State of Massachusetts—two legally.

Greg lost big and he lost fast. At first, he took the money from his own savings account. After that, he used his father's ATM card and made daily withdrawals. He figured he had a month to win it back before his parents caught up with him. It was just two weeks before the credit card company called his father about the daily transactions—long enough for Greg to drain $4,000 from his parents' account. From his first illegal bet to the phone call to his father, just two months had elapsed.

From the professional gambler in frontier America to James Bond in Monte Carlo, gamblers look glamorous. Advertisements for government-sponsored lotteries and multimillion dollar casinos, and elegant racetracks like Churchill Downs in Kentucky and Ascot in England intensify gambling's glittering image. In America's West in the 18th and 19th centuries, the professional riverboat gambler culti-vated his romantic image and was generally the best-dressed man around; he would surely have graced the cover of *Gentleman's Quarterly* had it been published in those days.

Such glamour was calculated; with this appearance, the gam-bler gained access to games on riverboats with wealthy men who would not otherwise have accepted him in their game rooms and clubs (Fabian 1990). Such calculations persist in today's advertisements for legal gambling, which emphasize glamour, fun, excitement, and potential for wealth. James Bond, impeccable in his tuxedo, and equally cool betting fortunes or engaging in life-threatening situations, displays disdain for the money itself as he wagers. This scornful attitude toward the money used for gambling has a long legacy from several centuries of European aristocrats through the Gilded Age in America (Fabian 1990). It survives today not only in the fictional life of James Bond but at fancy racetracks around the globe where most bettors lose their money while aspiring to the demeanor of the horse owner who graciously raises a symbolic trophy while quietly pocketing a huge purse.

The glamorous image of the gambler is as close to *everyday* reality as the Riviera is to Death Valley. Most people who gamble lose; most people who gamble a lot lose a lot. Most people who lose a lot live lives that are anything but glamorous. Yet the persistence of the myth that gambling is glamorous has two important negative effects.

First, it creates an unrealistic attraction to gambling. Although many people can gamble without problems, others, like Greg and Chris, are ill prepared to deal with the consequences of problem gambling. Second, the glamorous myth inhibits the mental health community from taking gambling seriously. Although there is a small but growing number of mental health professionals who are well-versed in problem gambling, many are not. Our research has shown that fewer than 10 percent of a nationwide sample of university medical centers, VA hospitals, and community mental health centers routinely look for problem gambling in their patients. This, despite the fact that one out of four of their patients will have had a problem gambling at some point in their lives. Moreover, our research has found that fewer than 2 percent of patients who have had a gambling problem have had this problem identified by their therapists and counselors—even among those who had been in treatment for years (Federman 1998). In short, the glamorous image of gambling ultimately translates into fewer professional resources for the problem gambler and his family.

Myth #3: Problem Gamblers Are Always Young to Middle-Aged Males

Marilyn and Joe had occasionally vacationed in Atlantic City or Lake Tahoe and one summer they had taken a cruise with an on-board casino. Joe liked the table games, particularly blackjack and roulette and Marilyn preferred the slot machines. They budgeted what they could afford to lose and always stayed within their limits.

After Joe died, Marilyn remained active, as she had been all her life. At seventy-five, she had been retired from teaching for more than twenty years, and her four children were grown. Nevertheless, she remained socially active and vigorously pursued the oil painting she had begun ten years earlier. When she reached eighty, her mind remained alert but a progressive and untreatable eye disorder (macular degeneration) was destroying her sight and she could no longer paint or drive. Only one of her close friends was still alive and she, too, was unable to drive. Marilyn had become isolated and despondent when she first decided to take a day-trip on the charter bus that went from the Senior Center near her home in southern Connecticut to the Foxwoods Casino.

Her anxiety about the new venture turned to nostalgic reverie as she thought about the times she and Joe had spent in casinos. She didn't hear her seatmate's initial attempt to strike up a conversation. A touch on the arm brought her back and she soon found herself deeply engaged in conversation with someone she had just met, an experience she hadn't had in years.

The slot machines were bright with large symbols and Marilyn could see them easily, a welcome change from her usual struggles with vision. She liked to pull the handle on the slots— that was part of the old experience and it transported her through time—transported her not only through the minutes of her day that had grown long with emptiness but through the years to the days when Joe was just across the way. Even when her arm grew tired, she could push the button and the bars and cherries still whirled and the bells still rung and the minutes passed.

That first day she lost more than she had budgeted, which surprised her because she had always been so disciplined in the past. On the bus ride back, she again had a lively conversation; overall it was one of the best days she'd had in months. Soon she would be on that bus each Wednesday when it left the Senior Center. Her discipline had deserted her but Wednesday had become the high point of her week.

At first her four children were pleased that she had found an activity she again enjoyed. Then they were amused by the notion of their "gambling grandma." And finally they became alarmed when they realized that she had lost more than $5,000 in one year. Her closest daughter was a two-hour car ride away, and the others were best reached by plane. So although they were attentive, and three of them had urged her to move in with them, they didn't get to see her very often. She insisted on remaining in her home of forty years and did not want them interfering with the one activity she could still enjoy. They all knew her funds were very limited and that she had only a very small income. Although each of the children were willing to help financially as much as they could, none were in a position to replace that much money.

Problem Gamblers Come from Every Segment of the Population

Our research has shown that most people tend to picture a problem gambler as a young to middle-aged male with a range of other problems (e.g., marginal employment, substance abuse) (Mello, Drebing, Federman, Krebs, et al. 1999). Although many problem gamblers do have such characteristics, most do not.

Increasing numbers of senior citizens, like Marilyn, who never had the remotest problem with gambling, are developing problems later in life. Women are far from immune; more than one-third of problem gamblers are women. We have already noted that 4 percent of adults develop problem gambling. Among adolescents, the rate of problem gambling rises alarmingly to three times that of adults and, in college, student problem gambling rates edge even higher. Finally, as Linda discovered, the notion that well-functioning individuals with good jobs and no other major problems do not develop gambling problems is also untrue. Problem gamblers come from every segment of the population and there are many who are the same age and gender, as well as having similar family, vocational, educational, and economic characteristics as your family member.

Recognizing the realities of problem gambling—as opposed to the three myths described above—will allow you to move past the complications imposed by the myths and to address directly the primary problems resulting from problem gambling.

Societal and Personal Impact of Problem Gambling

A study in Wisconsin estimated that each severe problem gambler costs society almost $10,000 per year in health care, welfare, work-related and criminal justice costs (Thompson, Gazel, and

Rickman 1996). The University of Chicago reported that health care costs for pathological gamblers are $1200 higher per year than for comparable individuals without gambling problems (National Opinion Research Center 1999). At the University of Illinois, Professor Kindt estimated "that for every dollar that states take in from gambling, they pay three dollars in costs, for social agencies and the criminal justice system" (New York Times 9/25/95). Considering that state revenues exceed 20 billion dollars per year from lotteries, this implies an astonishing societal cost of 60 billion dollars a year due to problems associated with gambling.

Considering that state revenues exceed twenty billion dollars per year from lotteries, this implies an astonishing societal cost of sixty billion dollars a year due to problems associated with gambling. Such staggering costs to society reflect the sum total of hundreds of thousands of painful stories of individual families; it is these individual stories and how gambling affects your family that is our primary focus.

The gambler personally faces financial losses and pressures, possible job loss, increased risk of depression and other psychiatric problems, as well as increased risk of substance abuse. In addition, problem gambling brings behavioral changes in its wake that may include increased risk of self-injurious (i.e., suicidal) behavior, aggressive behavior, and illegal behavior. These high-risk behaviors may occur in individuals who have never done such things in their past.

The first blows to the family are the loss of financial resources, broken bonds of trust, and decreased time and energy available from the problem gambler. These primary impacts lead to increased tension in the family, psychological distress, loss of material goods, loss of friends, and perhaps ultimately a breakdown in the family structure.

These are the general problems that families with a problem gambler confront. There is variation between families, of course. We will address the primary source of variation by considering, at key points throughout the book, your relationship to the gambler. Is the individual with the gambling problem your partner, like Chris, your child, like Greg, or your elderly relative, like Marilyn?

Although problem gambling can lead to bleak consequences, our book is designed to help you interrupt the downward spiral and to reset your family on a better course. We will address in detail the primary issues of resources (money, time, etc.) and trust as well as the emotional turmoil and family conflicts that have already taken place, or may ensue. We will help you to understand these issues and will provide step-by-step guidance for managing these areas to assist you and your family toward recovery.

Chapter 2

Recognizing Problem Gambling

Beverly consulted a psychologist, saying she had "suddenly" realized that her husband had a gambling problem. When asked how long she thought it had been going on, she replied "about seventeen years." It soon became clear that her husband had been gambling heavily throughout their seventeen-year marriage and for many years before that. The behavior had been there all that time, but she hadn't defined it as "a problem." To Beverly, her husband's gambling had been a hobby, a pastime, a bad habit he had learned from his father, a way to blow off stress, a waste of time, a personality flaw, but not a problem. After years of seeing it as something else, Beverly finally realized that his gambling was a "problem"—and the cause of many of the difficulties their family had been experiencing.

What we see is shaped by what we expect to see and what we want to see. If we expect our teenage sons to be having fun with their friends, playing poker, and betting on football games, we may define all the signs of a potential problem as evidence that "boys will be boys." If we want to believe our spouses when they say they aren't gambling much, or that the bank account is low because of business losses, we will tend to focus on evidence that confirms this conclusion and ignore evidence to the contrary. Both the gambler and family members may be motivated, consciously or unconsciously, not to recognize the problem (see chapter 5).

To accurately identify problem gambling, you must be motivated to look clearly at your relative's gambling and know what the signs and symptoms are. Problem gambling has two types or levels of severity: Severe Problem Gambling (also known as pathological gambling), which has been defined by the American Psychiatric Association by the criteria shown in Table 2.1 (DSM-IV 1994), and Mild Problem Gambling, which causes significant but less dramatic problems for the gambler and his or her family. Problem gambling as defined in chapter 1 encompasses both mild and severe problem gambling and is the definition we use in presenting prevalence rates.

Table 2.1:
DSM-IV Criteria—for Pathological Gambling

A. Persistent and recurrent maladaptive gambling behavior as indicated by five or more of the following:

1. Is preoccupied with gambling (e.g., preoccupied with reliving past gambling experiences, handicapping or planning the next venture, or thinking of ways to get money with which to gamble).
2. Needs to gamble with increasing amounts of money in order to achieve the desired excitement.
3. Repeated unsuccessful efforts to control, cut back, or stop gambling.
4. Is restless or irritable when attempting to cut down or stop gambling.
5. Gambles as a way of escaping from problems or of relieving a dysphoric mood (e.g., feelings of helplessness, guilt, anxiety, depression).
6. After losing money gambling, often returns another day to get even ("chasing" one's losses).
7. Lies to family members, therapist, or others to conceal the extent of involvement with gambling.
8. Has committed illegal acts such as forgery, fraud, theft, or embezzlement to finance gambling.
9. Has jeopardized or lost a significant relation, job or educational or career opportunity because of gambling.
10. Relies on others to provide money to relieve a desperate financial situation caused by gambling.

B. The gambling behavior is not better accounted for by a Manic Episode.

Severe Problem Gambling

Severe Problem Gambling, which is also known as "pathological gambling," is one of a number of "Disorders of Impulse Control," the hallmark of which is "the failure to resist an impulse, drive, or temptation to perform some act that is harmful to the person or to others" (DSM-IV 1994). (The term "pathological" refers to the destructive effect of the gambling. It is not a judgment about the person.) In these disorders, there is a growing level of tension or excitement, which precedes the problem behavior. Once the behavior begins, there is a release of tension or a sense of pleasure, in some cases followed by regret or guilt. These feelings are part of what makes the impulse to gamble so difficult to resist.

Pathological gambling has similarities to drug and alcohol addiction, including the stimulation which precedes the behavior, the pleasure or sense of relief experienced from the behavior, the difficulty in reducing the behavior, and the distorted thinking concerning the behavior. Treatment for pathological gambling shares features with effective drug and alcohol treatments. Many resources available for those with physiological addictions can be helpful for gamblers as well. However, pathological gambling is different from most addictions in at least one major aspect: no foreign substance is introduced into the body.

Mild Problem Gambling

Mild Problem Gambling has a range of negative consequences, but not enough to meet all the necessary criteria for a diagnosis of Severe Problem Gambling. It is typically less disruptive, but still troublesome enough to warrant efforts by the gambler and the family to find ways to solve it. Mild Problem Gamblers outnumber Severe Problem Gamblers three to one. There are several different subgroups within the broad group of Mild Problem Gamblers: those who are developing the more severe form of the disorder, those who are recovering from the severe type, and those who simply have a milder form of problem gambling.

Severe Problem Gamblers must exhibit five of the behaviors described in Table 2.1 to be diagnosed with the disorder. Mild Problem Gamblers need to satisfy one to four of the behaviors. The dividing line is somewhat arbitrary and the upper end of Mild Problem Gambling merges with the lower end of Severe Problem Gambling. For your purposes, distinguishing mild versus severe levels of gambling is less important than identifying the presence of a problem and responding effectively.

Identifying Mild Problem Gambling

The signs of Mild Problem Gambling are often difficult to distinguish from nonproblem gambling. Severe Problem Gambling is more dramatic and in its late stages it is typically quite apparent.

Nonproblem Gambling

The majority of people gamble and do so without experiencing any problems (Dickerson 1984; Shaffer, Hall, and Vanderbilt 1997).

* **Social or recreational gamblers.** These individuals enjoy gambling as a form of entertainment and social activity. They go to casinos or racetracks with friends the way others go to a movie or party. The gambling may add excitement to the time spent with others or provide a relaxing time alone. There is typically no problem in reducing gambling when needed, there is no tension when not gambling, and there is relatively little distorted thinking about gambling. Some may gamble frequently and regularly; others may gamble only on rare occasions. They may gamble and may even lose a lot of money—but they gamble the amount they plan to gamble and stop when they reach that amount.

* **Beginning gamblers.** It takes time to understand gambling and to form realistic expectations about winning. Some beginning gamblers, particularly adolescents and young adults, can be unrealistic about gambling and thus can suffer some large losses, leading their relatives to feel concern. Problem gambling is persistent and recurrent. A beginning gambler may make initial mistakes, but the behavior does not persist—the negative consequences of gambling lead to corrective action.

* **Professional gambling.** A small group of people are professional gamblers. They see gambling as a means of making money, and pursue it in a businesslike manner. They focus on games of skill such as poker or pool, because these games allow the possibility of winning over time. For them, gambling is not an uncontrolled impulse but a controlled, planned, and profitable enterprise.

Overview of Signs and Symptoms of Problem Gambling

With problem gambling the key areas of change take place in two categories: general behavior and behavior specific to gambling. Changes in general behavior occur in individuals with a gambling problem, but they are not specific to gambling problems. Problems such as mental illness or drug abuse can cause the same changes in general behavior, so gambling-specific behavioral change is necessary to pinpoint the problem accurately.

General Behaviors

You may not be with your relative while he or she is gambling so be alert for general behavioral changes.

1. **Change in home life:** As gambling grows in importance, other areas of life become less important. Typically, people invest significant time and effort in their family life and relationships. When the interest or effort put into these activities diminishes, it is always worth asking why. Where is that energy going? Relatives commonly notice changes such as decreased time spent with family, increased conflict in relationships, and increased emotional distance.

2. **Change in work life:** Similarly, a decrease in your relative's investment in work or education is cause for concern. Specific signs include poor attendance, decline in performance, diminished ambition or morale.

3. **Changes in finances:** Financial losses are the most tangible sign of problem gambling. In Mild Problem Gambling, the changes in finances may be relatively small and less easily noticed. They may include increased use of leisure money for gambling activities and trips, incorporation of gambling expenses into the family budget, or unexplained changes in cash reserves.

Gambling Behaviors

Because general behaviors can indicate many types of problems, it is important to identify gambling-specific signs to determine if the changes you notice are due to gambling. Problem gamblers in the early stages are the least motivated and skilled at concealing the problem. Often, they don't feel the need to lie about whether they are going to the track or the casino and where their money is going. They may even boast about the luck they are having as gamblers. This can present an opportunity for you to observe the specific changes in the gambling behavior itself.

1. **Increase in gambling:** Whether it is in the number of days spent gambling, the amount of time spent, the number of dollars

gambled, or the average size of each bet there will be some tangible increase in the gambling itself.

2. **Loss of control:** Losing more money than budgeted and gambling for longer amounts of time than planned shows loss of control. Other plans or activities may then be missed or canceled. At first, the loss of control can be surprising to the gambler who doesn't fully understand what is happening. He may feel remorse that he missed an important event because he was gambling, or because he spent money that was needed for something else. There may be apologies, efforts to make things up, efforts to avoid gambling. As a rule, most people do not like losing control and often the signs of this struggle can be seen most easily in the early stages of the problem.

3. **Chasing:** *Chasing* is the term for trying to regain money lost gambling by additional gambling and it is common among problem gamblers. It begins with a loss, whether small or large. The fact that they lost, that they are "down" so much money, becomes the reason to gamble further. "I just have to win back that fifty dollars." Not surprisingly, chasing typically leads to greater losses. These additional losses, instead of signaling a time to stop, often intensify the urge to chase. The cycle continues until they are out of money or until the cost becomes so high that they finally give up.

    Chasing is specific to problem gambling. In no other impulse control disorder nor in any addiction to drugs or alcohol does the problem behavior or substance have the potential to solve all the problems created by previous use. No one drinks alcohol thinking it will solve all the problems created by drinking. But additional gambling can be seen as a potential way to retrieve the losses of the initial gambling. The result can be periods of intense gambling resulting in severe financial losses.

4. **Continued gambling following wins:** "I'll quit while I'm ahead" is a common response for many people, who walk away from the blackjack table or the racetrack with some of their winnings. The problem gambler may find it difficult to walk away with money that could be used for gambling.

5. **Gambling as an escape:** For some, gambling is a way to forget problems or negative feelings (see chapter 3 for more on motivation). At times, all of us look for ways to temporarily forget our problems and escape feelings of anxiety, frustration, anger, or depression. Gambling can be a very effective way to forget our problems temporarily. It is exciting, interesting, and usually done

in a location quite different from the rest of our lives, with different people. Fantasies of immediate gratification can flow freely. Nevertheless, most people don't rely on gambling to escape problems because it does nothing to actually solve those problems and may lead to additional problems. For the problem gambler, these shortcomings don't outweigh the sense of escape they feel when they gamble.

You might notice this sign by identifying a period of discomfort, often in the form of depression, anxiety, frustration, or boredom, immediately before a period of gambling. While gambling, the gambler is different—excited, relaxed, or confident and seemingly oblivious to her problems. The end of the gambling means coming back to face the problems that were avoided, problems that have not changed for the better and may now be worse. The problem gambler is often tense or distressed after gambling.

6. **Gambling as a stimulant:** We've asked many problem gamblers why they gamble. The most common answer is "I love the excitement." One of the criteria listed in Table 2.1 is a level of arousal and/or euphoria associated with gambling. There is a physical response to the activity that is often so intense as to be observable to others. Nonproblem gamblers may also experience excitement but generally less frequently and less intensely than problem gamblers.

> **Case Example:** Chris, who was discussed in chapter 1, started out gambling as many adults do. He gambled for fun by putting a few dollars on the big sporting events each year. But the frequency of his gambling increased dramatically. He started gambling on other games, then every weekend, then during the week. It was exciting and he felt at his best when he had money riding on a game. His increased interest in gambling lessened his interest in his work. Linda noticed that he stopped talking about promotions. He seemed less excited about being a father and more distant as a husband. More emotional energy was spent with gambling friends: talking and thinking about gambling, past experiences, and future plans. Linda did notice these clues in general behavior and in gambling-specific behavior, but she did not recognize the problem. Chris had lost more than he had planned to gamble, usually by trying to regain some of his initial losses. He had felt concerned and considered talking to Linda about it. Yet he loved to gamble and increasingly he protected his gambling by being secretive about it.

Identifying Severe Problem Gambling

In the early stages of a gambling problem, the signs may be subtle and difficult to identify. Over time, the changes become more dramatic. Unfortunately, the amount of denial and deception often increases as well, sometimes making it difficult to see some of these changes. Here are the key signs to watch for when the problem has become severe.

General Behaviors

1. **Effects on family:** Gambling becomes more important to the gambler than family relationships. This is due in part to an increased interest in gambling and gambling-related relationships. It may also be related to the dishonesty and shame that accompany gambling problems. As the dishonesty needed to sustain the gambling increases, the trust within the family relationships deteriorates. Family members are often aware of the growing distance, and they may be developing their own lack of trust. Often interpreting the gambler's behavior as a sign of selfishness or lack of love, family members start to distance themselves emotionally.

2. **Impact on work:** Similarly, investment in work and school continues to decline during this stage. Efforts to pursue long-term goals, such as professional ambitions, are further eroded. Performance deteriorates further with lower attendance, higher use of sick leave, and poorer performance appraisals as common signs of a decline in commitment and interest. Sometimes the poor performance is due to distraction, depression, or chaos in the lives of problem gamblers. Sometimes it is more direct. For example, a physician began reducing his office hours so that he could spend more time at the track; he canceled appointments because he could not leave the track in time to see his patients.

   Although interest in work is low, some gamblers may increase time at work hoping to pay off their debts. Striving to increase income by working overtime or extra jobs makes sense for the gambler who is desperate to avoid impending financial disaster. You may notice that the added work is accompanied by a surprising lack of financial gain.

3. **Secrecy:** As the losses become more apparent, the gambler's concern that others will find out becomes more distressing. Dishonesty increases, not as a malicious plan, but to protect the gambler from the shame and additional obstacles to gambling she fears

will come with discovery. This increases the difficulty of identifying problem gambling. Lottery tickets are destroyed, receipts that can be linked to gambling are hidden. A pattern of talking carefully about gambling develops to avoid raising suspicion. The resulting evidence of evasiveness or dishonesty can be a valuable sign suggesting that the gambling has transitioned to a more serious stage. Common distortions include the following:

* denial that the financial losses are significant; * lies about where the gambler is while gambling; * defensiveness or lies about financial accounts.

Often there is an attempt to raise a boundary around financial records altogether. One client tried to convince her husband she was taking over all the finances for the family so that he "didn't have to worry about money so much." In reality, it was a means of hiding the evidence of her losses.

Gambling behavior is also a focus of secrecy. The increasing frequency at the track or casino has to be hidden, so cover stories are developed. The gambler is "out with friends," or "working extra hours." The explanations may have some truth to them but are vague. If the explanations are challenged, the gambler may react defensively or angrily to discourage any further pursuit. Again, this pattern is itself evidence of a problem.

4. **Change in mood and personality:** Your relative may seem like a different person. Common changes include increased irritability and anger, moodiness, diminished warmth or friendliness, and change in energy level. Often, the behavioral changes reflect a change in values—what seems important now was not important before. In general people do not change dramatically in personality or mood unless there is an underlying problem. Although in adolescents some changes are more common, clear changes in mood or personality should raise your concern.

5. **Unexplained change in finances:** As losses mount, financial indicators become more apparent. The gambler may put off paying bills or reduce spending. He may try to reduce his lifestyle expenditures in some ways. Calls from creditors become more common, as do repeated notices of unpaid bills. Credit ratings may decline. Borrowing on credit cards may become a way to put off dealing with debt. Some families may notice the steady unexplained erosion of the family savings, punctuated by large losses. You may see these signs without knowing the cause. Your relative may explain that these changes result from a business problem or unexpected expenses.

Gambling Behaviors

The gambling itself continues to increase in frequency and intensity. The characteristics of loss of control change. For example, in the early stages, the gambler may be surprised or puzzled by episodes of loss of control. Over time, the inability to solve this problem often leads to increased denial. The gambler may express less distress about the loss of control. He will make more efforts to stop gambling, but these are often not shared openly with others, lest they push for a stop to it as well. Chasing becomes more common and difficult to stop.

Signs and Symptoms in the Most Severe Cases

The final stages are often the most tragic, showing the dramatic effects of complete loss of control.

Case Example: A family member asked a physician to talk with his sister about her gambling problem. He brought her to the doctor's office on a pretense because she refused to see a therapist about gambling. She was a fifty-six-year-old single woman who had gambled at Keno and scratch tickets for many years. Over the past five years it had become a severe problem. She lived alone and was increasingly distant from her brothers and sisters. They discovered that she was in danger of losing her home and was in legal trouble. Her gambling losses had become so severe that she had remortgaged her home and promptly spent the mortgage money gambling. She had signed up for multiple credit cards and took cash advances. She began reporting the cards stolen, which led to an investigation. Her family found out that she had been briefly hospitalized after a failed suicide attempt.

When the doctor raised the topic, she denied anything more than "occasional" gambling. She described her financial and legal problems as lies made up by her siblings to take control of her money. She admitted to having been a little depressed in the past, but the suicide attempt was "nothing." She refused to admit having any problem and since, at the time of the evaluation she was not depressed or suicidal, the doctor was unable to provide any help.

1. **Denial/dishonesty:** At this stage, the consequences of the gambling have become so severe, they are impossible to hide. It is

difficult to avoid facing the problem directly, providing a greater chance to get help. Despite this, some will continue in denial.

2. **Impact on finances:** Gambling has devastated the financial resources at this point, savings are gone and credit is ruined. The gambler has borrowed from everyone possible and damaged relationships. When legal means are exhausted, a surprising number of gamblers in this stage will turn to illegal means to fuel their gambling.

3. **Impact on the family:** Relationships with other family members have been severely damaged. The lies, the secrecy, the loss in financial resources have all damaged the trust and care that hold those relationships together. Increased conflict and emotional distance are typical, as are divorces and separations.

4. **Gambling behaviors:** Gambling has become the controlling focus of the person's life and dominates thoughts, activities, and feelings. There is little pretense of control, as the person may often gamble to the last dollar.

Recognizing Signs and Symptoms

Age: Teenagers and young adults have rates of problem gambling that are three to six times that of the general population. In this age group, both impulse control and judgment are less developed. Typically, there is less experience with gambling and its long-term consequences. These factors may contribute to the high rates of gambling problems for this age group. Therefore, it is important that:

* careful attention be paid to the gambling-specific behaviors;
* less weight is placed on the criteria not directly related to gambling; * the consistency of symptoms over time is carefully considered.

Gender: Men and women have different rates of gambling and different patterns and preferences for gambling. Men are twice as likely to develop a gambling problem. They tend to start earlier in their lives and they gamble more often than women. Societal expectations for men and women may lead men to be more visible in their gambling than women. This may make it likelier that people will look for and find gambling problems in men while many women will go undiagnosed and untreated.

Gambling preferences: The variety of gambling activities have different signs as well as different levels of acceptability and visibility. For example, a growing form of gambling involves stock market trading on the Internet. Many people would not consider this gambling, and so may miss the classic signs. Some forms of gambling such as playing scratch-off lottery tickets can be very private, while others are done only in certain public settings, such as casinos.

It is important to ask about all gambling activities specifically. It is not enough to ask the general question, "Do you gamble?" Table 2.2 presents a list of gambling activities to help you ask more precise questions.

Gambling frequency also varies. For some, gambling is a daily activity, with the losses impacting the family finances every week. Others gamble only on the occasions they are in particular settings or with certain people. They may gamble only once a year when they visit a casino, but not at all when they are at home. Either way, it is important for you to focus on the way the person behaves when gambling and its impact on his or her life to determine whether it is a problem. Frequency alone is only part of the picture.

Table 2.2: Types of Gambling Activities

Playing cards for money

Betting on horses, dogs, or other animals

Betting on sports of any type

Playing dice games for money

Gambling in a casino

Playing the numbers or betting on lotteries (Keno, Megabucks)

Playing scratch tickets, pull tabs, or "paper" games

Playing bingo for money

Playing stock market, options, and/or commodities market (Internet trading)

Playing slot machines, poker machines, or other gambling machines

Internet gambling

Bowling, shooting pool, playing golf, or any other game of skill for money

Adapted from the South Oaks Gambling Screen (Lesieur and Blume 1987).

Culture: In some cultures gambling has a more socially accepted and central position, which can make it more difficult to distinguish problem gambling given the higher rates of nonproblem gambling. Despite this, the targeted signs of problem gambling and the impacts on the family will still identify those with a problem.

Psychiatric problems: People who have psychiatric problems, including addictions to alcohol or drugs, have much higher rates of severe gambling problems. At times, these other problems can over-shadow the gambling, making it less likely that family members or professionals will notice it. For others, the gambling emerges along with the psychiatric problem. For example, some people gamble heavily only when they are drinking or depressed. Given these factors, it is important to follow these guidelines:

* Look carefully for gambling problems in relatives who have substance abuse or mood disorders.

* Stay focused on the gambling behaviors themselves to determine whether problem gambling is present.

* Know if your relative has bipolar disorder, also called manic-depressive illness. He or she may gamble as part of the illness (see chapter 3).

Putting It All Together

Step 1: Know what to look for.

Remember to focus on objective behaviors and signs, both gambling-specific and general as described in this chapter.

Step 2: Collect information.

This is often a challenge because of barriers raised around this information. Typically, relevant data can be found in the areas of personal finances, work or school, family, and gambling behaviors.

* Get copies of financial records, including credit card records, savings and checking account statements, records of regular expenses (i.e., mortgages, utilities), credit reports, stock and mutual fund summaries, and any other documents related to the gambler's assets (see chapter 9).

* Look at patterns of behavior around work or school: attendance, sick leave, motivation, achievement (grades, promotions, performance appraisals).

* Look at the level of trust and conflict within your family (amount and quality of conversation, openness to talk about gambling and finances, number of conflicts).

* Find out what you can about specific gambling behaviors. How often does he gamble? How long does he gamble? How much does he gamble? What is the average bet? Does he ever chase? Does he show signs of losing control?

Step 3: Exclude other explanations.

As noted earlier, other explanations must be considered. Specifically, you should be clear that the problem is not any of the following:

* social gambling; * beginning gambling; * a psychiatric disorder, particularly bipolar disorder; * drug or alcohol abuse; * other secretive behavior, e.g., having an affair, illegal activities.

Step 4: Consider using a standard test for gambling problems.

These tests help to identify people with gambling problems. One of the most widely used is the Gamblers Anonymous 20 Questions. We have included it here, adapting the questions so that family members can take it. It can be found at the end of this chapter. If you answer "yes" to six or more questions related to your relative, there is a significant probability that he or she has a gambling problem.

Step 5: Consider consulting a professional.

Professionals can help you identify what the problem is, particularly when the signs and symptoms are not clear. See chapter 10 for a discussion about finding appropriate professional help.

Exercises

It will help you master this material if you take notes in a separate journal while you read. Then, before you fill in answers to any questions or checklists, consult your journal. Now, read the following vignettes carefully, looking for evidence to determine whether the person is a problem gambler. As an exercise in recognition, complete the checklist in Table 2.3 by placing a check mark in each row when you believe that sign or symptom is present. Also, consider the following three questions when you read each vignette. (The answers will be found toward the end of the chapter.)

Question 1: What evidence for and against a gambling problem do you see?

Question 2: What additional information (if any) would you try to collect?

Question 3: Does he have a gambling problem?

Vignette 1: Jason is a twenty-year-old college student who has recently called home to request $500 for books. His parents are puzzled because the semester is more than half over. He seems to need the money urgently and yet is evasive when asked why he would need money for books at this point in the semester. In general, his parents have been concerned about him recently. The previous semester he hadn't shown them his transcripts, which was a first for a kid accustomed to getting mostly A's and proud of it. He complains that his classes are much harder this year and the professors just won't give him a break. He seems more distant and calls home much less often. When he does, he always asks for money. He has always been an energetic and, at times, impulsive kid, but something feels different this time. He hasn't said anything about gambling or gambling problems.

His parents first ask Jason about drinking, drugs, and mood. He says that everyone drinks at school but that he doesn't have a problem. He denies having any depression or other problems. He does admit to some gambling but says he only bets on football games at school. His parents call his resident assistant at school, but without Jason's consent they are not able to talk.

His parents confront him about his money—where is it going? He continues to be evasive, but with increasing pressure, he admits that he has lost money gambling, but continues to insist that it is not a problem. He admits to owing another student $300 for a bet on a recent game. He was trying to recoup some losses from the week before. He is quick to point out that he won $200 on a game last fall. He says that all his friends gamble and he does it only because they do. At the same time, he says it's "a lot of fun" and he loves it.

He admits to gambling on a weekly basis, mostly with a bookie on college sports, until he lost this recent bet. He used to bet $10 or $20, but now bets $100-$200 each time. Everyone does, he insists. He says that all his friends bet on the games. He denies there is any link to his grades, which he admits have declined in the past year. Again, he claims the bad grades are due to the difficulties of this year's classes.

His parents remember that he used to play poker with friends in high school. It didn't appear to be a problem, but he did play most Friday nights for a year or two. His grades were good at that time.

Vignette 2: Bill is a sixty-eight-year-old retiree who remarried two years ago, after his wife died of cancer. His new wife approaches his adult niece confidentially, saying that she thinks he has a gambling problem. She gives the niece the following description of his behavior.

Bill gambles at the track with his friends three days each week. He spends $300 each week on the horses. He occasionally plays scratch-off lotto tickets, and he goes to Las Vegas about once a year. He has gambled for much of his adult life–everyone jokes about Uncle Bill winning big some day. No one has ever expressed any concern about his gambling previously. He was a hard worker all of his life—a sales manager for a car dealership—and he made enough money to become the wealthiest person in the family. He loved his first wife and doesn't seem as happy as he was before she died. He used to have an alcohol problem, but has been sober for six years and attends Alcoholics Anonymous. There has been no clear problem with mental illness, but he appears somewhat depressed.

His wife says that he doesn't want to go on vacation to the mountains or the beach with her unless it is somewhere near a casino. She thinks he is too interested in gambling and not enough in other things. She also thinks that the money he spends on gambling is too much and they could use it for other things such as a new car. There have been some arguments between them regarding money. She has asked him to stop gambling in the past but he refuses, saying it is one of the few things he really enjoys. She doesn't think he is spending more money gambling than before, but senses it is still too much. When his niece checks with other relatives they all say they still see him as much as ever. No one else in the family seems to be worried about him. When she talks with Uncle Bill, he seems to be a little less energetic. He says he is still going to the track, waiting for the "big one" to come in. He denies anything new in his life—he doesn't mention tension with his wife.

Table 2.3:
Checklist for Vignettes 1 and 2

Sign	Vignette 1	Vignette 2
General Behaviors		
Work:		
Diminished Focus/Ambition		
Change in Attendance		
Change in Performance		

Home:
    Diminished Focus
    Change in Time Spent at Home
    Increased Tension/Conflict		

Change in Level of Honesty/Openness		
Change in Mood or Personality		
Unexplained Change in Finances		
Gambling Behaviors		

Increased Gambling:
    Frequency
    Total Amount of Time
    Amount of Bets
    Total Money Bet		

Incidents of Loss of Control:
    Gambled Longer Than Planned
    Gambled More $ Than Planned
    Remorse After Gambling
    Gambled to Last Dollar
    Gambled Instead of a Planned Activity		

Chasing		
Continued Gambling Following Wins		
Gambling as an Escape		
Gambling as a Stimulant		

Efforts to Gain More Money to Gamble:
    Borrow Money to Gamble
    Take Money Needed for Other Expenses to Gamble
    Sold Possessions to Gamble
    Increase in Money Budgeted for Gambling
    Illegal Activity to Gain Money for Gambling		

Answers to Checklist for Vignettes 1 and 2

Sign	Vignette 1	Vignette 2
General Behaviors		
Work/Education:		
Diminished Focus/Ambition	?	No—Retired
Change in Attendance	?	N/A
Change in Performance	Yes	N/A
Home:		
Diminished Focus	?	Possible
Change in Time Spent at Home	No	No
Increased Tension/Conflict	Yes	Yes
Change in Level of Honesty/Openness	Yes	No
Change in Mood or Personality	No	No
Unexplained Change in Finances	Yes	No
Gambling Behaviors		
Increased Gambling:		
Frequency	Yes	No
Total Amount of Time	?	No
Amount of Bets	Yes	No
Money Bet	Yes	No
Incidents of Loss of Control:		
Gambled Longer Than Planned	?	No
Gambled More $ Than Planned	?	No
Remorse After Gambling	?	No
Gambled to Last Dollar	?	No
Gambled Instead of a Planned Activity	?	No
Chasing	Yes	No
Continued Gambling Following Wins	?	No
Gambling as an Escape	?	No
Gambling as a Stimulant	?	Possibly

Efforts to Gain More Money to Gamble	Yes	No
Borrow Money to Gamble	Yes	No
Take Money Needed for Other Expenses to Gamble	?	No
Sold Possessions to Gamble	?	No
Increase in Money Budgeted for Gambling	No	No
Illegal Activity to Gain Money for Gambling	No	No

Answers to Questions

Vignette 1

Question 1: What evidence for and against a gambling problem do you see?

Though available information is limited, there is evidence of a number of the key changes in gambling behaviors and general behaviors typically found in problem gambling. Despite Jason's denials, the increased gambling, large amounts of money lost, evidence of borrowing, and chasing all point to problem gambling. There is a clear change in school performance and some change in the way he interacts with his parents. There is little direct evidence against problem gambling, although there are areas where information is lacking including school attendance, evidence of loss of control, and gambling as an escape or stimulant.

Question 2: What additional information (if any) would you try to collect?

Grades, attendance records, bank account, any records from school, information about gambling behavior.

Question 3: Does he have a gambling problem?

It seems fairly likely that he has Mild Problem Gambling.

Vignette 2

Question 1: What evidence for and against a gambling problem do you see?

The amount of time Bill spends gambling and the amount of money he loses may suggest a problem. The key evidence is that he does *not* show the specific changes in his gambling behavior. He has not increased his gambling. He does not show any evidence of losing control, or of trying to find new ways to get money to continue to gamble. He does gamble a lot of money—possibly more than you would. But he apparently has a large income and the amount he gambles has not really changed. Gambling appears to be a stable part of his leisure. His wife may not like it—she may not think it is a good way to spend money—but this does not mean that he is a problem gambler.

Question 2: What additional information (if any) would you try to collect?

No additional information is necessary.

Question 3: Does he have a gambling problem?

Chances are very low that he has Problem Gambling.

Do You Have a Problem Gambler in Your Family?

Answer the following questions by circling "T" for True or "F" for False.

T F   1. Has he ever lost time from work or school due to gambling?

T F   2. Has his gambling ever made your home life unhappy?

T F   3. Has gambling ever affected his reputation?

T F   4. Has he ever felt remorse after gambling?

T F   5. Has he ever gambled for money to pay debts?

T F   6. Has his gambling ever been associated with a decrease in his ambition or efficiency?

T F   7. Has he ever felt some urgency to return to gambling to win back lost money?

T F   8. Has he ever felt some urgency to return to gambling after a win, in order to win more?

T F   9. Has he ever gambled until his last dollar was gone?

T F   10. Has he ever borrowed to finance gambling?

T F   11. Has he ever sold anything to finance gambling?

T F   12. Has he kept money separate for gambling and been reluctant to use it for other normal expenses?

T F 13. Has gambling appeared to cause him to be careless of his own welfare or that of other family members?

T F 14. Has he ever gambled longer than planned?

T F 15. Has he ever gambled as a way to escape worry or trouble?

T F 16. Has he ever committed or thought of committing an illegal act to finance gambling?

T F 17. Has he ever had difficulty sleeping because of gambling?

T F 18. Has he ever responded to arguments, disappointment, or frustrations by gambling or expressing a desire to gamble?

T F 19. Has he ever celebrated, or talked of celebrating good fortune by a few hours of gambling?

T F 20. Has he ever considered, talked about, or tried suicide or some other self-destructive act as a result of gambling?

Adapted from Gamblers Anonymous Questionnaire.

If you answered True to more than six questions, the probability that your relative is a problem gambler is high.

Chapter 3

Who Becomes a Problem Gambler

About eleven out of every 1,000 (1.1 percent) adults are Severe Problem Gamblers; an additional 2.8 percent are Mild Problem Gamblers. In all, about four out of every one hundred adults have had a gambling problem within the past year. The rates climb even higher if we consider those who have a problem sometime in their life, not just in the last year. By comparison, about 6 percent of all adults abuse alcohol and 5 percent have a serious clinical depression. Problem gambling is as common as many of the most common psychiatric disorders, affecting more than one out of twenty-five, or about eight million adults in the United States (DSM-IV 1994; Shaffer, Hall, and VanderBilt 1997).

Vulnerable Groups

Anyone can develop a gambling problem, regardless of his or her gender, age, race, cultural background, or economic situation. However, some groups are particularly vulnerable to problem gambling, either because they have an elevated risk of developing problem gambling or because the effects of problem gambling can be particularly destructive for individuals in these groups. Such groups include adolescents, elderly adults, individuals addicted to alcohol or drugs, and individuals with other psychiatric disorders including mood disorders, attention deficit disorder (ADD), and schizophrenia.

Adolescents and Young Adults

Teenagers' risk of developing problem gambling is almost triple that of adults. Among college students the risk increases to six times the adult risk. The teenage and young adult years represent the period of highest risk for developing gambling problems. More teenagers gamble than smoke marijuana or use other illegal drugs. Alcohol use barely exceeds the prevalence of illicit gambling (i.e., lotteries) among seventh- to twelfth-graders (*The WAGER* 1996). About 13 percent of adolescents and young adults—one in eight—will have a gambling problem (Shaffer, Hall, and Vanderbilt 1997).

Elderly Adults

Clinical evidence suggests problem gambling is rapidly increasing among seniors and may occur at higher rates than in the general adult population. Convergent factors put elderly adults at higher risk, including isolation, increased free time, reduced financial reserves, and life changes that may remove people or activities which restrain gambling.

A small but significant percentage of adults above the age of sixty have some type of cognitive impairment. This may be the result of a host of medical conditions, including strokes, Alzheimer's disease, and the long-term effects of alcohol. For a small group of these seniors, symptoms of their cognitive impairment include a reduction in their ability to reason clearly and control their impulses, rendering them more vulnerable to developing problems.

For example, one woman's sisters brought her to the hospital after she had gambled away her pension fund. She had never had a gambling problem before the age of sixty-five, but then she began playing Keno and the lottery until she lost more than $200,000. A complete physical examination revealed that long-term alcohol abuse had produced mild brain damage, which was very likely related to her gambling. In general, she was less inhibited, more impulsive, and more likely to use poor judgment than when she was younger.

The effects of problem gambling on seniors can be particularly severe. Problem gambling can exacerbate elderly adults' susceptibility to depression and anxiety. Vital financial reserves can be rapidly depleted, with no time or capacity to replenish them. Seniors can find their hopes and dreams of a comfortable retirement swiftly wiped out.

One elderly patient lost thousands of dollars on mail-in sweep-stakes. Although he had been an astute businessman when he was younger, his judgment had been reduced by a series of small strokes. He was easy prey for the marketing strategies employed by many sweepstakes companies. He was convinced that he was going to win and even tried to drive across the country to pick up his "winnings." By the time his daughter and son-in-law realized what was happening and intervened, he was virtually destitute.

Alcohol and Drug Abusers

People with alcohol and drug problems have rates of problem gambling some six times that of the general population. In addition, alcohol and drug abuse occurs at higher rates among problem gamblers than it does among the general population (Federman, Krebs, Drebing, et al. 1998). The reasons for the association are complex, including culture, common environments, early family exposure, and, possibly, genetics.

Perhaps the most easily understood factor is the presence of alcohol in many gambling locations and the availability of gambling opportunities in many places where people go to drink. Alcohol is literally given away at many casinos and is widely available at race-tracks and other gambling facilities. Similarly, pool tables, keno, and other gambling games are readily available in many bars, clubs, and lounges.

Problem gamblers who are addicted to alcohol or drugs may find that their addiction may interfere with their efforts to stop gambling. Similarly, gambling problems may impede efforts to stop drinking or using drugs. Together, the problems can be doubly difficult to resolve, creating a cycle of relapse and failure.

Other Mental Health Problems

People with a number of mental illnesses are at greater risk for developing gambling problems. Similarly, problem gamblers have higher rates of psychiatric disorders than the general population (Specker, Carlson, Edmonson, et al., 1996).

Mood Disorders

Bipolar disorder (also known as manic depression) is a disorder in which people fluctuate between periods of mania (characterized by high energy, extreme impulsiveness, and euphoric mood) and periods of depression (characterized by feelings of sadness, low energy, and low self-esteem). Impulsive, unrestrained gambling often occurs during mania. When gambling occurs *only* during a manic episode, it is not considered a separate disorder but rather is seen as a manifestation of mania. However, the symptoms and consequences can be identical, so gambling during mania may have a profound effect on the individual and the family.

The relationship between depression and problem gambling is complex and interactive. Depression increases the chance of developing problem gambling but it may also be a consequence of the losses associated with continued gambling activity. Problem gamblers have higher rates of major depression than the general population. Among problem gamblers in treatment, rates of depressions are three to five times that of the general population (Becona, Lorenzo, and Fuentes 1996; McCormick, Russo, Ramirez, et al. 1984).

Attention Deficit Disorder (ADD)

Almost 20 percent of adults with gambling problems have a disorder called attention deficit disorder, characterized by distractability, inability to maintain focus for long periods of time, restlessness, impulsivity, and learning difficulties. Individuals with ADD often appear hyperactive and overstimulated. Paradoxically, ADD may be associated with lower levels of stimulation or activity in the front portion of the person's brain—resulting in difficulty focusing attention. Stimulating situations can raise the level of activity in that portion of the brain, thereby rendering people more comfortable and able to focus their attention. For some, gambling may be risky enough to draw and hold their attention, temporarily relieving their symptoms.

This disorder appears in childhood but it is not always recognized. About half of the children with the problem will continue to have significant symptoms of poor attention, impulsivity, and high levels of activity in adulthood. ADD is associated with other impulse control disorders as well. Fortunately, treatment is often successful.

Schizophrenia

Our research suggests that individuals with schizophrenia have rates of problem gambling exceeding those occurring in the general population. People with these disorders face special challenges in dealing with the everyday problems of living and they confront severe symptoms including hallucinations, delusions, and disorganized or unusual behavior. Treatment, including medication, counseling, and a supportive environment, is often successful in moderating or eliminating many of these symptoms.

Problem gambling, however, can exacerbate many of the difficulties these individuals normally must confront. Because of gambling's negative impact on finances, relationships, and productive activity, it serves as an additional source of intense stress in the lives of those who frequently have only limited resources for coping with life's challenges. Gambling may also expose them to increased opportunities for alcohol and drug use. Finally, it can exacerbate the stress on family members, who may themselves have only limited resources available for coping with their relative's situation.

Motivations

Not all problem gamblers are alike, and the factors that contribute to their gambling also vary. Understanding your relative's constellation of motives is critical if you are to help that person identify effective ways to stop gambling and to meet his or her underlying needs in appropriate ways. There are basically six motivations that may lead people to engage in problem gambling.

1. **Action/excitement:** If you ask problem gamblers why they gamble, many will talk about the excitement. Both the potential for a big win and the risk of a loss can produce a thrill the gambler enjoys. For some gamblers, a high need for excitement and stimulation, sometimes called "sensation seeking," is a general personality trait. They are often risk takers in other areas of their lives, enjoying challenges and new experiences. They may find many ordinary situations relatively boring.

   This motivation is probably more common in adolescents and young adults and in people with attention deficit disorder. As mentioned above, people with ADD often report feeling more focused and comfortable when engaged in exciting or high-risk activities.

2. **Avoidance of depression, anxiety, and other negative feelings:** Many gamblers describe feeling as if they are in "another world" when they gamble. They forget about their daily concerns and focus entirely on the game they are playing. Some gamblers even describe feeling in a "trancelike" state, not fully aware of what is going on around them. For some, it is the chance to escape depressed moods or negative feelings like sadness, anxiety, anger, or fear. Typically, these individuals gamble, or gamble more often, when they are experiencing negative feelings. The gambling provides a few hours of escape, but, of course, it does not resolve underlying problems.

3. **Socializing:** Gambling can be the chief means by which an individual's social needs are met. Some people may develop a network of friends with whom they gamble regularly at the track or casino. Other gamblers find that being around others, even

without much personal contact, is an important motivating factor. Going to a crowded casino and gambling alone achieves precisely the level of social contact they desire. Socializing may be an important motivating factor for both the older gambler and the adolescent/young adult gambler.

4. **Identity and self-esteem:** Being a "gambler" provides a positive identity for some people as well as increasing self-esteem. This may surprise those who see gamblers in a negative light. However, our culture often views the gambler positively. The media frequently portrays the gambler as exciting, daring, fun-loving, glamorous, adventurous, and a desirable companion. Being a "winner" is a related image that is also attractive. Most gamblers enjoy telling about games they have won and how much money they have made, believing that others will be impressed. (And sometimes they are impressed.)

    Gamblers' beliefs about what characteristics are desirable vary greatly. Some want to be seen as a gambler because it is glamorous. Others will want the experience of being viewed as a "winner" and being envied by others. Still others may see being a gambler as something of a special characteristic, which sets them apart. The images people try to project may not actually reflect who they really are. For example, a shy, fearful adolescent may pursue gambling to prove that he is fearless and sophisticated.

    Even people who were not initially attracted by the gambler's image may enjoy their reputations as gamblers after years of gambling. Giving up gambling may mean giving up an important part of their self-image. Males in particular may feel greater social pressure to acquire and maintain these qualities that they perceive as "glamorous" as part of their identity.

5. **Interpersonal motives:** For some gamblers, the role that gambling plays in family relationships is an important part of the motivation to gamble. For example, Mathew is a twenty-four-year old who feels and acts much more like a fourteen year old. He dropped out of college and resumed living with his parents. His underlying fear of becoming an adult and his wish to have his parents continue to take care of him is a major theme in his life. His gambling problem plays an important role in helping him keep his parents' support. It is proof to him and his parents that he is too irresponsible and dependent to make it on his own.

    This is just one of many possible motives. For some young adults gambling can be a way of trying to break away, in contrast to Matthew who was eliciting parental support. For some, gambling is one way to express their anger or contempt either for themselves or their family members. For some couples, one partner's gambling may be a way to express hostility or to keep the other partner distant.

6. **Money:** Of course, virtually all gamblers consciously want to win money. Problem gamblers often resume gambling to recover previous losses—the phenomenon called "chasing." Seeking money is, along with excitement, the motive most readily identified and talked about by problem gamblers.

   Although the laws of probability dictate that the gambler will lose money in games of chance in the long run (see Appendix B), those with a limited income are more likely to see gambling as the only way to appreciably improve their lifestyle. Thus, many people with limited resources spend at least some of those resources gambling. Unfortunately, the most common result is simply a further reduction in their already limited funds. For this reason, the motivation for money is a particularly important one to consider in regard to gamblers from lower income brackets and those with limited incomes, such as the elderly.

Assessing Motivation

Problem gambling is often hidden from other family members. Once it is revealed, understanding a problem gambler's motivations for gambling can be helpful both for the gambler and for other family members. For the gambler, understanding motivation can be an important step toward treatment and an eventual halt to the gambling (see chapter 10). For you, understanding motivation can help make sense of why your relative is gambling in a way that undermines his as well as your family's psychological and financial well-being. It can also help you to open an effective dialogue and work with the problem gambler toward eventual recovery.

You may already have some ideas about why your relative gambles. But there is probably a good deal more you could profitably discover in this area. Problem gamblers themselves are often, but not always, unaware of the particular combination of motives which underlie their gambling. Some motivations—like money and excitement—are frequently more evident to family members and to the gamblers themselves. Others—such as interpersonal gains and avoidance of distressing feelings—may not be evident to the gambler nor to anyone else in the entire family. Because few gamblers directly consider this issue, one effective way to assess a problem gambler's motivation for gambling is to get him or her engaged in a wide-ranging, open conversation about his or her gambling. This is particularly the case if you are already engaged in a dialogue with the gambler about his or her gambling. (See chapter 7 for information on opening such a dialogue.)

Even if your relative's gambling is creating tension or problems that interfere with your communication, try to set these tensions aside temporarily. Allow yourself to be genuinely curious about your relative's gambling. Your goal—which you can explicitly convey to the gambler—is to better understand how and why your family member engages in this activity. If you are at the point where you suspect your family member has a gambling problem, but you have not yet approached him or her, you can still think about this issue, by reviewing whatever evidence has led you to suspect your relative of problem gambling. Later, after you have engaged your relative in dialogue you will have an opportunity for conversation on this topic.

There are a number of questions you can ask gamblers to better understand their motivation. The most direct route is to ask the individual why he believes he gambles. What does he get out of it? What does he achieve? What does he enjoy about it? Does it help him to feel better about things? Is he able to leave his worries and cares behind when he gambles? If you have not had an opportunity to observe your family member actually gambling in the past, ask him to describe a typical gambling episode from start to finish. How did he feel when he was gambling? What was he thinking about? Answers to these questions may help you to recognize when excitement or avoidance of negative feelings is a primary motivator.

Pay attention to whether he gambles alone or as part of a group of friends or acquaintances. If he gambles with others, ask him to talk about his gambling friends. Notice if your relative talks about these friends and the times they have together in positive or even glowing terms. Try to understand what gambling means to your relative in terms of his identity. Listen closely to your relative's accounts of gambling, focusing on how he talks about himself, what he seems particularly proud of, what he thinks others say or think about him, and how he describes himself. Ask him to describe his own personality, his reputation, what others like about him. All of this information can help you to ascertain whether an enhanced personal identity is an important motivator for your relative.

Identifying interpersonal motives can be difficult for other family members, since you are immersed in frequent, if not daily, interactions with the problem gambler. Many of these interactions may be so automatic and unconscious that you never reflect on them objectively. Often, an objective friend, relative, or other third party may help you understand underlying themes in family relationships. Also, consulting with a professional can be useful for understanding interpersonal motivation.

You need to understand what the person is trying to accomplish interpersonally by gambling. Are there predictable patterns in how people respond to the gambler when he is gambling? Include close friends and the gambler's peer group as well as family members in your considerations. Do people usually become more distant from the gambler or more involved? What does the gambler gain by gambling from family members? Does he garner attention, help, sympathy, freedom, and admiration, or emotional distance and disapproval?

Again, simply asking the gambler what he or she is seeking often will reveal whether money is a primary motivator. Another useful tactic is to discuss the meaning and emotional significance of money for the gambler and others in the family. In many families, this topic is seldom discussed openly. Problem gamblers often display some unusual, often subtle, distortions in their thinking about gambling and money. Common distortions to listen for include the following:

> * "The more I bet, the greater chance I have to win." * "I will eventually hit it big and make up for all my losses." * "When I win, I should keep going, so I can win more." * "If I have a lot of money, I am a better person." * "People care about me because of all the money I bring in for the family."

Putting It All Together

Problem gambling is a widespread and growing phenomenon. It is a behavioral disorder, which anyone can develop in any family at any age. Certain groups—the young, the elderly, people addicted to alcohol and drugs, and people with other psychiatric disorders—are particularly vulnerable, both in terms of developing the problem and in terms of suffering its most destructive effects.

Gambling problems are almost always complex. Many individual factors lie behind your relative's development of a gambling problem. However, he or she is most likely driven to gamble by motives common to many problem gamblers. Understanding and addressing these motivations can assist both the gambler and the family on the road to recovery.

Chapter 4

Problem Gambling: A Family Issue

Problem gambling can affect your entire family emotionally, financially, socially, and even physically. Many of these effects are subtle and hidden from view. Even when family members recognize the effects, they may not immediately think of gambling as the source of the difficulties. Taking into account how the entire family responds to the problem gambler helps to cope with these strains. Ignoring the family's role may make it easier for members to unintentionally contribute to the problem gambler's behavior.

We often take family life for granted as part of our everyday reality. It is a little like the air we breathe; most of the time we don't pay much attention to it. Only when we grow short of breath do we become alert to the atmosphere around us. By doing so, we prepare ourselves to take steps to improve our situation. In the same way, with your family facing a possible crisis in the form of problem gambling, you can reap big dividends from assessing your family's current circumstances.

In this chapter, you will learn to understand and address problem gambling as a family matter. The specific ways in which the gambler's behavior may be having a negative impact on each family member are discussed. We also point out some of the less as well as the more effective ways your family can respond to the presence of problem gambling.

Understanding Problem Gambling in Your Family

Problem gambling affects the family as a whole, as well as each and every member. In some families, problem gambling becomes a central organizing factor. Anything that happens to one member inevitably affects every other member. Like the body, the family is composed of individual parts, each of which affects the others. In the body, for example, a broken leg will lead to lack of activity, resulting in decreased muscle tone and decreased cardiovascular functioning. The family works the same way. The changes in one individual brought about by the presence of problem gambling triggers changes in other family members.

For example, if a woman becomes depressed about the family's financial troubles resulting from her husband's problem gambling, the children in the family may become depressed as well, not because the family is facing difficult financial conditions, but because their mother has become withdrawn and inattentive to their needs for affection. It is important to remember, however, that to respond effectively to the situation it is not necessary to track every possible effect of problem gambling on the family. A general appreciation of problem gambling as a familywide problem and an understanding of the major ways it may be currently impacting your family should help you to manage the situation.

Roles and Responsibilities

Most family roles and responsibilities are divided among family members. Parents are primarily responsible for caring for the younger members of the family and teaching them how to speak and act in various situations. Children may be responsible for learning, performing daily chores, and providing emotional support to other family members. The effects of problem gambling will vary depending on the roles and responsibilities of the problem gambler within the family and the relationship of other family members to that individual. The effects of a parent's gambling problem on the family will be quite different than that of a teenager's gambling problem, because their roles and responsibilities are different. Similarly, parents and children will be affected in quite different ways by a grandparent's problem gambling because parents' and children's relationships to that grandparent are different.

Family Life Cycles

Families go through predictable periods of change as individual family members age and families evolve. The general characteristics of the family life cycle are similar for most families. Typical stages include marriage, settling down, becoming parents, child raising, mid-life, and retirement, each with its own role expectations and tasks. In the early years of marriage, couples typically establish their own family identity separate from their families-of-origin. With the arrival of children, the emphasis shifts to caring for the young and transmitting cultural values to the next generation. During mid-life, the family may be focused on redefining the relationship between parents and their adult children and accommodating itself to new family members brought in by the marriages of their children and the arrival of grandchildren. Furthermore, toward the end of the family life cycle, parents typically become increasingly reliant on their adult children for practical and emotional support. Within this broad cycle, each family establishes its own unique course, depending on the particular events experienced by that family (e.g., adjusting to a divorce, an illness, or death, or a sudden change in social or economic status).

As families move through these stages of growth and change, the roles and responsibilities of individual family members change as well. Thus, a woman at mid-life who has spent two decades raising her children, now in their early twenties, may suddenly face an empty nest in which her maternal responsibilities are dramatically diminished. During such times of transition, family members go through periods of adjustment and perhaps conflict as they learn to renegotiate their relationships. This is a normal and expected development for all families.

Problem gambling usually disrupts the ability of the whole family and its members to perform the particular tasks appropriate to their stage in the life cycle. For example, one of the primary tasks for a recently married couple is to develop an identity independent of their families-of-origin. The loss of a well-paying job and several thousand dollars of debt forced one gambling client and his wife to borrow money from the wife's in-laws. But the money came attached with unwelcome strings: phone calls several times a week from the wife's parents, showering advice on the husband and private recriminations on the daughter for her poor choice of a marital partner. Both the client and his wife felt trapped in this new relationship with the wife's parents. In another example, an eighty-year-old retired postal worker, living alone, began running up sizeable debts with a local bookie. He bitterly resented the alarmed intervention of his adult children, viewing it as meddling with his independence, which, in any case, he had been gradually losing in recent years as his health had declined.

How Problem Gambling Affects the Family

Problem gambling disrupts family life through its negative financial consequences, the deterioration of basic trust between the gambler and other family members, and the loss of the problem gambler's ability to carry out his or her normal family roles and responsibilities. These developments in turn produce social, emotional, and even physical changes in the family's well-being.

Family members often respond to these effects long before they become aware of problem gambling in their family, making subtle changes in their routine behaviors, shifting family roles and responsibilities, alternating everyday patterns of interaction and communication, and reducing their contacts with the outside world. Because these changes occur gradually, family members may be unaware of them. As the problem gambling grows more severe and disruptive, however, the family's adjustments will necessarily become more dramatic, eventually forcing their way into the family's consciousness.

Financial and Social Effects

The obvious financial consequences of problem gambling include loss of income, depletion of savings, incurring large debts, damage to the family's credit rating, and decline in overall standard of living. Additionally, there are many other indirect effects that arise from such changes in the family's financial status. A lowered standard of living can produce a sense of deprivation, depressed feelings, and anger toward the gambler as the cause of the change in the family's fortunes. Family members may be involuntarily cut off from important social relationships when the problem gambler herself alienates extended family, friends, neighbors, or co-workers by borrowing money and not repaying it.

Families of problem gamblers often choose voluntarily to withdraw from social contacts with extended family, friends, neighbors and co-workers. They do so partly to focus their energies on addressing the increased stresses within the family, but largely to avoid situations where they might reveal details of the problem gambler's behavior and the family's current financial troubles. For example, an adolescent son of a client revealed in a family session how he had been avoiding close friends at school for months because he was ashamed that his father's gambling debts had forced the family to sell their house and move to a small apartment in a neighborhood several miles away.

Family members often reinforce and add to their depressed feelings after they pull back from regular contact with extended family, friends, and neighbors. These contacts are essential for emotional health; without them, some families turn inward, become overly involved in each others' lives and adopt an "us versus them" attitude.

Loss of Trust

The psychologist Erik Erikson observed that the formation and nurturing of basic trust is the first fundamental task in human development. Trust is essential in family relationships. It extends to nearly every aspect of family life. When we say we trust a family member, we mean not only that we trust them to be honest in their words, but honest in their deeds. In other words, we know we can depend on them in large and small ways, from providing child care, to emotional support, to handling money responsibly, to taking a phone message. A violation of trust—betrayal—is considered one of the worst transgressions any relationship can endure.

When a family member conceals and lies about his problem gambling, he introduces distrust into family relationships. Although this distrust is most evident between the gambler and family members, the problem gambler's deception also may create subtle doubts in the minds of other family members about their ability to trust each other. If children, for example, learn that one parent has lied to them about gambling, they may wonder how much they can depend on the honesty and reliability of the other parent. Betrayal of trust can produce profound feelings of depression, anxiety, sadness, and anger among family members. It can also make it more difficult for the family to organize effectively to address the problem and can inhibit family members from reaching out for social support outside the family.

We often think of trust as an all-or-nothing phenomenon. However, viewing trust in this manner makes the restoration of trust in family life very difficult. Any significant betrayal appears to leave little in the way of foundations on which to begin rebuilding trusting relationships. In reality, most families will find they can still rely on an individual who has betrayed them—to some degree and in some areas. Adopting this more flexible view can be an important first step toward recovering trust within the family.

Impairment in Roles and Responsibilities

The problem gambler's ability to perform her normal roles and responsibilities in the family declines as she becomes more preoccupied with winning back her losses and erasing the negative consequences of her gambling. This often leaves other family members feeling they cannot depend on the gambler to act responsibility and live up to family commitments and expectations. A young mother who repeatedly fails in her promise to pick up her children at the end of the school day may use excuses to conceal the real reason for her tardiness—playing the slot machines at a local club. Her young children may grow increasingly anxious and angry, without truly understanding why their mother is late.

Family members are often forced to take over many of the roles and responsibilities at which the gambler has failed. Taking over new roles may leave them feeling anxious and resentful toward the gambler for having forced them into a new and uncomfortable role in the family. In one family, a wife who had developed a gambling problem brought in a critical second paycheck which helped cover the family's monthly expenses. Distraught over her gambling problem, she grew seriously depressed and lost her job. Her husband had to moonlight at a local convenience store in the evening in addition to his day job. On weekends, he spent most of his time looking after their two young children. Within three months, he desperately needed counseling, explaining he felt exhausted, angry, and depressed.

Paradoxically, for some individuals, taking over new roles may have a positive effect, at least initially. An adult daughter with a cognitively impaired mother who had always dominated her was placed in charge of her mother's financial affairs after a judge declared her mother legally incompetent for having gambled away her life savings on the state lottery and magazine contests. In therapy, the daughter confessed that she had mixed emotions about this new arrangement. On the one hand, she was secretly enjoying the reversal in roles, but, on the other, she felt guilty about her pleasure in such a sad and destructive situation. Her ambivalence disappeared quickly, however. Within a matter of weeks, she became thoroughly irritated by her mother's constant complaints and the time required each week to go over her mother's accounts.

Pessimistic Beliefs

The longer problem gambling goes on, the more likely family members come to believe they are helpless to change the situation. If the problem gambler is concealing the problem from the family, family members will fail to understand the source of their difficulties. No matter what the family does to try and improve conditions, things will stay the same or get worse, because the true source of the problem remains hidden. Even after the family suspects the truth, or the problem gambler has confessed her situation, the problems may seem insurmountable, particularly when the gambling family member continues his gambling or returns to gambling after having stopped for some weeks or months. Thoughts of helplessness may give rise to feelings of intense sadness and despair, frustration, and anger. These beliefs can spill over into other areas of family life, making it harder for family members to take on new roles and responsibilities to keep the family functioning.

The Impact on Physical Health

Family members are often unaware of the indirect effects that problem gambling can have on physical health, but those effects are often significant. Physical difficulties result from negative changes in emotional functioning, reinforced by social isolation. Chronic anxiety, anger, and sadness can impair the healthy functioning of the immune system, interrupt normal routines, and make it more difficult to obtain adequate sleep, nutrition, and exercise. Family members may respond to added stress with increased vulnerability to infectious disease and a variety of symptoms including headaches, gastrointestinal difficulties, backaches, asthmatic symptoms, cardiovascular difficulties, allergies, and skin problems.

Disruptions in physical health can compound disruptions in other areas. One client developed debilitating headaches around the time his wife's problem gambling became increasingly severe. He was forced to take time off from work and lost a promotion that would have eased the financial pressures on the family considerably. Of course, nongambling factors also may contribute to family stress and to physical ailments. Whatever the cause, if your health or that of other family members is suffering, we advise you to seek appropriate medical care and to discuss your family situation with your regular physician.

Position of the Gambler in the Family

The position of the problem gambler in the family—whether parent, spouse, child, or older relative—will influence how problem gambling affects the family, how the problem gambler relates to other family members, and how other family members respond to the problem gambler.

If Your Partner Has a Gambling Problem

If your partner has a gambling problem, the effects on your family are pervasive because of his or her central role in the family's life. In a well-functioning family, adult partners play multiple roles, including breadwinner, nurturing parent, marital partner, and social representative of the family to the outside world. Problem gambling behavior disrupts your partner's ability to perform each of these roles. As these disruptions become obvious (e.g., overdue bills piling up, friends and neighbors avoiding family members, loss of interest by the gambling spouse in sexual activity, lack of attention to the children), your stress will grow, likely resulting in feelings of depression, anxiety, anger, and perhaps a sense of betrayal. One woman in treatment spoke of feeling "alone and abandoned" by her problem gambling husband. She was angry that her husband had let her wonder for more than two years why things had gone wrong in their relationship. When he finally admitted to gambling, she was tempted to retaliate by starting an affair with an attractive co-worker.

Partners of problem gamblers often compensate by taking over the responsibilities abdicated by the gambler. They may feel the need to become a "super parent" for the children or a surrogate parent for the gambling partner. For example, a husband whose partner has a gambling problem may run himself ragged leaving work early each weekday to be home when the children arrive at the end of the day, cooking dinner, putting the kids to bed, and attending school sports events on the weekend. Similarly, the wife of a problem gambler may need to get a second job and take over managing the family finances, traditionally handled by her problem gambling husband. This approach may buy her a sense of control but it will likely result in more stress on her and the rest of the family at a time when the problem gambler is less available to meet any of the family's needs.

If you have children, any increased stress on you will likely affect the lives of your children too. Children are particularly vulnerable to the effects of stress, because they are less well equipped intellectually and emotionally to deal with disruptions in family life. Moreover, children are intensely dependent on their parents for emotional as well as practical support.

Young children are less able to reflect on their feelings and more likely to act on them. Children's distress often shows up as

declining performance in school, neglect of household chores, or misbehavior. Younger children often have idealized images of their parents that they try to preserve in the face of evidence to the contrary.
They may resist acknowledging any problem associated with the
gambling parent and may, instead, offer explanations and rationalizations for their parent's erratic behavior, both to other family members and to friends and neighbors.

Older children may feel subtle pressures to take on some of the
roles and responsibilities neglected by their gambling parent, becoming a little "Mom" or "Dad" to younger children in the family or a
surrogate spouse for the nongambling parent. Older children in particular may feel intense embarrassment and shame about their gambling parent's behavior and the consequences for their families. They
may avoid social contacts with friends or relatives, where such contacts might lead to questions about Dad's being laid off from work,
or the repossessing of one of the family cars, or the angry arguments
between their parents.

If Your Child Has
a Gambling Problem

Discovering that your adolescent or college-age child has a
gambling problem can be a devastating experience. Adolescents and
many young adults continue to play a central role in the emotional
life of the family, and to a lesser degree in the social life of the family—even if they have physically left the household to attend school
or to work. In many families, children may also remain integrated to
some degree in the economic life of the family. They may be living at
home, working, and contributing financially to family expenses or
receiving financial support from parents for school or living arrangements elsewhere. Consequently, an adolescent or college-age child
with a gambling problem can disrupt both the emotional and financial life of the family.

Adolescent children are in a transitional stage between childhood and adulthood. Although they seek increasing independence
from family life, they still require parental support and guidance.
Parents are involved in a transition of their own: from full-time parents to independent adults free of parental responsibilities. Problem
gambling may play a central role in a child/parent struggle over
redefining the adolescent or college-age child's relationship to parents and other members of the family. A desperate adolescent may
turn to parents for emotional support or to be "bailed out" of debt.
Alternatively, parents may intervene on their own initiative if they
suspect their child is in serious trouble. Either way, parents may take

on increasing responsibility for the child's psychological and financial welfare just when the child is expected to be doing more for himself or herself.

Both parents and child may feel strong ambivalence. Parents will be concerned for their child's welfare, yet irritated and frustrated by the adolescent's irresponsibility. While some parents will be tempted to rescue their children, and release the child from all financial responsibility, others may blame the child for not heeding past advice and guidance. They may angrily decide to let the child suffer the consequences of his or her actions. They may also harbor secret doubts about their adequacy as parents, feeling guilty and self-reproachful, wondering where they went wrong and what they could have done differently. The child, on the other hand, may openly resent the intervention of his parents, even as he covertly feels grateful for it. Parental intervention may arouse simultaneous feelings in the child of shame, guilt, and relief. If the adolescent or young adult had left home and now returns, both parents and other children must adjust to the child's reentry into the daily life of the family. In situations where the gambling child has accumulated significant debts, the financial impact on the family can be significant. Depending on the financial status of the family, all family members may be affected by the financial burden.

If Your Parent or Older Relative Has a Gambling Problem

The effects of problem gambling on your family members will vary depending on the degree to which an older parent or relative is physically and socially integrated into your family's affairs and everyday family life. If an older parent is living in the same household with you, the effects of problem gambling on the household will be immediate and unavoidable. But even when older adults are living at some physical distance from the family, the development of a gambling problem still can affect your family's emotional, social, and financial functioning significantly.

Helping an older relative with a gambling problem can take many different forms, from simply offering advice all the way to petitioning a court of law for control of the elderly family member's financial affairs. Such interventions may re-ignite old struggles between you and your parent over power and control of finances, daily living conditions, and discretionary life choices, which you may have thought resolved decades earlier. Aging relatives want to maintain their capacity for independent living as long as possible, including decision-making control over their personal and financial affairs. Your parent is likely to experience your concerned efforts as a direct challenge to his or her autonomy and competency.

Such struggles can be emotionally volatile and stressful for both you and your older relative. Your parent may feel angry at you, guilty and ashamed about his gambling problem, and anxious about losing control over personal matters. You may feel frustrated and irritated that your relative is not more appreciative of your concerned efforts. You also may find yourself anxious about challenging your parent's authority—an emotional holdover from earlier struggles when you were an adolescent. These battles and their attendant emotions can be exacerbated in those situations where your family has a direct financial stake in the affairs of your older parent. This can happen if you feel financially responsible for the older individual or if you are counting on receiving a share of your older relative's inheritance—an inheritance which you may see dwindling from gambling losses.

If you have other siblings, you may have difficulty coordinating your actions vis-à-vis your elderly parent. Siblings may have different emotional reactions to an elderly parent's problem gambling, depending on their relationship with the parent. They may also have different ideas about what should be done. Siblings often live at varying distances from the parent; the burden of taking care of the situation may fall on those siblings who are geographically closest. You may feel resentment if you end up more involved with your parent and you may feel guilty if others take on the lion's share of the effort. Working with siblings may bring up old conflicts and rivalries, particularly those involving competition as children for the attention and favor of your parents.

If there are younger children in the family, they can be affected in a number of ways by the uncontrolled gambling of a grandparent or other older relative. As adults become stressed and preoccupied dealing with the behavior of their elderly relatives, this stress and inattention will be passed on to their own children. Just as they idealize their parents to some degree, children may idealize their grandparents as well. Grandparents and parents may vie for the loyalties of grandchildren, trying to convert the child to their point of view about the gambling of the grandparent. This may be the case especially when grandparents live in the same household or nearby. Being placed in this position represents a no-win situation for younger children, since, in effect, they are asked to take sides in a struggle that they may understand only vaguely and have no way of resolving. If parents continue to be preoccupied over an extended period of time with a grandparent's gambling problem, younger children may be asked to become more self-sufficient and to take over new tasks for the family unit, such as helping in the preparation of meals or caring for the youngest members of the family. If attempted interventions result in the alienation of the grandparent from the adults in the family, then children may be deprived of the emotional presence and support they previously enjoyed from a close relationship with the older relative.

Ineffective Family Responses

Every family has a unique pattern of response to problem gambling. All families respond effectively in some ways and less effectively in others. Knowing how to recognize and address *ineffective* family responses will help you to develop a sound and effective approach to dealing with problem gambling.

1. **Denial:** Almost all families respond to changing conditions with some degree of denial, particularly in the early stages of a gambling problem. Denial refers to the tendency to neither notice nor acknowledge the behavior of the problem gambler and the effects of that behavior on the family. It can take many forms. Some family members simply may act as if the problem doesn't exist. Some may refuse to talk about it. Some may become openly angry if you bring up the subject and assert that your family member needs to seek help. Other family members may fail to notice any changes in their emotions or their behavior attributable to the problem gambling. Even when the gambler's behavior and its impacts on the family can no longer be ignored, family members may persist in denial by downplaying the severity of the situation.

   In the shortrun, denial may be an effective response (see chapter 5), insofar as it allows family members to maintain smooth family relations, continue functioning in their daily lives, and avoid disruptive feelings of depression, anxiety, anger, guilt, or shame. In the long run, however, denial becomes ineffective, because it allows all family members (including the problem gambler) to pretend that the gambling behavior does not exist or pose any significant problem for the family, or to persist in the belief that it will eventually "fix itself."

2. **Co-dependence:** A co-dependent family member unintentionally supports or reinforces the problem gambler's dysfunctional behavior. Co-dependent responses develop slowly over time as well-meaning family members take steps that seem appropriate, logical, and even necessary without recognizing that their behavior generates unintended consequences.

   Co-dependent responses include enabling and rescuing. *Enabling* is generally done to keep the family functioning but also makes it easier for the gambler to gamble. For example, a wife may step in and start taking her son to his weekend Little League games because "Dad is just too busy at work these days and we don't want to bother him." *Rescuing* is done to minimize short-term damage to the gambler but often carries more severe negative long-term consequences. For example, children may bail out an elderly father from his frequent losses at the casino because allowing him to continue gambling seems to help him cope with the recent loss of his lifelong spouse. After all, they reason, he's on a fixed income and he always seems excited and upbeat the day after his weekly trip to the casino, doesn't he? (See chapter 6 for a more complete discussion on enabling and rescuing.)

Co-dependent responses can include decision making, ways of thinking, and emotional responses. A wife may share her husband's excitement when he comes home with $500 in lottery ticket winnings while ignoring the $3,000 he lost over the previous four weeks. A co-dependent partner may blame herself for "causing" her husband to play poker five nights a week. A father may feel secret enjoyment from hearing his son's stories of nights of big wins and big losses. Family members may avoid social contacts with friends or relatives who might challenge the problem gambler's behavior. In these cases, the family member's co-dependent behavior may be driven by the emotional benefits that he or she derives, while the larger context of the gambling's impact on the family is ignored.

Sometimes, as gambling dominates the family landscape, a family member's life may be increasingly devoted to keeping the family functioning, minimizing short-term pain to the gambler while enjoying the few emotional benefits available in this environment. In this case, with her life revolving around gambling, a family member may understandably find her very sense of self defined only in relation to the gambling behavior.

3. **Blaming:** Blaming responses are common in families dealing with problem gambling. It is often easier to blame the problem gambler than to take the initiative to improve the situation. Divided and upset, family members may also blame each other for acting in ways that fail to relieve the crisis. In the family of one elderly problem gambling client, two sons and a daughter fell into repeated bickering about the best way to intervene to "protect" their father—and what was left of their potential inheritance— from his addiction to lotto scratch tickets. When one of the sons finally petitioned a judge for legal guardianship of the father's affairs, the other two siblings were outraged and testified that their brother was violating their father's rights as a

competent adult.

Blame is a natural response when we perceive someone has fallen short of our expectations, violated our rights, or failed to meet social obligations or responsibilities. It involves a thought—in which we designate someone as responsible for some action—and an emotional component—usually anger. Blame shifts the burden of responsibility onto the other person for some perceived failure. It relieves the blamer of anxiety from any concerns about failing in his or her responsibilities. It allows the blamer to feel self-righteous about his or her own actions.

Although blame may make the blamer feel better in the shortrun, it usually results in the blamed person feeling anger, resentment, and/or shame. Often those who are blamed respond with defensiveness or denial. Blame does little to promote dialogue or collaborative problem solving.

As previously noted, sometimes family members end up blaming themselves for the gambler's problem, a form of co-dependency. Family members may also blame themselves for ineffective responses or for failing to make things right in the family in spite of the gambler's behavior. This is also ineffective, as it may result in depressed mood, shame, and sadness, immobilizing family members instead of motivating them to take effective action.

4. **Withdrawal and isolation:** As stated previously, many families respond to problem gambling by withdrawing from social contact and isolating themselves from their friends, neighbors, and others who could be of assistance. But family members may also withdraw and isolate themselves from the problem gambler and each other. This is a natural response when emotional resources are overtaxed. It is designed to protect an individual from exposure to stressful encounters, anxiety, and conflict and the demands of other family members to do something to meet their needs or rectify the situation. Isolation also occurs when family members have been taught they must solve their problems "on their own," or they are too anxious or ashamed to seek support from others. Family members may also find themselves isolated if the family disagrees about the reality of the situation or the best course of action to address the problem. For example, you may have a sense of isolation if you are alone in suspecting or acknowledging problem gambling in the family.

   There are three forms of isolation: *physical, interpersonal,* and *emotional.* Although it's possible to be physically isolated from your friends and neighbors, you're likely to be surrounded by your family. In spite of this, if family members communicate poorly with each other, you can be interpersonally isolated. And if no one talks openly about their feelings in the family, you will be emotionally isolated.

Withdrawal and isolation are ineffective ways to deal with problem gambling because they divide family members and prevent them from openly acknowledging the problem, discussing the issues, providing each other emotional support, and seeking support and information from outside the family. It also prevents the family from adopting a unified approach to dealing with the problem gambler and denies the problem gambler access to family support. Isolation also can make it easier to adopt co-dependent behaviors that actually reinforce the problem.

Putting It All Together

The important thing to remember about denial, codependency, blaming and shaming, and withdrawal and isolation is that almost no family confronting a gambling problem will escape them entirely, for these types of responses often appear to yield short-run benefits for individual family members and the family as a whole. But the *persistence* of these responses is counterproductive. Early understanding and recognition of these ineffective responses will help you to develop an effective set of family responses.

Effective Family Responses

1. **Work together as a family:** Since each family member is affected by problem gambling, each should be involved in a way that is consistent with their age, ability to understand, and appropriate responsibility for family affairs. Even the youngest family members can be offered explanations that they can understand. Older children can be enlisted to support measures the family chooses to take to address the problem.

   How the family works together to resolve the situation will depend on which family member is the problem gambler. When the gambler is a spouse, much of the effort will be confined to discussions and activities involving the married couple, particularly where younger children are involved. When older adolescent children form part of the family, they can be brought into general discussions and planning—and should certainly be informed of major decisions affecting their lives—but the decisions should remain in the hands of the adults.

   In the case of an older relative with a gambling problem, coordination between adult siblings who may be living in separate households will be critical to ensure that all agree on the nature of the problem and on the appropriate measures for resolving it.

When an adolescent or college-age child is the gambler, both parents and the gambling child need to work closely together to coordinate their activities.

2. **Openly acknowledge the existence of a problem:** Families who successfully deal with problem gambling overcome their initial denial. Often, speaking candidly will make a gambling problem seem less formidable. Families who address a gambling problem openly are better equipped to take realistic stock of their situation and to develop adequate measures in response. Open discussion promotes involvement of all family members in developing solutions, including the problem gambler. Candor reduces the pressures on the family to maintain the gambling problem as a secret from the extended family and the outside world. Once problem gambling is no longer a secret, family members' sense of shame is often dissipated, and they are able to reach out to others beyond the family for emotional and practical support.

3. **Restore basic trust:** Family trust involves honesty in communication and dependency in roles and relationships. Trust must be restored between the problem gambler and family members and, if necessary, among other family members. The tendency to think of loss of trust as completely undermining a relationship is often most pronounced in our closest relationships. If someone violates our complete trust, it is easy to conclude that the absence of complete trust is no trust. We often hear people say when they have been lied to by someone close to them, "I'll never trust him again."

As stated earlier, the key to restoring trust is recognizing that it is not an all-or-nothing phenomenon. Close examination will usually indicate that family members continue to trust each other to varying degrees in many family roles and relationships.

Although trust can be disrupted overnight, it neither develops nor is rebuilt overnight. As your family struggles to rebuild this essential foundation of family life, you must understand that a successful effort often takes as long as a year. In the early stages, you will want to focus on those areas of trust that are most critical for addressing problem gambling and beginning the healing process. See chapter 12 for guidelines for restoring trust in family relationships.

4. **Communicate clearly and caringly:** Active listening strengthens the emotional bonds between family members and reassures them

that others in the family care about them, respect them, and are interested in what they have to say. Speaking clearly and openly ensures that others fully understand the meaning behind your words. You can draw on many techniques to improve communication within your family—we discuss several of these in chapter 7. Perhaps most important, though, is the skill of listening and speaking from the heart as well as the mind.

5. **Provide emotional and practical support to each family member:** Because each member of the family will be affected by the presence of problem gambling in different ways, support for each family member may take widely differing forms. Each family member should try to identify the kinds of support he or she needs and not be hesitant to ask for it. For children, emotional support might be as simple as offering reassurance that the family will successfully work through the current crisis, or it might involve a parent or an older sibling devoting extra time to reading, playing, or talking with the young child. For adults, it might take the form of a husband listening to his wife's fears about the well-being of their college-age daughter who has become involved in frequent sports betting. For a couple coping with the problem gambling of one of the partner's elderly parents, it might involve the other partner planning a surprise weekend away—just for fun and relaxation. Similarly, practical support may take many forms. For example, an older child might offer to relieve his mother, from having to prepare dinner on those nights when she attends Gamblers Anonymous meetings.

6. **Seek support from others outside the immediate family:** Support from others may come from relatives, friends, work colleagues, spiritual counselors, members of Gamblers Anonymous, and professional counseling. Try to make use of a wide variety of these resources, for information, advice, emotional backing, and practical aid. Initially, many families feel isolated when forced to deal with a gambling problem. Overcoming that initial isolation is key to solving the problem successfully in the long term. Among friends and relatives—and even among many clerical and mental health professionals—this may require educating them about the nature of problem gambling and its effects before they are able to adequately provide needed forms of support (see chapter 5).

Chapter 5

Coping with the
Emotional Fallout

You may be confronting a range of intense emotions including anxiety, sadness, anger, shame, and guilt. This chapter is designed to help reduce your emotional distress and thereby enable you to deal more effectively with the other problems you are confronting. Before turning to managing your emotions, however, we will examine their role and importance.

The Nature and Function of Emotions

Emotions are both natural and vital to survival. The primary emotions—anxiety or fear, anger, and sadness as well as love and joy—serve to organize and motivate behavior. Anxiety, for example, alerts us to danger and propels us to reduce it by prompting us to avoid or escape a threatening situation. Anger energizes us to respond rapidly to a threat. Sadness emerges in response to a loss; its function is to bind us to others and reinforce social ties to our family, friends, and community. Anxiety/fear and anger are essential for the survival of the individual and sadness is essential for the survival of the community.

Strong emotions also leave complete and permanent imprints on memory. There are events that cause strong emotional reactions that remain in the memories of virtually every member of an entire culture. For example, if you are an American over the age of twenty-five, you will probably remember precisely where you were when the Challenger exploded; if you are over fifty, you will remember where you were when John F. Kennedy was assassinated, and if you are over seventy, you will remember where you were on Pearl Harbor Day. Such memories, sometimes called "flashbulb memories," are permanently imprinted by the strength of the emotions that accompanied the event. Each of us also has experienced many emotionally powerful events in our individual lives that remain burned into our memories. Emotionally powerful experiences often occur in dangerous circumstances; thus permanent memory serves as protection against future mishaps. (In this discussion we are not addressing the question of trauma and memory.)

Although emotions are both necessary and natural, they can be disruptive when any specific emotion is too intense or lasts too long, or too many emotions are present at once (of course we are not speaking of the pleasant emotions like love and joy). With a problem gambler in the family, most people experience intense, long-lasting, and complex emotional experiences such as sadness about the emotional and financial losses and anger at the unfairness of it all. Such feelings may be both painful and disruptive.

Blocks to Emotional Experience

Some individuals may experience the discomfort and disruption caused by intense and complex emotions and yet not be directly aware of the specific emotions. Sometimes people develop physical symptoms instead (e.g., headaches or gastrointestinal difficulties) or they just have general feelings of discomfort and distress which they do not understand. For example, someone may be clearly behaving in an angry manner yet when asked may reply honestly that he does not feel angry. Since emotions generally seem so tangible, immediate, and easy to recognize, you may wonder how emotions can be blocked. This can occur in two ways.

1. **Early learning:** Many families teach their children that they shouldn't feel certain emotions or they should be "strong" enough to overcome them. For example, children may be taught not to feel angry ("How dare you be angry with your mother?") or that sadness is unacceptable and a sign of weakness ("I'll give you something to cry about"). Sometimes, children learn not to experience and identify *any* emotions directly perhaps because they are taught that all emotional experience is unacceptable. Possibly they experienced traumatic events and they "turned off" (or

dissociated from) their emotional experience.

When children are taught not to directly experience their basic emotions of anxiety, sadness, and anger, they may feel shame and guilt when such emotions are evoked. Here's how that works. Shame results from a failure to live up to your expectations of yourself. Guilt results from a failure to live up to deeply held values. If you believe, "I should be strong enough to handle this without getting upset (anxious, depressed)," or, "Only weak people get depressed," then it is likely that you will be ashamed if you feel anxious or depressed and less likely that you will be able to acknowledge these feelings directly. If you believe, "It is wrong to be angry," or, "Only bad people get angry," then you are likely to feel guilty if you experience anger, and again, less likely to acknowledge your anger.

These beliefs, though common, are based on an incomplete understanding of the nature and purpose of emotions. It is also a "double whammy": the unpleasant feeling state is itself compounded by self-criticism, shame, and guilt for having the feeling in the first place.

2. **Denial:** Most people go through an initial period during which they see the evidence of a problem but don't fully appreciate the implications of that evidence. This is common when confronting many problems in life including gambling and is often referred to by the term "denial." Denial can refer to an inability to accept or admit observable facts, the implications of those facts, or responsibility for the implication of those facts (Winn 1996). Although denial is a natural process, it generally has a negative connotation because its negative consequences are more well known than its benefits.

Denial's primary purpose is to protect against being overwhelmed by intense negative emotions. This defense is essential in catastrophic or traumatic situations during which excessive emotion can limit urgently needed effective action.

Yet denial occurs regularly, not only in traumatic situations. Understanding this basic human response to short-term outcomes will help you see why denial is so commonplace. Although we have the capacity to foresee, contemplate, and be influenced by future events, we are by nature more influenced by what will happen immediately than by long-term outcomes. Our ability to see ahead gives us the potential to value long-term over short-term outcomes, but it is frequently difficult to do so. "Do I have dessert?" "Do I exercise today?" Jerry Seinfeld illustrates this dilemma by saying "night guy" doesn't care about "morning guy." Night guy says, "The heck with morning guy, I'm staying up late and having those extra drinks." Then morning guy wakes up with a hangover and is furious with night guy.

Since we respond more to short-term reinforcers and denial protects us from negative emotion, we use denial to protect us from short-term negative emotions even when they are not overwhelming and even when the long-term costs outweigh this short-term gain.

Did you notice that denial refers to an inability to believe something (accept *facts*) but its purpose is to protect us from overwhelming *emotion*? This makes sense because *beliefs lead to emotions*. The primary way denial works is by influencing beliefs to prevent the development of painful emotions.

Magical Thinking

How can we honestly believe one thing when the facts are plainly otherwise? We are all born magical thinkers and only through experience do we learn logical connections about the world. Magical thinking is illogical and creates (or dissolves) connections between events that don't (or do) exist in reality. One example of this would be the child's notion of "If I wish it, it will happen." We all practice magical thinking to some degree. If you experience some medical symptoms and resist going to the doctor because at some level you think, "If it's not diagnosed, then it doesn't exist," you are practicing magical thinking.

At times, we are all unable to confront problems that are staring us in the face and believe instead, despite substantial evidence, that the problem is not there. Sometimes, information is so hard to accept that we briefly forget a facet of reality we know to be true. For example, people may believe for a moment that a person whom they know to be dead is still alive. This phenomenon occurs more regularly soon after a death and becomes less common as time passes and the living person more fully accepts the death of the loved one. Can you see that this is comparable to believing that a family member does not have a gambling problem? "If I don't believe it, it's not a problem."

Gambling and Denial

We often associate denial with the gambler (see chapter 4) who consciously may use denial to mislead or lie about certain facts ("I wasn't gambling"), to deny the clear implication of those facts ("Sure I gamble a little but not at a problem level"), or to minimize responsibility for certain outcomes ("It's the pressure and the demands from your family, not my gambling, that causes all the tension in the family").

Since denial is a natural process that everyone employs occasionally, it is likely that you and your family also use it to some degree. Perhaps it has been hard for you to believe that your relative has a gambling problem and perhaps the other nongamblers in your family also find this hard to believe. For example, the gambler may be out four nights a week but you haven't been "keeping track" and think she is out less often. Or you may know that the gambler is wagering in increasing amounts that have reached $500 per week, but you think that she generally breaks even or loses only a little money each time she gambles so her losses are not a problem.

When you understand how denial works, it is easy to see why many people find it hard to accept that his or her family member has a gambling problem when the gambler denies the problem. Believing something that a family member insists in false means her is lying or deliberately being misleading. For many people, this would lead to a breach of trust, which could undermine the relationship and lead to intense sadness. Because denial protects us from intense sadness, it also undermines the ability to believe the ideas or facts that would produce that emotion.

Here is another example: Someone who accepts the fact that her relative has a gambling problem may feel compelled to do something about it. She may feel that she should *confront* him about the problem, which would lead to increased conflict and anxiety in the short term. Again, we would expect denial to limit her ability to accept the fact that he has a gambling problem because the results of the confrontation will be so emotionally difficult

Overcoming Emotional Blocks

1. Remember that emotions are both natural and vital to our survival. They alert us to important information and motivate us to act. They are not a sign of any weak or bad characteristic.

2. Recognize that your situation is realistically challenging and you are probably confronting multiple stressors (see below). It is normal to have strong and complex emotions such as anger, sadness, and anxiety in such situations.

3. Keep alert for any signs of general emotional distress or discomfort. If you are having increased physical symptoms, *first* check with your physician. If she believes they may be partly stress-related, give thought to whether the situation with the gambler could be evoking emotions that are hard to pinpoint.

4. Look for potential areas of denial. If you or other nongambling members of your family can identify some beliefs about the gambler that might be open to question (about how much he is gambling, for example), think about how you might feel emotionally if you changed your belief. If that changed belief would produce a disturbing emotion, then it is possible you are employing denial as a natural defense against this. This insight may help you to challenge some of your beliefs that are the product of denial.

Following these steps will help you see the situation and your emotions more clearly and reduce any secondary layer of shame and guilt you may be experiencing. By doing so you will free up energy and resources to reduce, manage, and tolerate the original painful feelings.

Managing Your Emotions

We generally experience our feelings as emerging immediately in response to a situation. Actually, as shown in figure 5.1, our thoughts intervene between the situation and our feelings, evaluating and interpreting the situation very rapidly outside our conscious awareness. Our feelings then emerge in response to these thoughts Our perception, interpretation, and understanding of a situation lead to our emotional reaction. (Although there are scientific [see J. LeDoux, *The Emotional Brain*] and theoretical [see W. James, *The Principles of Psychology*] reasons to question whether this useful model is *always 100 percent accurate*, such technical points make little difference for our current purposes.)

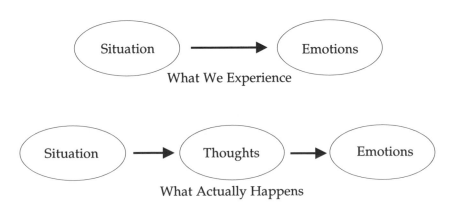

Figure 5.1   A useful model of thoughts and emotions.

To illustrate this process, let's suppose that the gambler has been moody and uncommunicative. You might have a range of emotional reactions including anxiety, sadness, and anger. How would each of these emerge? If the gambler's behavior left you uncertain about whether he might increase his gambling or whether arguments in the whole family might increase, then it is quite likely that you would feel anxious. If his behavior evoked the thought that you would lose his closeness and support, then you would be likely to feel sad. Finally, if you thought it was unfair for him to behave in that manner after all you've done for him, then you would likely be angry. You might have all three of these thoughts in evaluating his behavior, which would lead to a complex and varied emotional response.

This example also illustrates that specific emotions characteristically emerge in response to specific types of interpretations. The following table identifies the characteristic connection between specific thoughts and specific emotions.

Thought	⟶	Emotion
Uncertainty, risk, danger	⟶	Anxiety/fear
Loss, helplessness, hopelessness, personal shortcomings	⟶	Sadness/depression
Unfairness, injustice	⟶	Anger

Identifying the specific stressful situations you face, your thoughts about them and the way you respond emotionally will provide the foundation for specific action steps that will help you to manage your emotional distress.

Identify Your Stressors

You may clearly recognize the pressure you are under but may not have specifically identified each of the many types of stressors in your life. These may include interpersonal, financial, legal, and work-related stressors as well as the vital issue of safety for you and your family.

Each of these general categories of stressors may themselves contain multiple individual stressors. For example, interpersonal stressors alone might include tensions with the gambler, your nuclear family, your extended family and friends, as well as with members of your broader community.

When confronted with multiple stressors, we tend to see them as one overwhelming package. By identifying each one, you can break down an apparently overwhelming problem into more manageable parts. If you were faced with only one of these situations, you'd probably be able to manage it. Therefore, it makes sense to identify and tackle each stressor one by one. Remember the old proverb that a journey of a thousand miles begins with a single step.

Problem gambling adds many difficult situations to the stressors that were already a part of your life. To help identify the specific stressors in your life, refer to table 5.1 which is organized hierarchically into gambling and nongambling-related stressors with broad categories of stressors (e.g., *Interpersonal*) within each of these areas. We have listed specific examples of stressors that occur frequently.

First, check the corresponding box for all the stressors that you are currently confronting. Leave the third and fourth columns (Priority and Emotions) blank for the time being. We will complete these as we proceed through the chapter. Then, write down any additional specific stressors you may be experiencing in your life in the separate journal you have been using to take notes.

Filling out this table may be difficult and may even temporarily increase your anxiety level as you list all the stressful situations that you are facing. Nevertheless, completing this exercise is an important first step for coping with these stressors.

Table 5.1:
Identifying Specific Stressors

Stressor	Check if stressor present	Priority	Emotions
Gambling-related			
Interpersonal			
Gambler is moody, uncommunicative,			
Gambler has been less than truthful			
Child having behavioral problems			

Damaged relationships with some extended family members			
You think friends and neighbors are critical of you			
Community (e.g., church) is unaware of the problem, but you think they will be critical			
Financial			
Rent or mortgage payments overdue			
Unable to meet expenses			
No money for discretionary activities			
Damaged credit			
Substantial gambling debt			
Legal			
Gambler faces legal charges			
If caught, may face legal charges			
Safety			
Gambler possibly at risk for self-injurious behavior			
Gambler may present risk of harm to others			
Nongambling-related			
Work			
High pressure environment			
Change in work status (laid off, transferred, etc.)			
Medical			
You are ill			
Family member is ill			
Interpersonal			
Parents require care			
Relative is having a hard time and needs support			

Loss of a valued relationship			
Other			
Volunteer activities			
Duties at child's school			

Action Step 1: Prioritize

Although not easy, generating this list of demands and stressful situations is an important first step. Probably almost every one is important. Even so, some will stand out as more urgent than others. For example, if you have included issues of safety, you will probably agree that these take the highest priority followed closely by ensuring that your family's essential needs for housing and food are maintained. Now return to table 5.1 and assign each of your current stressors a priority rating of A (the highest), B or C. Try to limit the number of stressors to which you assign a priority of A. Prioritizing helps you to figure out where you should devote your efforts first.

Action Step 2: Reduce the Demands on Yourself (If Possible)

After prioritizing these multiple demands and stressors, you probably will see that most of them form an essential and unavoidable part of the fabric of your life. However, you probably have some discretionary responsibilities that you can handle comfortably in normal times but not during periods of acute stress. For example, perhaps you have duties as part of the parents' organization at your child's school. You have generally enjoyed this activity and believed it was fair for you to contribute your share. However, it may be that during this critical period in your life you do not have the time to manage this responsibility as well as all the additional ones you now confront. Review the list of stressors in the table above. See if there are any that you might temporarily discontinue while you wrestle with the immediate problems you currently face, knowing that in the long run you will actually have more energy to devote to such less urgent tasks.

Identify Your Thoughts

As figure 5.1 shows, we generally experience our feelings immediately in response to situations. Thus, it intuitively seems that we have little control over the emergence of our feelings. Yet in fact, our thoughts intervene rapidly to evaluate the situation; it is our thoughts that produce our feelings. Since our interpretation is potentially open to change, it follows that it is possible to prevent or change the emergence of emotions by changing our thinking.

This is not to suggest that you can change your thoughts easily and your painful feelings will just go away. Realistically, you are likely facing many difficult situations that naturally lead to painful emotions. However, there are characteristic ways that people think that *unnecessarily increases the intensity* of painful emotions. The three most common types of counter-productive thinking are overgeneralizing, engaging in all-or-nothing thinking, and excessive self-blame.

Overgeneralization

The ability to generalize is a hallmark of human intelligence. But just as denial can create difficulties, so too can generalization. Because you have so many stressors, you may have the tendency to conclude "Everything's in upheaval." Such a general statement is likely to lead to thoughts of "I'm overwhelmed, I can't cope, everything is uncertain," which characteristically will produce intense anxiety. By identifying stressors specifically, as above, and by simultaneously resisting the tendency to overgeneralize about the entire situation, you can reduce the intense and extra overlay of feelings that will be produced by this interpretation.

You may also find yourself generalizing from your current situation into the indefinite future. For example, you may have suffered financial losses—a *fact* that would produce sadness in most people. You may overgeneralize and conclude, "We'll never recover." This overgeneralization, consistent with hopelessness, may lead to intense sadness and possibly even depression.

All-or-Nothing Thinking

All-or-nothing thinking is black and white; there are no grays. For example, if the gambler has lied, all-or-nothing thinking concludes that he is a bad person. The reasoning would go like this: people are either good or bad; since he engaged in bad behavior, he is no longer good and must be a bad person. There is no room for the idea that essentially good people can engage in bad behavior. In chapter 4, we saw that all-or-nothing thinking is often applied to the element of trust in a relationship, thus intensifying the already painful feelings. Many people apply all-or-nothing thinking to themselves.

Excessive Self-Blame

Excessive self-blame generally results from unreasonable standards combined with all-or-nothing thinking. Faced with formidable stressors, many people have a tendency to blame themselves. For example, if your son is gambling, you might think, "I should have seen this coming; I could have prevented this; I should have spent more time with him. It's my fault and I am a worthless parent." There may or may not be any truth to the first three statements. At any rate, you can take a careful look to see where you might have made mistakes that you can learn from, and where you did things well that you can build on. The conclusion that you are a worthless parent, however, would likely be based on the extremely unreasonable standard that you should be a perfect parent combined with all-or-nothing reasoning that one is either a perfect parent or a worthless one. Drawing such a conclusion is likely to lead to feelings of intense sadness and even depression, a common by-product of excessive self-blame.

Action Step 3: Challenge
Counter-Productive Thinking

These three counter-productive methods of thinking—overgeneralizing, all-or-nothing thinking, and excessive self-blame—will produce ideas that intensify your difficult emotions. You can recognize the results of this type of thinking by the broad, categorical, and hopeless conclusions they produce. When you feel intense disruptive emotions, be alert for these counter-productive thoughts and challenge them. Are these thoughts realistic and logical? If not, replace them with more realistic and productive thoughts as illustrated in Table 5.2.

Table 5.2
How to Challenge Counter-Productive Thoughts

Counter-productive thought	Productive thought
There are so many problems, it is useless to try to solve any of them. (Overgeneralization)	I have many problems; I will address them one by one. I will tackle what I can directly, and get help and guidance on the problems that I can't address by myself.
My relationship with my entire family is permanently ruined. (Overgeneralization)	A number of my family members are angry with me; some are supportive. I will seek support from those who are available and work to repair the other relationships over the long term.

I should be able to care for and protect my mother now. She always took care of me when I needed it. I should be able to fix this problem now. (Excessive self-blame)	I can rally my siblings to try to convince my mother to stop gambling. We can also try to convince her to put her major savings in a place she can't access so quickly and easily. However, she is mentally alert and not depressed and we cannot control her life at this point. I will get professional help to see if there is another way to keep her from losing all her money.
My son is doing terribly in his life now; his future is certainly ruined. (Overgeneralization)	This is a very bad period for him. We are getting professional help and we will keep working to get him through this. Although no one can predict the future, many adolescents go through tumultuous periods and ultimately do okay. I'll do everything I can to help him achieve that outcome.
My partner is a good-for-nothing bum. (All or nothing thinking)	My partner has done several very bad things. He continues to have some good qualities. I will continue to explore whether we can resolve this sufficiently to preserve our relationship in the long run.

Keep an eye out for such counter-productive thoughts, which lead to a downward spiral of increased emotional distress and decreased behavioral effectiveness. When you spot them, do your best to replace them with more accurate and productive thoughts that will alleviate the downward spiral of emotions and may reverse it.

Identify Your Emotions

To help identify the specific emotions you experience in each stressful situation, now turn back to Table 5.1. In the fourth column fill in the emotion(s) that you experience in each situation. Also try to identify your interpretation (thoughts) about each situation. Are these thoughts consistent with your emotions? For example, in response to "payments overdue," if you felt anxiety, then you might discover that thoughts about future uncertainties are present. If you felt anger, then you might realize that you were thinking how unjust it is that the gambler has squandered your money.

When doing this exercise, remember two key points. First, there are five primary negative emotional states—anxiety/fear; sadness/depression; anger; shame; and guilt. Although there are many different words for negative emotions, they can be categorized under these five primary ones. For example, worried, apprehensive, tense, jittery, fretful, and alarmed all fall under the general heading of anxiety/fear. Second, remember that we can experience several emotions at the same time so be sure to consider the full range of your feelings.

Action Step 4: Express Your Emotions

In chapter 7, you will learn how to express your emotions to the problem gambler appropriately. However, when taking care of your own emotional state, it is most helpful if you can express your feelings to others in a supportive and open manner. Is there a friend or family member with whom you would feel comfortable doing this? Is there a support group available? Perhaps there is a Gam–Anon in your area that is a support group for family members and is distinct from Gamblers Anonymous (see Appendix A). Can you find support through your church, temple, or community organization? Should you consider seeking professional guidance in order to manage these feelings? Later in this chapter, you will find detailed information on how to get this support (see also chapter 10).

If none of these resources is available to you, consider, at a minimum, writing down your thoughts and feelings, in a daily or weekly journal. Writing helps many people to clarify their thoughts and feelings as well as enhancing effective problem solving. Expressing your emotions in writing also can help to calm yourself (and could be included under Action Step 5) but it is listed separately here because it has widespread benefits.

Action Step 5: Calm Your Emotions

In this action step, we will briefly describe a number of methods that will help you to calm your emotions. See the end of this chapter for books that provide more detailed information. Different calming techniques appeal to different people. In addition, different techniques are often more suitable for specific basic emotions.

* **Slow, deep breathing (to help decrease anxiety, anger)**

Our minds and bodies are fully connected. When our emotions intensify, our heart rate, blood pressure, muscle tension, and rate of breathing increase as well. Anxiety or anger in our minds is accompanied by tension in our muscles. Relaxing our muscles and slowing down our breathing has the opposite effect: our emotional arousal decreases. This means that we can achieve a psychological benefit (anxiety or anger reduction) by making a physiological change (relax muscles, slow breathing).

There are other examples of this mind-body connection that you may already know. For instance, have you ever found that physical activity such as a walk or a run decreases your anxiety or improves your mood? Using medication to achieve a psychological benefit or drinking alcohol to calm down (although alcohol is less constructive) is based on the same principle: You can achieve a psychological change by means of a physical intervention.

There are many different relaxation techniques for which slow, deep breathing forms the foundation. Breathing is a natural process we do without conscious thought or effort but we can also voluntarily control it. By consciously breathing slowly and diaphragmatically, we can relax our bodies. Diaphragmatic breathing, often called belly breathing, is the way we breathe normally when we are completely relaxed. The diaphragm is a muscle in the stomach region that controls breathing. When it moves down and out (the stomach area visibly puffs out), it allows the lungs to expand. As the diaphragm moves up and in (the stomach area appears to contract), it compresses the lungs, thus forcing the air out.

So, when we breathe in, our belly expands, and when we breathe out it falls back in. If you have ever watched someone sleep on his or her back, you may have observed this. Sometimes, however, when we breathe deliberately, we use our chest muscles to breathe and suck in our stomach as we inhale. Check to see if you are belly breathing by placing your hands on your stomach. If your stomach puffs out as you breathe in and falls back as you breathe out, you are belly breathing. If not, just let your hands rest on your belly and follow your breathing for a minute or so. Don't breathe in any special way, just allow the regular process to continue and follow it. You should find after a short while that you are belly breathing.

When you are comfortable with belly breathing, you are ready to move on to the exercise. To practice, find a quiet place and place your hands on your stomach. Allow yourself to focus on your breathing for a minute or so. Follow your breathing as the air moves in and out of your body. After a short time (about a minute, but don't time it), let yourself take a breath that's just a little slower and a little deeper than usual. Breathe out slowly. Notice how the tension leaves your body as you breathe out. Now repeat that slow breath about four more times. That's it. The whole exercise should take less than two minutes. Most people find that if they practice this breathing about five times per day, that they become increasingly skilled at calming their bodies. This calms the mind and the emotions.

* Visualization (to help decrease anxiety, anger)

Do you ever have vivid daydreams during which you fully imagine that you are in a certain situation? Do you experience emotions during these daydreams that are consistent with the situation you are imagining? This natural process can be harnessed to help manage your emotions.

To do so, imagine a place you find calm and peaceful. It can be anyplace—somewhere that you have been to, or read about, or a place you only imagine. It can be the seashore, the mountains, the city, anyplace you like—indoors or outdoors. You can be alone or with other people. It's up to you. Pick a place and circumstances that you find calm and peaceful. Now close your eyes and imagine yourself there. See yourself there as clearly and vividly as possible. Try to see clearly all the things that are there. In your mind's eye look all around. Let yourself be there and feel all the feelings that come from being there. Stay there for a while and allow calm feelings to envelop you. When you are ready, gently open your eyes, remaining calm and relaxed and knowing that you can return to this special place when you choose.

* Activity (to help decrease anxiety, sadness, and anger)

Being active in some engaging, meaningful, or fun way when your emotions are aroused is helpful but can be challenging to accomplish. For example, if you are feeling blue, you are likely to notice an improvement in your mood if you do something you find meaningful or if you exercise (in accordance with your fitness level and doctor's recommendations). However, often when you are feeling sad, you won't have the energy to think about preparing for the activity. For example, if taking a walk outside would be your chosen activity, you might not want to locate and change into walking shoes and suitable clothing.

If you prepare in advance, you will find it easier to have the activity available as an active coping method when you are anxious, sad, or angry. To do so, first create a list of activities that you like and that are available to you. This might include walking, jogging, gardening, shopping, reading, watching a movie, painting, or exploring the Internet. Next to each activity, note what practical preparations you need to make so you can move readily into the activity (e.g., have gardening clothes and tools easily accessible). Now anticipate that you may be feeling anxious or sad at some point in the coming days and plan (while you are feeling *relatively* better) to do that activity when you start to feel anxious. This minimizes the necessity for active decision making and preparation at the time you are acutely distressed.

Getting Support from Family, Friends, and the Broader Community

There is a wealth of literature demonstrating that support from other people improves physical health, prolongs life, and decreases depression and anxiety. Social support has these profound benefits in ordinary times and is even more important in times of acute stress. Social support yields these broad benefits by providing help in many areas including the following:

* expressing your feelings; * thinking through practical solutions; * accessing additional resources; and * helping with tasks during a time that your burdens are heavy.

There are three steps to getting this support: (1) identify potential sources of support, (2) allow yourself to access that support, and (3) ask for support.

Action Step 6: Identify Sources of Support

You can do this exercise alone or with other members of your family. It involves preparing a separate list for each family member of all-important relationships (see Table 5.3). For each family member, list any and all individuals with whom each family member has had supportive contact, either on a regular or an infrequent basis. The contact could be face-to-face or by telephone, e-mail, or letter. How often you or other family members have contact is less important than the quality of that contact.

Supportive contact can take many forms. People can give or lend money or the use of possessions. They may help the family member with carrying out a task or doing a project. This could range from giving a family member a ride to school, to a co-worker helping you to meet a deadline on a work project, to a friend dropping by to help you clean out your garage. Another kind of support involves advice, guidance, or information received from others. Still another kind of support involves sharing thoughts and feelings in conversation. And yet another kind can involve doing something together for leisure, like going to the movies, watching TV together, or going for a drive in the country (Keane, Scott, Chavoya, et al., 1985). Frequently a relationship will involve several of these forms of support.

Often when we think of important relationships, we think of a few close relatives, our closest friends, perhaps our next-door neighbor, and maybe a few colleagues at work. Thinking of relationships in terms of these kinds of supportive contacts should stimulate you to cast your net more widely. We encourage you to consider including members of your nuclear family; extended family such as aunts, uncles, cousins, nephews, and nieces; in-laws; friends; neighbors; co-workers; and any others in the community who provide emotional or practical support, including teachers, clergy, co-worshippers at a place of worship, and fellow members of clubs and community organizations. We have listed each of these categories in Table 5.3. (We have left space on the sample table if you wish to use it to prepare your own list, but you may need additional pages.) There are also several lines for you to fill in categories of individuals or groups that we haven't included.

Since you are listing the important relationships for each family member, it's a good idea to include the gambler and other family members, including children, in this activity. Even young school-age children can be asked to suggest names for their lists. You can introduce them to the task by simply explaining you are putting together lists of all the important people in the family's life who support and care for family members. You can do this as a group, or you can ask individual family members to put together their own lists. If you think creatively and include *all* who have provided support to your family in one way or another, the number of names on the lists may amaze you by the time you and other family members have finished. One important by-product of doing this exercise is often a newfound appreciation for just how many people contribute something positive to your family life in one way or another.

Once you have completed the list of people with whom you or other family members have had past supportive contact, think broadly to identify possible new supportive resources as well. In addition to acquaintances, neighbors, co-workers, and others, these could include support groups like Gam-Anon, an employee assistance program at your workplace, or professionals who provide either psychological or financial counseling. Review the list of resources for problem gamblers and their families in Appendix A to identify resources that you could access in your area by phone, mail, or via the Internet.

Table 5.3: Important Supportive Relationships

Possibilities	List Specific Individuals or Groups
Current (nuclear) family	
Family-of-origin	
Extended family	
Friends	
Work friends	
Neighborhood friends	
Other friends	
Support group (e.g., Gam-Anon)	
Clergy	
Contacts from church, temple, etc.	
Organizational support groups	

Employee assistance program	
Professional counseling	
Financial counselor	

Once you have identified some resources you can access, objectively weigh the pros and cons of each (it is helpful to write these down), and identify those that are most appropriate for you. Don't rule out any resources because you don't think you are entitled to support or don't know how to ask for it.

Action Step 7: Allow Yourself to Seek Support

Earlier in this chapter, we addressed the commonly held, but unhelpful ideas that you must be strong enough to handle everything by yourself, that you shouldn't be a burden to others, and that you are "not entitled" to get social support. We encourage you to challenge and correct these mistaken ideas. At times, we all need help in meeting life's challenges. The need for support is all the greater during times of increased stress such as you are now confronting.

Because people tend to keep problems secret, it might appear to you that few families you know include a problem gambler as a family member. However, keep in mind that about 4 percent of the population experience gambling problems. If, on the average, each problem gambler has another 2.5 people in his or her immediate family, then 10 percent of people will confront this problem in their immediate families.

Other families have different problems. For example, some 12 to 14 percent of us will have at least one major depression in our lives; more than 10 percent of us will have a substance abuse problem (DSM-IV 1994).

Problems are not rare—only hidden.

In most cases, people will be understanding. Of course, this is not universally true; a small percentage of people will be critical. If you do seek support from some who turn out to be critical, listen carefully to what they have to say. In many cases, you will find that their criticism tells you something about them—not about you or your family. It may tell you that they are not well-informed about this particular area or that they hold strong views which limit their ability to provide support.

For example, imagine that you tell someone you are anxious because your spouse has a gambling problem and you are in a financial bind. If that person replies, "Gambling is wrong and you should just leave him," you have gotten a lot of information about that person. In such a case, it offers no insight into you, your spouse, or your situation. By anticipating ways that people might be critical and by thinking through what that criticism might mean to you, you are less likely to fear the results of that encounter and more likely to allow yourself to seek the support you, like all of us, need to receive.

Nevertheless, your concerns about possible criticism might limit your willingness to seek support if you have one of the following beliefs:

1. Most people will be critical of you.

2. Someone will be critical of you *and* it is unacceptable to you if anyone is critical of you.

Again, our experience has shown that most people will not be critical if given a chance to understand the situation. The second belief is another example of a counter-productive belief.

In this case, it is likely to lead to feelings of shame that can block you from seeking support. To the extent that you are able to adopt beliefs that set a reasonable rather than excessive standard, you will be able to reduce feelings of shame and allow yourself to seek the support that you need. For example, your thoughts might move toward the productive idea that "Some people will probably be critical of me, and although this may not be desirable, it doesn't mean I am a bad person just because they are critical. I will do my best to repair relations with them but I cannot control how they will respond."

Action Step 8: How to Seek Support

The basic guidelines below will help you to actually ask for support. You can make minor modifications depending on which individual(s) or group(s) you approach.

1. Inform them you have a problem you'd like to discuss.

2. Ask if it would be okay to do so and, if so, when.

3. Give an overview of the situation that includes the general problem, a specific practical impact and a specific emotional impact. If you are also asking for help with a specific responsibility, then include that as well. For example, "My son, John, is spending

many hours every week gambling (*general problem*), he is missing school (*practical impact*), and I am frightened about what will ultimately happen (*emotional impact*). With all that is going on, I need to spend more time with John and wonder if you could help out looking after my daughter Rose from twelve to four for the next two Saturdays."

4. Allow the person to respond. There are a number of different responses that can be helpful including sympathetic understanding, asking for more information, agreeing to your request and working with you to explore other ideas and resources that can be brought to bear on your situation. Although they may not be able to help in just the way you've suggested, they may help in some other way. Stay open to suggestions and be flexible.

5. If you find their initial response supportive, you may more comfortably go further in your conversation.

6. If you find their initial response nonsupportive (e.g., "I told you that kid would come to no good"), you may elect to discontinue the conversation (having learned something about that person), or you may elect to give it one more try and let them know that a more sympathetic and understanding response would be more helpful. They may have many valid reasons for being unable to meet your request, including greater demands in their own lives than they can manage.

Putting It All Together

Managing your emotions includes the following steps:

1. Understand the relations between your stressors, thoughts, and emotions.

2. Identify your stressors; when possible reduce them.

3. Identify your thoughts, challenge counter-productive thinking.

4. Identify your emotions; express and calm your emotions.

5. Identify and access resources to provide emotional and practical support and to help you solve problems.

Let's look at an example to see how these steps can be turned into specific action plans to help with managing your emotions and with moving toward problem resolution. Suppose that Jane's husband has been gambling heavily for two years and denying it for most of that time. In addition, they have lost their savings, many of their possessions, and have significant debt. Jane's initial view of these circumstances is, "Everything's in upheaval. We have a huge financial debt. I've lost many of my treasured possessions, and my husband lied to me and others." These views are listed in the stressor column. Under the column labeled Thoughts, you will see Jane's initial thoughts about these stressors. The emotions these thoughts evoke are listed in the third column. In the fourth column, we summarize how Jane can turn the information from this chapter into an action plan.

Table 5.4:
How to Create an Action Plan

Stressor	Thoughts	Emotion	Action plan
Everything's in upheaval	I can't cope; I'm overwhelmed. Our family is ruined.	Anxiety, sadness	1. Be more precise about the situational stressors. 2. Reduce stressors if possible. 3. Replace counter-productive thoughts with more specific, accurate, and productive ones. 4. Calm emotions. 5. Seek support.
Financial debt	We are in financially perilous waters with uncertain outcome.	Anxiety	1. Establish financial action plan. (See chapter 9.) 2. Use anxiety reduction techniques.
Financial and material losses	We have lost a great deal. We will never recover.	Sadness	1. Recognize necessary grieving for loss as natural (and time-limited). 2. Use sadness reduction techniques. 3. Challenge counter-productive idea that you will "never" recover. 4. Establish financial plan. (See Chapter 9.)

Gambler lied	I can't trust him at all. This damages our relationship. He has been unfair to me.	Anger, sadness	1. See the sections on trust in chapters 4 and 12. 2. Establish the extent and limits of violation. 3. Honor sadness as appropriate for damage to relationship. 4. Practice sadness reduction techniques.

We have covered a lot of material rapidly in this chapter. Books that provide more in-depth coverage of some of these areas are shown below. Remember, too, that stressful situations and intense emotions suggest that exploring whether counseling would be a wise course, might be appropriate with a professional.

Suggested Readings

Greenberger, D., and C. A. Padesky. 1995. *Mind Over Mood: Change How You Feel by Changing the Way You Think.* New York: Guilford Press.

McKay, M., M. Davis, and P. Fanning. 1998. *Thoughts and Feelings: Taking Control of Your Moods and Your Life.* Oakland: New Harbinger.

Chapter 6

What You Can and Can't Do to Help

Understanding all of the issues pertaining to self-control and responsibility for gambling is challenging for family members and controversial among clinicians. Do people control their behavior? If so, why do gamblers seem unable to stop even when gambling threatens to ruin everything they care about? If gamblers are not in control, how can we hold them responsible? But if we don't hold them responsible, don't we make it more difficult for them to learn and practice self-control? Unfortunately, there is no single, widely agreed upon model to aid us in understanding this issue of responsibility. Nevertheless, although we cannot settle this complex matter once and for all, we have developed a balanced model of responsibility to provide a framework for interacting with your family member.

Assuming people are responsible for their behavior allows us to work together and influence each other in positive ways. This *everyday model* of responsibility is exemplified in our legal system. The law holds each of us responsible for our behavior unless we were too impaired to differentiate right from wrong. Only a tiny minority of defendants are judged not guilty for their actions because they were unable to control their behavior due to "insanity."

Generally, holding individuals responsible works well, but it has its limitations. When applied to some behavioral problems in the areas of mental health or addictions, the result can be harmful.

Therefore, the *disease model*, with its origins in medicine, has been used to explain behavioral problems. In this model, an internal force acts on an individual causing the illness and victimizing him. He suffers the results of the illness and must fight to find a remedy. The patient is not considered in control of the symptoms but he is expected to seek treatment.

The disease model of behavior is so different from our everyday model of responsibility that we can become confused as to which to use. Do we hold ourselves and others responsible for certain behaviors, or do we try to understand those behaviors as the result of factors outside our control, maybe even outside our awareness? Looking at the long-running nature versus nurture debate suggests that this question poses the alternatives too starkly. For many years, the controversy in that debate centered on this question: are we primarily influenced by our genetic makeup and biology (nature), which is generally considered outside our control, or by experience and learning (nurture), more commonly seen as within our control? After many years of heated argument, it is clear that *both* the factors not in our control, such as genetic predisposition, and the factors within our control, such as our views of right and wrong, govern the vast majority of our behavior.

Tom is a sixteen-year-old who has been in Gamblers Anonymous for about a year. Both his parents were problem gamblers who have been abstinent for more than five years. When Tom first began gambling with friends after school, he loved it immediately. He began to play for larger amounts of money, with school and family problems following quickly. Within two years, he had attended his first Gamblers Anonymous meeting with his parents and had started on the road to recovery.

It is likely that this young man has a biological predisposition toward gambling as his family history and his early response to gambling suggest. That is only part of Tom's story. He had a choice of how to respond to this problem. With the informed support and guidance of his parents, and the help of a professional counselor, Tom joined a self-help group and stopped gambling. If he is like most gamblers, his recovery will include some lapses (see chapter 12), but with persistent effort and the support of others, he probably will gain mastery over gambling. His experience illustrates certain basic truths about responsibility, self-control, and gambling.

A Balanced Model of Responsibility

It is undeniable that many variables outside our control affect our behavior. Genetics plays an important role in a wide range of human experience, from shyness to depression to substance abuse. Learning during the first few years of life also has the power to push us toward some actions. Although many of the resulting behaviors— including gambling—are affected by factors outside our conscious choice, they can be brought within our control. When behaviors arise that threaten our interests, we are usually motivated to find ways to gain control over them. The process of taking control of a problem behavior such as gambling depends on many factors, including how strongly the behavior is driven by genetics and other biological variables, the resources the person has for learning to control this behavior, and her motivation. The degree to which a person believes that she is responsible for gaining control over her gambling is directly related to her motivation to change.

The gambler's belief that he is responsible for his own behavior is highly influenced by the beliefs of those around him. Holding someone responsible for gambling helps to motivate him to gain control. It communicates confidence that the person can change. Communicating the view the gambler is not responsible for his behavior— that he is a victim of factors outside his control or that he is not capable of gaining control—diminishes his motivation to change.

In some cases, there is a limited capacity to be responsible. This is true for young children, sometimes true for the mentally ill, and sometimes true for those older gamblers whose gambling is related to an illness that impairs self-control. When the capacity to be responsible is limited, family members must look for ways to assume responsibility.

What You Can Do

The balanced model of responsibility can serve as a framework for understanding what you as a family member can and can't do to help.

Be responsible for yourself. Hold yourself responsible for your own life including the choices you make and how you interact with the gambler. Remind yourself that you are always making choices: choices to be around the gambler, choices about how you view the problem. Like the gambler, you may not have made the initial decision to do things the way you are currently doing them. You may even think that you cannot change yourself; but you can. This is the same challenge the gambler faces—to gain control of a problem area—but it is your choice.

For example, a young woman told a psychologist that her boyfriend was driving her crazy. He had been gambling uncontrollably for two years and had resisted all her efforts to get him to stop. She complained that his gambling was causing her to lose her health, her life savings, and her self-respect. She had become obsessed with his gambling and didn't know why she stayed with him. The psychologist asked her, "Who are you here for, him or yourself?" She was surprised by the question. "For him of course. He has the problem. I don't gamble. I don't need the help—he does." The psychologist replied, "He is not here—he is not seeking help. I cannot help him. . . . You are here, and though you may not think so, you appear to need help. I could help you if you want to change something in your life." She realized that in truth she was there for herself. She did want to change how she felt. She then focused on her problems: her obsession with his gambling, her decisions to allow him to control her health, finances, and self-image. Eventually, she began to find solutions.

Be clear that the gambler is responsible for gambling and the problems it causes. Many factors may tempt you to place the responsibility elsewhere—on gambling friends, on your relative's stress at work or school, on fate, or maybe on yourself. Although, these factors may contribute to the gambling, and understanding their role may be helpful, they cannot be ultimately responsible.

Exercise 6-1: Responsibility is communicated in very subtle ways. Listen carefully to yourself to understand what you are communicating about responsibility. In your journal, write down the statements you have made about the following topics. Think about what these statements may be communicating to your relative:

1. What are the causes of your relative's gambling?

2. Who is responsible for finding a way to stop the gambling?

3. When the gambling causes problems for you, do you get angry, and if so, with whom?

4. What reasons, if any, do you give for the gambler having trouble stopping?

5. What excuses, if any, do you make for your relative?

6. Do you feel guilt or a sense of failure with respect to the gambling? What do these feelings indicate about how you see your role?

Provide support. Support can take many forms including listening, encouraging, providing specific help, at times even prodding or confronting. Support does not take away the responsibility from the person; it enhances it. Support communicates the belief, "I know you are working on a difficult problem and I will help you meet your goal."

Know and express what you feel and need. Your feelings and thoughts are important to communicate and will be of value to you and your relative. Your feelings about the situation provide important information the gambler needs to make decisions about his or her gambling. One of the gambler's responsibilities is to participate in the relationship with you. Perhaps you expect less and less from the gambler: less expression of love and support, less help solving problems, less communication , less of everything. This is not helpful either for the gambler or you. She needs to know what you feel about the situation. She needs to know what you want and need from her so that she is clear about what your expectations are in your relationship with her.

Help identify resources for the gambler. Often when gamblers are ready to change, they don't know where to turn or what resources are available. Even for the highly motivated gambler, accessing the needed resources can be a challenge. Without taking responsibility for the problem, you can help identify resources such as information about gambling, sources of professional treatment, support groups like Gamblers Anonymous, and other help such as financial counselors. (See Appendix A.)

Set limits and stick to them. In all relationships, rules are important guides for behavior. They are necessary to ensure that the relationship stays healthy for everyone. Gambling can tempt people to begin breaking rules and crossing boundaries. Maintaining the rules in the face of problem gambling can be a challenge. It takes persistence, assertiveness, and unflagging hope for the future of the relationship. One common mistake is to set limits but not to enforce them consistently. This communicates that the rules are not actually important. By consistently pointing out where your relative breaks the basic rules in the relationship, you will help him change.

In cases of reduced capacity to be responsible, take responsibility. If a young child or impaired older adult is at risk because of gambling, you can and should step in to ensure safety and to restore order to her life.

What You Cannot Do

Don't take responsibility for the gambler. To act as though *you* rather than your relative will be the one who is going to stop her gambling simply doesn't work. You cannot control someone else, and you certainly can't control something she isn't controlling. In addition to setting yourself up for failure, you inadvertently send the wrong message. When you act as if you can control her problem, you imply that she is not able to or does not have to control it. Such a message undermines her motivation to change and is demeaning. Your attitude implies that the problem gambler is less capable than others of controlling and being responsible for her own behavior.

Don't rescue the gambler from the consequences of his actions. Instead of focusing on helping the gambler gain control of his gambling, many relatives find themselves working hard to rescue their relative from the consequences of that gambling. This can include such efforts as helping to pay off gambling debts or trying to intervene in relationships damaged by gambling. More subtle efforts, although well-meaning, are not constructive. Such efforts typically take the form of family members trying to relieve the immediate distress of the gambler by denying their own anger or damaged trust in the gambler, or downplaying the importance of the losses caused by the gambling. Family members may see short-term benefits in fixing the most immediate problem caused by the gambling. They may think that the consequences are the only part of the picture they can change. They may think, too, that helping the gambler escape his predicament may improve their relationship with him. Unfortunately, these motivations fail to reflect the central truth: *gambling is the root of the problem.* The consequences, in all their varied forms, actually make continued gambling undesirable for the problem gambler. Rescuing him from the consequences often reduces his motivation to change.

Don't enable the gambler. In chapter 4, we defined enabling as any action that makes it easier for the gambler to gamble. This group of responses by family members is one of the most destructive and least understood. Typically, family members must work hard to recognize ways in which they make gambling easier for their relative. Sometimes enabling is very direct. Examples include providing money or transportation for gambling or gambling alongside the relative. Often, however, the dynamics of enabling are more indirect. Some relatives provide subtle encouragement to gamble. A parent may feel that his teenager's gambling is beneficial because of the friends the child now has. When feelings such as these are communicated to the gambler, and this is often done indirectly, they reinforce the gambling. Finally, mixed messages about the ultimate responsibility for gambling and its consequences can encourage further gambling.

Co-dependent behaviors, which include rescuing and enabling, are often difficult to identify and change. Often they are unconsciously motivated. Becoming aware of co-dependent behaviors is therefore an important goal for all relatives. Exercise 6-2 is designed to help you begin identifying signs of co-dependency. Often, a professional counselor is needed to help unravel the complex pattern of motives. Co-dependent behaviors are your responsibility and you should learn how to discontinue them.

Exercise 6-2: Self-review is the first step in identifying co-dependent behaviors. In your separate journal, answer the following questions to draw out possible clues. Think about how your answers may support or encourage your relative's gambling.

1. List the items your relative needs to continue gambling (e.g., money, transportation, etc.)

2. For each item identified in question 1, identify anyone, including yourself, who helps provide that resource.

3. List any positive feelings you have ever had about your relative's gambling. Here are some examples to stimulate your thoughts.

   a. Positive feelings about what the gambling means about him (e.g., he is fearless, exciting, intelligent, wealthy, fun, popular, etc.)

   b. Positive feelings about what the gambling means about you (e.g., you are living an exciting life, you are proud of having a relative who is well liked, you are needed by the gambler, you are a "better person" than the gambler.)

   c. Positive feelings about what the gambling gives to you or your relative (e.g., money won, friends, excitement, prestige, opportunities to help him.)

   d. Any beliefs the gambler may have about what you like or liked about his gambling.

4. List some consequences of his gambling that you have helped him avoid, e.g., debts, conflict with others, guilt.

5. List some ways you may have communicated to your relative that he is not responsible for his gambling.

Don't ignore safety issues. Problem gambling can lead to increased risk of self-harm and harm to others. The risk is real and action may be necessary. If you think your relative may be a danger to himself or others, turn to chapter 11.

Don't give up. Although in some situations, giving up on the relationship may be appropriate (see chapter 12), more often family members feel the urge to give up when it is in their best interest to persist. Recovering from problem gambling is often a long process. It has many ups and downs. To be a supportive family member to a person with a gambling problem is like climbing an emotional Mount Everest. It is daunting. It takes great problem-solving ability and emotional fortitude, but above all, it takes persistence. Avoid giving up because of short-term trials. Persevering for the long-term benefits must be a central goal of each family member who is committed to helping.

What to Do When the Gambler Is a Child or Teenager

Generally, we don't hold children to the same level of responsibility as we do adults and for good reason. They do not have the capacity for self-control that adults have. They are less likely to be able to gain control over problem behaviors as quickly as adults. And yet, the temptation to hold a young gambler less responsible for his or her gambling is ill-advised. The truth is that youngsters, like their adult counterparts, can overcome their gambling only by finding ways to control it. Parents can, and in some situations, should step in to eliminate possible opportunities for gambling, but typically this is a stop-gap solution. The youngsters will still need to develop the skills and supports to stop by their own choice.

Given that perspective, parents must strive to maintain their children's safety (see chapter 11) but also to help their children establish internalized patterns of good behavior. The gambler's age will determine what degree of parental control and responsibility is appropriate. The older the teenager or young adult, the more the parent will want to focus on helping the gambler gain his or her own control over the problem.

Prevention: The Best Approach with Children and Teenagers

There are a number of ways to intervene with your children before they have an opportunity to develop gambling problems. First and foremost is to educate your children. Gambling is an attractive but potentially dangerous activity that will be a part of many children's lives. Like drugs, alcohol, sex, and other similar topics, parents and other caring relatives should provide children with the information they need to make informed decisions about gambling. By the time children are twelve, they will be exposed to many advertisements for lotteries, casinos, racetracks, and other gambling opportunities.

When to approach them. There is no set age to talk with kids about the dangers of gambling. Research suggests that many twelve-year-olds have already begun gambling (The WAGER 1996). Moreover, they may be gambling in surprising and illegal ways. In New York, a study conducted by the City Council found that 11 percent of businesses that were investigated sold scratch-off lottery tickets to teens aged fifteen to sixteen (New York Times, 8/19/1999, p. B6). Therefore, talk with your children early in ways that are appropriate to their age. Children may or may not raise questions about gambling, so you should not wait for them to ask.

How to approach them. Be casual and conversational. Engage in dialogue with your child rather than lecturing. You might want to ask some questions first, to gauge their understanding. Does your child know what a lottery is? Has he or she ever bet on anything? If so, what kinds of gambling did your child do? Card games, sports betting, a lottery? Did she bet money? Have your child's friends ever bet money?

Content to Discuss

* Discuss basic terms and concepts, such as betting, gambling, and chance or probability (e.g., how gambling games work and how probability works to ensure that in most games money is lost—particularly over time [see Appendix B]). Compare the probability of winning at gambling and the probability of other events. Use vivid examples. For example, the chance of being struck by lightning is thirty-five times higher than that of winning at powerball.

* Discuss who gambles (many people, including some teenagers and children) and why they gamble (most people gamble because it is entertaining).

* Describe problem gambling (see chapter 2), and who becomes a problem gambler and why (chapter 3). For younger children, you can explain that some people have a problem. They start gambling and have trouble stopping. Some of these people are kids.

For adolescents, you might want to explain that kids are at greater risk than most adults for gambling problems.

* Explain about the laws on gambling in your state. Most states prohibit children from most forms of public gambling. It's illegal for children to play the lottery or to get someone to play for them.

* Explain that as your child gets older, he or she will need to make his or her own decision about gambling. You want to make sure that your child knows enough to make an informed choice. Go over the pros and cons of gambling:

Pros	Cons
Gambling can be fun.	Some forms of gambling are against the law.
It can be a good thing to do with friends.	Most people lose money gambling.
Many forms of gambling are legal when you get older.	Some people lose a lot of money—the more they play the more they lose.
Most people don't have a problem with gambling.	Some people develop serious gambling problems.

* Talk to your child about what to do if someone asks them to gamble. Also discuss what to do if he or she knows someone who is gambling and getting into trouble.

* Finally, make sure they can talk with you anytime they have questions or concerns. And revisit the issue with them on occasion. Don't let this be a one-time conversation.

A second thing you can do to prevent your children from developing a gambling problem is to teach them about self-control and judgment. Recognize that adolescents tend to have fewer resources to deal with gambling. They have limited experience with money and responsibility, as well as with the people and industries who may take advantage of them. They may be less aware of danger and have limited impulse control and judgment.

Teaching self-control and judgment can be a challenge with teenagers. Often they cannot be taught directly, but a conscious effort on your part to help your teenagers develop good judgment and control is vital. Keys to success include the following:

* Talk directly about self-control and judgment. What does it mean to have self-control and good judgment? How would a child recognize it? Discuss examples of good and bad judgment and

effective and ineffective self-control that your child may have observed.

* Provide a good role model. Children follow examples more than instructions. Speaking about your judgments and why you make certain decisions helps them to understand the way to think through their own decisions.

* Help them to reason through situations they face in their daily lives. This is a particular challenge that requires mutual trust. Generally, your role should be to ask questions, not give directions. Help them to see that exercising good judgment and self-control is in *their* interests, not just yours.

A third way to help your children avoid gambling problems is to recognize that normal adolescents have a need for stimulation and excitement and a need to explore and try new things. This often translates into a willingness to take greater risks. Adolescents also are trying to find ways to connect with others and establish a personal identity to which others will respond. Risk taking is a valued avenue for connecting with others in adolescent culture. Generally, these are normal, healthy aspects of being a teenager—but these needs also can contribute to increased risk for gambling problems. You can take a number of steps to help them meet these needs while minimizing the risk of gambling problems.

* Provide healthy outlets for stimulation, excitement, and new experiences. Play an active part in channeling where they find stimulation. You should have some influence in directing the domain of their exploration. Work with their need to explore. Exploration, when combined with reflection on the new experience, leads to good judgment. Help them get involved in new activities that channel their energies into productive directions.

* Similarly, try to work with their need for risk taking, and not simply fight it. Recognize that the goal for children is not to avoid all risks but to take reasonable risks for worthwhile goals.

* By speaking with your children at an early age about gambling, you will set the stage for closer communication during the adolescent and young adult years when children's increased independence often decreases the information they give to their parents. Since the adolescent and young adult years are also when the frequency of many high-risk behaviors rise, including substance abuse and unsafe sexual behaviors, as well as problem gambling, a *history* of open conversation provides a strong foundation for continued dialogue. Yet you must recognize the limits of your influence as your child progresses through these years, so

try to monitor from a distance appropriate to your child's age, respect her independence, and maintain open lines of communication.

What You Can Do When the Gambler Is an Elder

First, be sure you understand the motives behind your relative's gambling. Socializing, avoidance of painful emotions, and the hope of "easy money" are among the most common motivators for this group of problem gamblers. Older adults often use gambling as a way to expand their social lives. The loss of loved ones, which is a natural consequence of growing old, may trigger depression, grief, anxiety, or loneliness, motivating some older adults to find temporary relief in gambling. Finally, for many elderly people living on reduced or fixed incomes, gambling is sometimes viewed as the most likely way to improve their finances.

Second, recognize that the issue of independence is very important to older adults. Their need to remain independent often makes it difficult to define gambling as a problem before serious losses have taken place.

* Be respectful of their independence while trying to be involved in a constructive way.

* Carefully consider strategies of approaching elderly relatives about the presence of a gambling problem or its treatment. Our experience with families suggests overly aggressive approaches can alienate the gambler, reducing the opportunity for influence.

* An indirect approach is sometimes best. Focus on the things they need for gambling (e.g., transportation, mailings from sweepstakes marketers) and factors contributing to their gambling (e.g., time alone). These can suggest ways to limit and lower the frequency of gambling.

Third, for some elderly people, gambling can have a passive quality; their gambling is initiated by other people, other events, or by contacts from gambling industries such as sweepstakes firms. There is fairly clear evidence that some companies target the elderly because they are vulnerable to gambling. Sometimes the marketing is unscrupulous. Although this can lead to major problems, the passive aspect of this type of gambling also can provide opportunities to intervene.

* Take a very active approach toward other people, particularly marketers, who may be targeting your relative for gambling. Many are actually responsible businesses that will respond to a request to remove your relative from their sweepstakes "lottery" or whatever it is called. More aggressive approaches may be needed with some businesses, for example, letters from lawyers.

Fourth, as discussed in chapter 3, in a select group of older adults, gambling is part of a medical illness. Often these illnesses are forms of dementia, such as Alzheimer's disease, and they are usually linked to diminished ability to control one's impulses.

* If you suspect that your relative's medical condition plays a part in her gambling, you need to educate yourself about her condition. There are many excellent medical references both in libraries and on the Internet.

* You also will want to consult with her physician. With your relative's consent, most doctors welcome the input and questions of concerned family members and may be able to give good counsel regarding ways to address the gambling problem. Creating an alliance with the doctor may be crucial for intervening—many adults listen to their doctor more willingly than to friends or family.

* Discuss your relative's medications with her physician to see how these may be related to her medical condition as well as to mood, impulsivity, and ultimately her gambling.

Finally, medical problems change the picture of responsibility. Your perspective on responsibility should be the same for older adult gamblers as it is for other adults. If the gambler no longer has the ability he once did to develop ways to control problem behaviors, then it will not help to hold him responsible. He will be unable to stop. The results can be disastrous and, at times, hard to avoid. The key is for family members to adjust the way they think about responsibility so that they can provide some of the control that their relative has lost. To be effective, this must be done carefully and respectfully. At the same time, family members need to ensure that the gambler receives the medical attention he needs. In such situations, seeking legal control over an older gambler's financial affairs may make sense. However, the legal system provides strong protections for the independence of elderly adults. These valuable protections can limit the ability of others to step in when a gambling problem is present. The primary legal issue is whether your relative is considered "competent" to handle his or her financial affairs.

The term "competent" does not refer to skill, but to the basic ability to understand and make decisions. Courts tend to consider anyone who is generally aware of what is going on around them and the meaning of those events as "competent." In the area of finances, many people are deemed competent by courts although their relatives would not agree. In our experience, most elderly gamblers are considered legally competent to manage their own affairs unless there is clear evidence of impairment. If you think that your relative is no longer competent, contact a lawyer or a legal assistance clinic that deals with competency to provide expert advice.

What You Can do When the Gambler Abuses Alcohol or Drugs

People who struggle with drug or alcohol problems often develop an understanding of how the problem affects them. This understanding can be a very useful basis for quickly understanding the dynamics of a gambling problem and for taking action to address it. For example, many people have attended Alcoholics Anonymous or Narcotics Anonymous, two very popular peer support groups. People with experiences in those groups may be able to work within Gamblers Anonymous more quickly and effectively.

* First review the connections between your relative's gambling problem and drug/alcohol addiction. Look at when they drink and gamble. Does one lead to the other? Do they always go together?

* If they are both active problems, try to deal with both at the same time. This is a challenge, but it is possible. Addressing one problem while ignoring the other is often a strategy for failure.

* When you talk with your relative, talk about the two problems in similar terms, emphasizing the similarities of problem gambling to alcohol and drug abuse. Use these similarities to help your relative recognize and understand her gambling problem more quickly.

* Find out about gambling and substance abuse treatment resources in your community. This should include self-help groups such as Gamblers Anonymous and Alcoholics Anonymous, outpatient services such as psychotherapists or therapy groups, and hospital resources such as substance abuse rehabilitation programs. Encourage your relative to use these resources. (See Appendix A.)

What You Can Do When the Gambler Has a Mood Disorder

Broadly speaking, mood disorders fall into two categories: depression and bipolar disorder, sometimes referred to as manic-depression. Problem gambling can co-occur with either of these types of mood disorders.

The relationship between problem gambling and depression is interactive and complex. Depressed persons can turn to gambling as a source of temporary relief from the pain associated with depression. Regardless of what triggers gambling, mounting gambling losses often lead to depression, even in individuals who were not previously depressed. Frequently, sorting out the relationship between the two is not easy. In some cases, there is a clear onset of depression followed by problem gambling. In other cases, it is virtually impossible to sort out whether a current depression is the cause or the result of coincidental problem gambling. Because depression's complications include social withdrawal, suicidal ideation, and increased risk of suicidal behavior, it is imperative that attention be paid to treating a person's depression regardless of its relationship to gambling activity. (See chapter 11 for safety issues.)

Gambling during the manic phase of a manic-depressive mood cycle is typically part of a group of self-destructive behaviors displayed by individuals who frequently cannot control their mood or their activities without appropriate medication. These behaviors include excessive spending and unusual work and social behavior—combined with gambling these activities can wreak financial havoc on an individual's life and the life of his or her family. Sometimes attention will be paid to the gambling problem or other prominent behaviors while the underlying mood disorder is left untreated.

Thus, when gambling is present *only* during periods of mania or depression, the first step is to help your relative address the mood problem. Treatments for mood disorders, which can include medication and counseling, are generally effective. In this case, successfully treating the mood disorder should eliminate the gambling problem.

Sometimes problem gambling will occur coincidental to a mood disorder, but independent of a person's mood state. In other words, even though the person is depressed or has manic-depressive episodes, he or she continues to gamble even when in a normal mood state. For such individuals, abnormal moods can exacerbate the gambling problem, but the gambling clearly exists as a problem separate from the mood disorder. In some individuals, mood disorders last a long time and/or reoccur frequently. Depression, particularly low levels of depression, sometimes lingers for long periods. Some individuals may cycle into abnormal mood states frequently despite treatment. In all these cases, it is important to treat the problem gambling independently of any treatment intended to alleviate the effects of the mood disorder.

Your relative may not be responsive to getting help with his problem gambling while his mood disorder is present. Mania will almost certainly limit his responsiveness to resolving a range of problems, including gambling. Depression may compound the usual difficulties of getting someone to work toward resolving gambling problems but there is a far better chance of working collaboratively with a depressed individual than with a manic one.

When individuals with a mood disorder are well (neither manic nor depressed), their judgment is usually sound. During periods of wellness, your relative is likely to have a clear understanding of the need to protect herself from future risks associated with her mood disorder, including gambling. If she is, then you can collaborate to minimize the risks. Here are some specific steps you can take toward that end.

* Plan to limit her access to funds and credit during high-risk times. To do this may require her to voluntarily transfer more authority over her financial affairs to you when she is well.

* Work together to learn as much as possible about her mood disorder including early warning signs. (Check the resources at the end of this chapter, in libraries, bookstores, and on the Internet.) Write down these early warning signs and agree on the specific actions to take if they appear (for example, to call her doctor right away).

* Anticipate that her mood disorder might reoccur and write down specific steps to minimize gambling involvement. (This particular step is unlikely to be effective if she has entered a fully manic state, which underscores the importance of early intervention.)

If your relative does not think it is necessary to minimize future risks, then you can try to increase her motivation in a step-wise fashion. We will explain this in greater detail when we discuss the stages of change later in this chapter. Until your relative is motivated to collaborate with you, try to find out if she is engaging in high-risk behaviors other than gambling. Ask your relative, but also seek other sources of information such as friends, co-workers, and financial records. When possible, take action to protect your relative from such risks.

At the same time, do what you can to minimize future risk (for example, establish your own financial independence [see chapter 9]) and be prepared to act quickly and independently if the mood disorder and gambling reoccur.

What You Can Do When the Gambler Has Attention Deficit Disorder (ADD)

First, understanding ADD is a crucial task that requires significant reading on your part, interaction with your relative, and possibly professional help. The way that the deficit in attention influences the person's life may be subtle but pervasive. It will take time and hard work before you and your relative understand the way in which he or she is affected and how to intervene effectively.

* Educate yourself. There are many excellent books on this topic. In many places, there are professional talks and educational support groups.

* Discuss what you have learned with your relative.

* Help her to become educated as well. Give her the books and articles you have read.

Second, it is appropriate to be optimistic but you must also be persistent. There are effective treatments for ADD, but it usually takes time to implement them fully. Typically, they involve medication and/or a combination of education, counseling, and family work.

* Be aggressive in pursuing treatment. You will want to see a specialist trained to recognize and treat ADD. Ask your primary care doctor for a referral. Patient groups such as Children and Adults with Attention-Deficit/Hyperactivity Disorder (CHADD) can help with referrals as well (see Resources at the end of this chapter).

* Be persistent and patient in reaching your treatment goals. It often takes several trials of medication before the best medication and dosage is found. Other forms of treatment also take time before they are successful. Accept that you and your relative are in for a long-term solution, one that may take several years to implement fully.

Third, many people with ADD find that they do better with regular help from family members. Usually, the family members help by providing extra support in keeping the person organized, providing reminders, feedback, and encouragement.

* As you help your relative structure his or her life, restrict the opportunity and resources for gambling. This will be easier with adolescents, but it can be done to some degree with others, too. To gamble, they need money, time, and access to gambling. Find ways to ensure that these resources are less available.

Fourth, for many gamblers with ADD, it is the desire for excitement and risk that will be the primary motivation. The high level of stimulation that gambling offers can result in more focused attention—temporarily. Help your relative to substitute less risky and costly activities that provide stimulation. Also, appropriate medical treatment for ADD will reduce the need for high levels of stimulation.

What You Can Do When the Gambler Has Schizophrenia

First, for some people with schizophrenia, problems with thinking and judgment make it more difficult for them to control the urge to gamble. For others, distorted thinking may be a factor in their gambling. Gambling is often obscured by the other serious problems experienced by those with schizophrenia.

* Work closely with your relative's mental health providers to form a plan to address his gambling problem. You will need their involvement and they will need yours. Together, you will have a much better chance of intervening effectively.

* Ask your relative about gambling behaviors specifically. Don't assume he does not have a problem. When we first began making these inquiries of our patients with schizophrenia, we were often surprised by those who had gambling problems that we hadn't known about or even suspected.

* Even if the person has limited money, don't assume that he doesn't have a gambling problem. Many of our patients are unable to work and have very limited incomes, yet they spend a large percentage of their incomes on scratch tickets, leaving them little else.

Second, some individuals with schizophrenia are unable to work. Consequently, they may have a great deal of time on their hands. Our experience has been that gambling is often a focus of their attention.

* Find out if issues such as excessive free time are relevant to their gambling.

* Help your relative to find other activities that will meet his needs and be incompatible with gambling.

What You Can Do When the Gambler Is Motivated by a Need for Action/Excitement

First, recognize and accept her need for excitement. Be persistent in trying to help her see the pattern of risk taking—it will be the foundation of her own efforts to change. Talk with her in a nonjudgmental way about her interest in exciting activities. Show her that you recognize the rewards that gambling has for her while helping her to appreciate the risks.

Second, address safety concerns directly. She may be aware of danger, but is likely to be more comfortable with a higher level of risk than seems wise to you. Listen carefully to ensure you understand what other risks she is taking. Gambling topics to inquire about include gambling with large amounts of money, gambling on credit or with borrowed money, frivolous betting with things that are important to her life. Ask about nongambling activities as well, such as substance abuse, drinking and driving, and unsafe sexual behavior. Suggest pursuing excitement in a "smart" way. If you focus only on safety, your relative is unlikely to listen. If you support her interest in excitement but emphasize the importance of doing it in a "smart" way, meaning a safe way, she is more likely to listen.

Third, help him channel his need for excitement and sensation constructively. There are many activities that are exciting like mountain biking and wind surfing. Typically, organized groups that do these activities emphasize safety and judgment. Your relative could get the level of excitement he enjoys while learning to do these activities in a *relatively* safe way. Pursue a long-term goal of helping him substitute other activities for gambling. Introduce him to new activities while providing support to keep him involved over time. When appropriate, participate with him—making this part of your regular activities together.

Fourth, recognize what giving up gambling may mean for your relative. Perhaps nothing else feels quite as exciting. Talk with him directly about his feelings of loss. Ask the following questions:

* What will you miss about gambling the most?

* What will it be like to not feel that level of excitement anymore?

Remind him why he is trying to give up gambling. Help him identify and review the long-term benefits of quitting gambling, including restoring or maintaining the love and respect of family and friends, opportunities to improve finances and ensure a stable lifestyle, and freedom from the problems and stress caused by gambling.

What You Can Do When the Gambler Is Motivated by Relief from Negative Feelings

First, both you and your relative need to understand the feelings she is trying to avoid. Often, gamblers are so intent on avoiding unpleasant feelings they may not recognize them or be able to talk about them. Family and friends may be unaware that the gambler is depressed or anxious. Getting someone to talk about uncomfortable feelings can be a slow but ultimately rewarding process. For some, it is a matter of learning to talk about feelings that they have never put into words. Others must overcome the stigma they believe is associated with negative feelings. Often, the time to begin to talk directly about feelings is when the uncomfortable feelings are not as intense. Work up to helping the gambler talk about his or her feelings while they are actively experiencing them.

Second, you can help your relative to change the ineffective strategy he is currently using to deal with these feelings. Taking a short-term strategy of blocking out the feelings provides immediate relief but it is not a long-term solution. Learning to manage and tolerate the feelings while working to resolve the problems causing them will result in long-term, lasting relief. You should recognize that your relative may need professional help to accomplish this goal (see chapter 10.)

What You Can Do When the Gambler Is Motivated by a Need for Socializing

First, help your relative to recognize his or her need for socializing and its relationship to gambling. Talk about his or her friends. Try to understand why your relative has few nongambling relationships. Is she shy? Does she feel inadequate? Does she lack conversational skills? Is she concerned she will not fit in with nongamblers?

Second, help your relative to identify and develop social contacts in nongambling settings. Don't rush to suggest that your relative should drop all of her gambling friends. Instead, support her in exploring nongambling-related activities with people she knows from gambling who are not frequent or problem gamblers. There is, however, some risk that continuing these relationships will support continued problem gambling, so explore this with your relative.

Encourage your relative to spend time with nongambling-related friends and look for structured social activities in which she can participate. Try to match the type of activity with your relative's interests. Many groups and activities are available for the adolescent/young adult gambler. Similarly, there are many activities oriented toward older adults, such as travel groups, senior centers, and community-service organizations. For middle-aged adults, structured activities are often the most difficult to identify. However, with a review of your relative's current interests and a little investigation of the activities available in your community, you should be able to come up with a range of options.

What You Can Do When a Gambler Is Motivated by the Need for Positive Identity and Self-Esteem

First, find out what gambling means to your relative in terms of his or her identity. You may already have a sense of how closely he or she identifies with the image of the gambler. Even so, since many aspects of self-identity may be outside your relative's awareness, you may have to explore this area. To do so, ask your relative to describe his or her personality and reputation. What does he think others say or think about him? Listen for characteristics related to gambling (daring, wild, courageous, irresponsible) or the opposite (fearful, cautious, foolish, overly responsible).

Second, encourage your relative to think about how gambling affects his identity and whether this is helpful or accurate. Feedback from you and others can often correct unrealistic thinking. Giving your relative positive feedback about nongambling-related qualities of his personality can also be helpful for boosting self-esteem. You can also encourage your relative to engage in nongambling-related activities that express the same qualities that he finds admirable in the gambler's image.

What You Can Do When the Gambler Is Motivated by Interpersonal Motives

First, review the section on assessing motivation in chapter 3 if you suspect this motive. You may have difficulty accurately understanding what your relative is trying to accomplish in this regard, since you are a participant as well as an observer of your relative's interactions with family members. Often consulting another relative or a professional can be helpful in gaining understanding in this area.

Second, if you are confident you have a reasonable understanding of the interaction patterns between your relative and other family members, start a dialogue with your relative about your observations. Avoid the temptation to lecture her about the "insight" you have developed. Instead, introduce your observations—particularly the connection between her gambling and the way that family members respond to that gambling—and ask her whether she agrees or disagrees with their accuracy. By all means, avoid making judgments about your relative's behavior.

You should not expect that your relative will immediately agree with all (or any) of your observations. We recommend that you continue to point out over time repeated situations where her gambling results in a similar response from other family members. In this way, you may assist your relative to develop a greater appreciation for the way in which gambling serves to meet important interpersonal needs.

What You Can Do When the Gambler Is Motivated by Money

First, discussing the role and significance of money with your relative can be revealing. Engaging in a dialogue will almost always be more productive than "interviewing" or interrogating your relative. Thus, you should be prepared to discuss your own views on this subject as well. Your goal is to better understand what your relative wants to obtain by winning money. For most people, money is a means to some other end: a more lavish lifestyle, a feeling of success or achievement, praise and attention from others, or simply happiness.

Once you understand how your relative hopes money will help to attain other goals, you will be in a position to inquire about the actual results obtained through gambling. How much money has been lost through gambling? What could he have done with that money? Are there other, more effective ways to acquire money in pursuit of those goals? Are there other ways in which your relative might achieve the same goals, even without additional money?

Second, correcting inaccurate thinking about the probability of winning money through gambling can help your relative to better understand the futility of continued gambling. This is a task that will usually require several conversations and may benefit from the intervention of a professional clinician or financial counselor. Review the introduction to probability in Appendix B. Point out to your relative that continued gambling at games of chance over time will increase the odds of losing to a near certainty. Often, it is helpful to compare the astronomical odds of winning a large amount of money with the odds of other unusual or unlikely events, such as being struck by lightning or a meteor striking the earth.

Third, if your relative identifies self-worth and satisfying relationships with having money, discuss the many ways in which family members and others value him. You can also point out many ways to build satisfying relationships that have nothing to do with money.

Fourth, if your relative has a limited income, be prepared to work with him or her either to find alternative ways to increase income or to learn how to manage within an existing budget. You may wish to refer your relative to a financial or credit counselor offering low-cost or free advice and assistance with finance management (see chapter 9).

The *Stages* of *Change*

Problem gambling is not resolved in one step. Instead, people go through a series of steps as they make changes of any kind. It doesn't matter if the goal is to stop smoking, change careers, or be more supportive of a spouse; people generally make changes in a predictable way. Understanding that process will give you a road map to understanding how your relative is proceeding in giving up gambling.

About twenty years ago, two psychologists, James Prochaska and Carlo DiClemente, began to look at patterns in how people change (1995). Their work has revolutionized the way people think about change, becoming a model for therapists and lay people across the United States. We will briefly review the six stages of change that they describe and then use these stages to examine your role as a family member across the process of change.

Stage 1: Precontemplation

As the name suggests, the first stage is identified by the lack of reflection about the problem. The person does not see gambling as a problem. He may see some of the consequences of gambling but does not consider gambling to be the cause of the problem. He may blame these consequences on other factors, for example, bad luck, bad decisions, you or other relatives. This may reflect his investment in not giving up his gambling or it may simply indicate the early stage of his awareness.

Stage 2: Contemplation

Once someone begins to recognize that her gambling has resulted in consequences she wishes to avoid, she begins to think about gambling as something she may wish to change. How the gambling connects to the consequences and what is required to change are common areas of reflection. This process of review is a prerequisite for the following steps.

Stage 3: Preparation

In this stage, the gambler has decided to change in the immediate future. Her task is to formulate a plan for that change. This involves questions of when to change, how to talk about this change to others, and how to gain needed support to sustain the change. This is an important, though typically brief period of planning that has important implications for overall success.

Stage 4: Action

This is the stage most people associate with the idea of change. The gambler takes steps to stop gambling and begins to reorganize her life without gambling. She may begin attending Gamblers Anonymous. She may limit contact with gambling friends or settings. She may begin filling her weekends with other activities. This is typically the most active and most demanding stage, although all the stages play crucial roles.

Stage 5: Maintenance

Change often requires sustained effort over months and years. Many gamblers and family members are surprised the first time a gambler lapses. The gambler expected to work hard at changing for several weeks or months, and then be finished with the change process. Long-term success requires continued work to sustain the initial changes.

Stage 6: Termination

At this stage, gambling no longer represents a temptation or problem. The gambler no longer has to make any special effort to avoid the gambling and can focus all of his or her attention on other areas of life. Many therapists as well as many "ex-gamblers" believe that problem gambling never reaches the termination stage.

Pacing Your Efforts Using the Stages of Change

Understanding the stages of change leads to insights about what you can do to help your relative at any point in the course of dealing with problem gambling. The stages are really about what your relative is doing, but they provide a framework for you to understand how you can support change. We will review the first five stages focusing on the attitudes and responses that are generally helpful at each stage of change.

Your unique situation may limit the desirability of responding in ways that are fully consistent with your relative's stage of change. Sometimes, the urgency of the situation or the gambler's behavior will prompt you to move more rapidly and independently. In addition, your relative's feelings as well as your own might limit your ability (or your willingness) to provide the response that a particular change stage suggests. In chapter 7, we will suggest one way that the attitudes and responses described below can be turned into concrete goals at each stage of change.

Precontemplative Stage

At this stage your relative is not actively considering whether gambling is a problem. Your efforts should be aimed at supporting him or her to move to the contemplative stage. To do this, you will want to find ways to encourage your relative to review her gambling and its consequences. Typically, gamblers have psychological defenses against thinking about the links between their gambling and its consequences, so your efforts must be done very carefully (see chapter 7 for help).

The most common mistake made at this stage is to use confrontation and accusation to coerce contemplation. The natural response to what feels like an attack or coercion is to respond defensively, which results in little real contemplation. A more effective approach is to view contemplation as a joint effort. You invite the gambler to think and talk about the problems you suspect are caused by gambling. Most problem gamblers are unhappy with the consequences of their gambling. Helping them tap into their discomfort will often prompt meaningful contemplation of the problem.

Contemplative Stage

In the contemplative stage, your relative reviews the problems she would like to change and tries to understand the links those problems have to gambling. She weighs the costs and benefits of her gambling to decide whether she really wants to try to change, which is something that most gamblers typically are convinced they may not be able to accomplish. So how can you help her in this process? Here are a few specific tasks:

* Help ensure that she has some place she can speak openly without fear of judgment. It is in open discussion that her contemplation will become more accurate. You may be able to help her just by being a nonjudgmental sounding board for her thoughts and feelings (see chapter 7 for help in doing this). For some relatives, however, this is an impossible task. You are not the best person to provide this kind of support if you are so angry and resentful that you cannot listen nonjudgmentally, or if your relative is not able to talk openly with you due to past conflict or guilt. Friends, other relatives, or professional counselors would be a better choice.

* Provide information for her review, including information about the consequences of her gambling. If she is trying to decide whether to try to change, your relative needs to know all the consequences of her gambling. It is here that the failure of some family members to be direct about what they see as the consequences of gambling makes it less likely that the gambler will move to the next stage. Remind her of what has been lost as well as what life could be like without gambling. For those who have been gambling for many years, the idea that they would have extra money to spend on other things is hard to imagine. Others may need help imagining what a closer more trusting relationship might be like. The trick is to do this without being heavy-handed or inducing unmanageable guilt or defensiveness.

* Help the gambler review her beliefs about her own ability to change. Many gamblers want to change and will move more readily into the preparation stage when they gain some confidence that they can do so.

Preparation Stage

Your relative is getting ready to stop gambling. This is a critical time for him. He is making plans and dealing with last-minute fears and hopes about changes. You probably have strong feelings as well: excitement about the change, fear of being disappointed, and possibly anxiety about what the change may mean for you.

To be supportive you need to be available to provide reassurance to your relative. After working hard to get the gambler to be responsible for the problem, some relatives make the mistake of giving in to the temptation to try to control the gambling at this point. They allow their anxiety about real change to drive them to pester or coerce the gambler. Ask yourself, "Is this the type of support that will be most productive?"

Action Stage

At this point, your relative has changed her gambling behavior and is actively seeking ways to consolidate this change. This is a major accomplishment that deserves a great deal of credit. Now the work of change is even more demanding and your role shifts significantly.

* First, you need to support the change. This may seem like a "no-brainer," but many family members actually impede change at this point. Sometimes it is overt, such as a husband who refuses to let his wife attend Gamblers Anonymous meetings. Often it is more covert. We are creatures of habit, and even the unhealthiest patterns in our life have the benefit of being predictable. In contrast, change almost always arouses some anxiety and resistance. There will be plenty of resistance both inside the gambler and out in the environment. You want to ensure that you are not creating any additional resistance.

* Since your relative will be doing the lion's share of the work, you need to be supportive. This includes being available to help in any reasonable capacity that your relative requests. Sometimes, this will mean very concrete assistance. More often, what she needs is encouragement, recognition for what she is trying to do, and someone to listen to her. She may need help in thinking through how to change. The more you know, the more help you are able to provide. The Action stage can involve many setbacks. It is simply part of the process of learning to control problem gambling.

* Be sure to distinguish what your relative needs in the face of setbacks and what you need. Many relatives confuse these issues, forcing help on the gambler which is not what she needs or wants. The wife of one of our clients was so anxious after he had lapsed and gone to the track after twelve months of no gambling that she threatened him with divorce. Later she revealed that she thought that this was what he needed to "get serious" about his problem. If she had been more careful to distinguish his needs from hers, she would have recognized that he needed encouragement and that she needed a way to express her fear and disappointment.

Maintenance Stage

As your relative consolidates his gains, your role may change again. Hopefully, you will be able to continue offering support and encouragement, as well as a listening ear. There may be short-term setbacks, but it is persistence over time that determines who ultimately succeeds. Family members occasionally find it harder to maintain the long-term perspective than do problem gamblers. Family members are so afraid of being disappointed that they may react to any lapse as though it is the final failure, which is not helpful. Setbacks are a normal part of recovery. They should come as no surprise and should not be interpreted as signs of long-term failure.

Finally, one of the critical tasks of the Maintenance stage is to develop a satisfying lifestyle, which can be a challenge for the gamblers as well as for family members. When gambling has ceased, time and money can be put to good use in rebuilding a more rewarding life. Some spouses, assuming this process will take place without effort, sit and wait to become "happy." Unfortunately, happiness takes more work than that. You have to focus on rebuilding trust in the relationship, rebuilding activities and outside relationships with family and friends, and returning to your efforts at pursuing a life you find meaningful. Occasionally, this means solving some problems that are hiding behind the gambling (see chapter 12). Your role will almost certainly include working with the gambler to resolve these problems and rebuilding your lives.

Urgency

In general, you will make a strong contribution by pacing your actions according to the gambler's current stage of change. Yet what if you sense an urgency for the gambler to change more rapidly? External developments that might lead you to take action inconsistent with the gambler's current stage of change include the following:

1. Threats to the safety of the gambler or others (including indebtedness to loan sharks) [see chapter 11].

2. Acute financial distress (including insufficient resources to meet life's vital functions such as for housing and food) [see chapter 9].

3. Vocational or academic disruption (including potential or actual loss of job, potential or actual expulsion from school).

4. Social disruption (including breakdown in family structure with potential for separation or divorce) [see chapter 4].

5. Increased symptoms of mental illness or other disorders in the gambler (including anxiety, depression, substance abuse, or other high-risk behaviors).

6. Increased symptoms or other disorders in you or other family members (including anxiety, depression, or substance abuse).

7. Illegal behaviors to support gambling or other potential or actual legal issues.

In addition to these objective circumstances, tolerance for delay varies across individuals and within individuals over time. For example, let's say that John finds that his wife Jane has been losing moderate amounts of money to gambling. Jane's losses prevent the family from doing any recreational activities, but all of their other needs are met. Suppose also that John knows that Jane is under intense pressure from work as well as from caring for her ailing, elderly parents. He recalls that ten years ago, she drank excessively for six months during a period of intense stress. If Jane's gambling doesn't escalate, John might tolerantly support Jane in working through the stages of change over a period of six to twelve months

Perhaps two years later, if Jane's gambling remains at the same level, John's sense of urgency might be much greater. So his tolerance changes over time, although the level of gambling and its impact remain constant. Another spouse might have had no tolerance for delay from the outset.

When reviewing your sense of urgency, distinguish between the circumstances and your tolerance for delay to determine the basis for that urgency. This recommendation does not imply that any particular degree of tolerance, whether greater or lesser, is a virtue. Rather, understanding the basis for your urgency will help you to make better informed decisions about what actions to take.

Seeking professional counsel is always a good idea.

Putting It All Together

This chapter is about a simple truth: your relative is responsible for his gambling and you are responsible for yourself. It seems so easy, so obvious, and yet for many people this truth is often elusive. We recommend that you revisit this issue regularly during the recovery period. The struggle with problem gambling often results in subtle distortions in how people view responsibility. Like traveling in a new city, you want to return to your map often to ensure that you are staying on course.

Resources
Attention Deficit Disorder

1. The National Institute of Mental Health has excellent information at their website: http://www.nimh.nih.gov/publicat/adhd.cfm

2. Children and adults with attention-deficit/hyperactivity disorder (CHADD). Contact information (to locate a chapter near you) for the national office is:
8181 Professional Place, Suite 201
Landover, MD 20785. Phone: 301-306-7070, 1–800-233-4050
Web-site: www.chadd.org

———Books

Hallowell, E., and J. Ratey. 1994. *Driven to Distraction*. New York: Pantheon Books.

Silver, L. 1993. *Dr. Silver's Advice to Parents on Attention-Deficit Hyperactivity Disorder*. Washington, DC: American Psychiatric Press.

Mental Health

Center for Mental Health Services
Office of Consumer, Family, and Public Information
5600 Fishers Lane, Room 15-105
Rockville, MD 20857
(301) 443-2792

———Books

Burns, D. 1999. *Feeling Good: The New Mood Therapy* New York: Avon.

Copeland, M. E. 1992. *The Depression Workbook: A Guide for Living with Depression*. Oakland: New Harbinger.

Chapter 7

Building a Dialogue

The best way for a family to solve the problem of gambling is by building a dialogue and working together. Initiating this complex process often falls to the relatives of the gambler because problem gamblers tend to deny that anything is wrong. This chapter examines the nature of dialogue and explains how families can begin to construct a productive dialogue, whether the problem gambler is your spouse, your child, or an older relative.

Key Elements

Basically, a healthy dialogue consists of the following elements:

1. It is interactive to the extent that each person is influenced by the other—both parties should be able to alter their thoughts, feelings, or (verbal) behavior in response to the other person.

2. Communication is good, meaning that the message sent is the same as the message received. Blocks to good communication include the speaker not expressing himself clearly and/or the listener not paying attention.

3. Information is conveyed both verbally and nonverbally. Nonverbal messages include how people say things (tone of voice, for example) as well as how they behave. We send and receive messages on all these channels.

4. The dialogue occurs over time because change requires time. Successful dialogue and healthy change are intrinsically connected.

5. Messages are sent on two levels: one is the literal content of what is said and the other is an emotional message.

The goals of the dialogue are linked to the stage of change that is being attempted.

Setting goals helps you get where you want to go. With an understanding of the stages of change and an eye toward the urgency and other demands of your situation (see chapter 6), you can develop goals step by step.

Here is one way of translating the generally helpful attitudes appropriate to each stage of change into concrete goals that will help you to move sequentially toward your ultimate goal of helping the gambler to stop gambling completely.

Stage 1: Precontemplative

Major goal: Reach agreement that a major problem exists.
Subgoals:

* Begin a dialogue. * State your concerns. * State in concrete terms what the problems are. * State in concrete terms what things would look like if the problems were resolved. * Give your relative the opportunity to express his or her views.

Stage 2: Contemplative

Major goal: Agree that changes need to be made.
Subgoals:

* Help the gambler to recognize your concerns. * Modify your understanding based on your active and realistic listening. * Reach an understanding of the specific problems. * Recognize the need for change. * Make a joint commitment to initiate change.

Stage 3: Preparation

Major goal: Develop a concrete plan of action.
Subgoals:

* Establish concrete goals (also in stages). * Establish a process by which those goals can be achieved. * Identify the role each of you will play in resolving the problem. * Identify the resources (in and outside the family) that will move the

process forward. ✳ Establish the parameters of a timeline for reaching these goals.

Stage 4: Action

Major Goal: Resolve the problems.
Subgoals:

✳ Implement the plan developed in Stage 3. ✳ Employ and manage the resources. ✳ Measure progress toward goals consistent with the timeline. ✳ Update as necessary (consistent with broad goals).

Stage 5: Maintenance

Major Goal: Stay on course.
Subgoals:

✳ Continue to monitor and measure progress. ✳ Establish resources necessary to maintain gains. ✳ Establish lifestyle to make maintenance more likely. ✳ Establish plan to address lapses.

How Long Should the Dialogue Take?

Your current circumstances and your personal tolerance for delay will be the main factors here. If your situation is desperate (e.g., further losses will result in the loss of your home), then action must begin at once. If the external pressures are less catastrophic (e.g., you have had to cancel your vacation), you might allow some time to progress through the various stages.

Of course, "some time" is still vague. We recommend that you specify a realistic time frame for accomplishing each stage based on your personal circumstances. Such a time frame should not be so short as to make goals impossible to accomplish, nor so long as to undermine the importance of establishing limits. For help in grounding your efforts toward a specific time frame, review the section on urgency in chapter 6.

Your time frame should include a chance to assess each goal before moving on to the next; further action should be contingent upon whether or not the previous goal was met. This will give you a sense of control over your situation which, in turn, will help alleviate depression and anxiety.

Establishing limits is not the same thing as "giving an ultimatum," however. Ultimatums are often greeted with resentment and opposition because it implies that you have control over the other person's behavior. As discussed in the previous chapter, you cannot control how much time the problem gambler will require to move through the stages of change. But if you are clear about your time frame, goals, and alternate plans, he or she will have freedom of choice with full knowledge of the consequences of various actions.

Each Stage May Require Multiple Discussions

Before approaching the gambler, have your goals for that discussion clearly in mind. This means knowing what you want to accomplish as well as the limits of what can be accomplished. By "limits" we mean the following: which goals are beyond the reach of the current discussion, how much time to allow for the current discussion, and what the red flags are that would signal the discussion should be concluded?

How to Make Discussions Work

The techniques for making each discussion work remain the same with each new goal. Here are some general guidelines.

Aim for a Win-Win Outcome

The most likely outcome of your dialogue is a win-win or a lose-lose. (Although we will show you how to protect and take care of yourself even if the gambler does not change, it is very difficult for you to win if the gambler loses.) If you and the gambler are able to work together as a team, you have the best chance of success. This means that your goal is to solve the problems, not to exact revenge, shame the other person, or prove that he or she is a bad person.

Goals for a Win-Win Outcome

To achieve a win-win outcome, you must express your point clearly without attacking the other person and you must listen sensitively yet realistically to the other's position. You need to do the following:

* Stay focused on achieving a solution beneficial to all. * Be committed to developing a true working alliance with the other. * Be nonjudgmental. * Be cautiously optimistic. * Be firm and yet open.

Remember to point to actual behavior and observable events as the problems; although gambling is the overall problem, it should be discussed in concrete, specific terms.

Keep the Other Person's Goals in Mind

Achieving a win-win solution means that both of you meet your goals to the fullest extent possible. Your goals should be clearly outlined, but what about your family member's goals?

Perhaps the gambler's ultimate goal is to keep gambling; although this is directly opposed to your ultimate goal for him or her to stop gambling, remember, there are many different motivations for gambling (see chapters 3 and 6). Try to understand which of these motivations apply to your family member. If these reasons for gambling can be satisfied or managed in another way, which may require professional assistance, the drive to gamble will diminish or disappear.

Don't Assume You Are 100 Percent Right

Everyone around you may agree that your family member's behavior is self-destructive. However, it is a mistake to assume that your various points of view are all 100 percent accurate. Another aspect of this issue is assuming that if someone doesn't understand your point, then he or she is at fault. Both the speaker and the listener share responsibility for accurate communication. You might address a misunderstanding constructively by asking, "Am I saying this clearly?" rather than "Don't you understand?"

Find the Right Time for a Discussion

If you search for the perfect time to talk, you may never find it. But if you are not careful about choosing the time, you may decrease your chances for success. Although anxiety, frustration, and anger may affect your behavior, with proper planning logical thought can guide your actions in finding the right time to talk.

What conditions should you look for? First, it must be a time when the two of you are alone. It is counter-productive for a couple to have children present or to raise the issue in a public setting (unless there are safety issues—see chapter 11) where other interpersonal dynamics, such as embarrassment, contribute to unpredictable outcomes. By approaching your child privately, you will show her you respect her developing independence and you will not compromise her (perhaps fragile) self-esteem, as you might if you were, for example, to bring this up in front of her siblings. Similarly, you will minimize any possible perception of assault on your older relative's dignity by addressing him or her individually.

Second, it is essential that other issues not be pressing so that attention can be focused on the discussion. It is not a good idea to start this discussion while you are doing the bills, for example, when financial pressures and related emotions are heightened. Ideally, you should set aside a specific amount of time to talk—perhaps forty-five minutes—in a quiet place where you will not be interrupted. This means that if you are home, you should agree not to answer the phone. If there are children, they should definitely be out of the house for a known amount of time or in bed for the night.

If you can't find such a time, now or in the near future, at least find a few minutes to tell the gambler that you'd like to schedule a time for later discussion. Suggest some specific times and be open to other possibilities, but make it clear that this is an important matter that will require about forty-five minutes. Do not delve into the topic at the time. If the gambler insists on knowing what is on your mind before he or she agrees to a time for discussion, state that you don't wish to go into details until there is sufficient time for a good discussion. You should say only that the topic is the impact of gambling upon the family. Be firm but not argumentative as in the following example.

You: I'd like to find a time to talk to you about something important. We'll need a quiet time when we can concentrate on talking for about forty-five minutes. How about Wednesday night or Saturday night about nine o'clock after the kids have gone to bed?

Family member: What's this all about?

You: I'd rather save the whole topic until we can really sit down and talk. Would it be all right to set a time for Wednesday night or Saturday night at nine?

Family member: I'm not agreeing to anything unless I know what it's about.

You: I see your point. I'm concerned about the impact that I believe your gambling is having on the whole family. I'd like to have a chance to talk about this together and see if we can reach an understanding of the situation.

Family member: Let's do it now and get it over with.

You: (If there are forty-five quiet minutes to do this) Okay, that sounds fine to me. (If there is not enough time) We only have about five minutes until the kids come downstairs and I know we won't be able to cover this. Will you please consider discussing this for about forty-five minutes on Wednesday or Saturday night? That will give me a chance to express my concerns and to listen carefully to your viewpoint. My goal is to reach an understanding and achieve a positive outcome for both of us—I am not going to criticize or berate you. Can we set up that meeting?

At this point many people would agree to a meeting, but if your family member does not, you might say, "I see you do not want to set up a meeting time now. I'd like you to think over whether such a meeting would be acceptable to you and I will raise the idea again in a few days." If the gambler is your minor child, you may firmly and respectfully insist on a meeting, particularly on your second request.

How to State Your Position

Begin by thanking the gambler for agreeing to set some time aside to talk to you. State directly that you want to talk about the impact you believe the gambling is having on the whole family. Acknowledge that to talk about this may be difficult for both of you, but emphasize that your goals are to work together to reach an understanding that will lead to a win-win situation. State explicitly that you do not intend to criticize or berate him or her.

Express Your Concerns

Information sources. The impact your family member's gambling is having on the family are generally based on three sources of information: (1) the gambler's behavior and observable events; (2) your own feelings; and (3) the inferences you make.

Behavior and other observable events. These are things you and others can see or hear that are not open to logical contradiction. A video camera could record these events on its video or audio track. Examples are the fact that the gambler only ate dinner with the family one night last week or the fact that your savings account has gone from $10,000 to $500 over the last six months.

Your own feelings. Reporting your feelings is legitimate but tricky. The most constructive way to report an emotional response follows this form: "When (name an observable event) occurs, I feel (name emotion)." For example, "When you don't come home until two in the morning, I feel angry." Do not say, "When you neglect the family and show you don't care about me, I feel angry." The latter contains many inferences: i.e., what does neglect mean and how is he showing he doesn't care? These questions are open to interpretation. However, coming home at two in the morning is an observable fact.

There are two important points to keep in mind as you report your feelings: (1) your feelings are valid and (2) your verbal and physical behavior should remain under control. Becoming angry, sad, or anxious is acceptable but screaming, insulting, or becoming physically aggressive is not. You should also refrain from bringing up tangential matters such as old hurts: "It's just like the time you bought that motorcycle" (which took place twenty years ago). This is an extraordinarily difficult situation and improving your skills at this type of communication may require professional assistance. We do not mean to suggest that the problem is your own fault or that the gambler may not be provocative. Rather, raising your personal communications skills to a new level can only aid you in achieving your goals.

Inferences. Conclusions that may or may not be accurate are inferences. You may infer that your family member is selfish. You may be correct but the inference is not constructive in a dialogue and to express it is to issue an invitation to contradictions.

Inferences include the following:

1. Interpreting the other person's behavior ("You did that to hurt me").

2. Interpreting the other person's motivation ("You're afraid of success").

3. Comparing him or her to someone else ("You're just like your father").

4. Making any kind of negative generalization ("You're no good; a liar; insensitive, etc.").

Be careful not to disguise an inference as a personal feeling by misusing the word "feel" when you mean "think." For example, if you say, "I get the feeling you are insensitive": That is not a feeling; it is a thought, conclusion, or inference that you have drawn. Just putting the word "feel" at the beginning of a sentence does not make it a feeling. "I feel you're an idiot" is not a feeling; it is a thought and an inference. This distinction is vital because in presenting your concerns you must stick to data that cannot be logically disputed.

Exceptions to the rule. Two exceptions exist to the rule against using inferences: (1) when the observable facts point to a gambling problem (see chapter 2) although the gambler denies it completely, and (2) when you are honestly using inferences as a way to build an alliance with your family member by understanding his or her thoughts and feelings. For example, "You appear angry. I wonder if you think I am being unfair." You are making inferences about his feelings and thoughts but you are doing so to build an alliance. In all cases, be careful to recognize inferences and to present them as hypotheses rather than truths.

Example: Expressing Your Concerns

So, what is the best way to express your concerns? Keeping in mind what you now know about observable events, feelings, and inferences, take a look at table 7.1. The Observable Facts in the second column relate to each problem area. Stating those facts would be a good way to open a discussion because they are nonjudgmental, constructive, and have the best chance of leading to a good outcome. However, the listed Inferences can be disputed in the Comment column and are not constructive. They lead to increased shame, counterattack, and increased argument.

Table 7.1: Observations versus Inferences

Problem Area	Observable Facts	Inference	Comment
Gambling consumes your family member's time and energy	"You go to the track three times a week and play cards twice a week. Counting travel time, that takes about 25 hours per week."	"You spend all your time at the track and playing cards and don't care about me and the kids."	Notice that the gambler may well care about his family and feel guilty about the situation but has not been able to reestablish balance. By claiming he doesn't care, you would be making a determination about his internal state that only he knows.
Negative emotional and behavioral changes in gambler including substance abuse	"Since your gambling has increased (as above), you have been drinking an average of 3-4 drinks per night, you eat less and have lost 10 lbs., and you told me that your sleep has been much poorer."	"You're depressed, irritable, and addicted to alcohol."	Inference can be refuted.

Impairment in work or school	"Your grades have declined over the last two quarters; you went from a 90 average to a 78 average."	"You are becoming a bum who is doing terribly in school and you'll never amount to anything."	Inference is shaming.
Financial hardships	"We owe $17,000 on our credit cards and are two months behind on the rent."	"You have squandered all our money."	Even the word "squandered" can be refuted. Your family member may believe that he lost $2,000 gambling (in a mildly irresponsible way) and $50,000 more because he wanted to get the $2,000 back for the family.
Increased tension in family	"You used to go to all the kids' events but have missed the last three of Jane's performances and all of John's games this year. We also cannot buy the kids any new clothing because of our debt. They have each said to both of us that they are distressed about this."	"You have lost all interest in the family and only care about yourself and your lousy gambling."	Inference is shaming and can be refuted.
Impaired relations with others outside immediate family	"Both Jack and Art are refusing to have anything to do with us until we pay back the money we owe."	"Both your brothers think you're awful and everyone looks down on us."	Shaming and can be refuted (e.g., not "everyone" looks down on us).
Legal problems	"You are facing prosecution for theft."	"You are a liar and a thief."	Inference is shaming and likely to produce a counterattack.

Exercises: Expressing Your Concerns

Step 1. Practice making constructive statements about observable events and your feelings. Table 7.2 below has one column for the problem area, a second column for observable events that manifest the problem, and a third column for your feeling state. The seven most common problem areas have already been entered and there is space for you to fill in other problem areas. First, add any areas in your life that are not included. Then, try to record observable events that demonstrate this is a problem, and the feeling states that result from the problem.

Table 7.2: Expressing Feelings Constructively

Problem Area	Observable Event	Your Feeling State
Consumes gambler's time and energy		
Increased tension, symptoms, or other problems in gambler including substance abuse		
Impairment in work or school		
Financial hardships		
Increased tension, symptoms, or other problems in family members		
Impaired relations with others outside immediate family		
Legal problems		

Step 2. Now, in your separate journal, write a concise and constructive statement that indicates your concerns in concrete terms. Be sure to include both observable events and your own feelings.

Step 3. Developing the skill to state your concerns in a constructive way is vital. This ability will be enhanced by clearly understanding both constructive and nonconstructive comments. Therefore, we'd like you to do some experimental writing in your journal deliberately stating your concerns in a nonconstructive way. In this exercise, draw inferences and make negative comments. Compare the other person in unfavorable ways to other people. This exercise is designed to help you understand the components of nonconstructive statements and to thereby further the goal of limiting their intrusion into your actual dialogue with your relative.

State the Changes You Would Like to Happen

You must be clear about the changes you want to bring about. Desired changes, like concerns, are best expressed in terms of behavior and observable events. For example, with the observation from table 7.1, "You used to go to all the kids' events but have missed the last three of Jane's performances and all of John's games this year," you should state what you want in concrete terms: "I would like you to go to all of Jane's performances and all of John's games, unless you are out of town on business."

Although it is legitimate to disclose your feelings, you cannot ask your family member to change your feelings. However, you can ask him or her to change the observable event that precedes your feelings.

When discussing financial matters, you must go further than specifying the observable changes that you want; you must discuss the process that will lead to those changes. To illustrate, again using an earlier example: "We owe $17,000 on our credit cards and are two months behind on the rent." Suppose the specific change you want to bring about can be stated as, "We should bring our rent up-to-date within two weeks and decrease our credit card debt at the rate of $150/month." This follows the guidelines of staying with observable events.

What if your family member agrees with that goal but thinks the best way to achieve it is to win the money back by gambling? In this case, you need to address the process of achieving the goal as soon as it is articulated. This is covered in detail in the section on "How to Respond to Objections" later in this chapter.

Listening Sensitively But Realistically

Good communication requires listening skills as well as speaking skills. Not only does constructive listening give you the data you need to understand the gambler and respond appropriately, it promotes a model of respect and understanding in the dialogue and increases the chances that your family member will listen carefully to you. The essentials of good listening are as follows.

You are trying to gain information. Your goal is to create a productive dialogue, not to deliver a monologue. If you are not listening and really absorbing new data from the gambler, you cannot have a dialogue and you are really trying to change the other person's behavior in a lecture format. What are the chances that a lecture will accomplish your goals? If you tune out what the other person says, you will not create a dialogue.

You are an active listener. Active listening will get you the most information and increase the chance that your family member will listen to your points. There are a number of guidelines for active listening. As with so many aspects of communication, they're straightforward but not always easy to adhere to during a discussion. Basically, active listening means paying attention, putting aside preconceived ideas (as much as possible), listening on multiple levels, and validating your understanding. Table 7.3 details specific behaviors covering each of these general points.

Table 7.3: Active Listening

General Point	Specific Behaviors
Pay attention	Don't talk, don't interrupt
	Don't rehearse what you will say next
	Don't be defensive
	Show attention through nonverbal behavior (eye-contact, nodding)
Don't hold onto preconceived ideas	Don't judge the person
	Don't be critical of the person
	Be aware of mental filters (e.g., "he always lies")
Listen on multiple levels	Be aware of the content of the words
	Try to understand the feeling state behind the words
	Try to understand what he/she wants to accomplish
Validate your understanding	Ask for additional information
	Ask for clarification
	Summarize and paraphrase your understanding of what the other person has said, and ask whether you understood. If not, ask what you missed.

Suggesting that you listen on multiple levels is asking you to make inferences, a practice we generally discourage. However, in this case these are *hypotheses* that the other person must validate before you treat them as truths.

Communication has two levels: content and emotion. Most people tend to be less aware of the underlying emotional level of communication than of the overt content. Nevertheless, we continually react to our perceptions of emotional messages and we continually send messages on the emotional level. Understanding someone's emotional state is a vital part of understanding what he or she wants, what they're going through, and what steps might lead to a solution. It is likely that the problem gambler will feel supported if you accurately understand his or her feelings, which is an important step toward a productive dialogue.

At times, you may resent trying to understand the problem gambler's feelings, particularly if his behavior causes so much difficulty and he appears to pay little attention to your feelings. Keep in mind that understanding his feelings does not imply that you have to "fix" any bad feelings he may have. However, if you choose to do that, you do have the option of offering assistance.

Remain alert to your own feelings because they might influence your perceptions and choice of responses.

Be aware of your own reactions. Everyone has sensitive areas that require only mild stimulation to evoke a strong emotional reaction. These areas are commonly called "buttons," and were "installed" during strong emotional experiences earlier in life —often during childhood but sometimes during earlier interactions with this particular person. Although current stimulation might activate these buttons, the intensity of our reactions is driven by earlier learning. For example, if a person is sensitive about his/her intelligence, and even oblique reference is made to this ("You don't get the point"), a strong (at least internal) reaction is likely. If you understand that the intensity of such a reaction is related to an earlier time, not the current situation, you will be better able to stay focused on the current interaction and reduce the chance of derailing the discussion.

Behavior communicates. Remember, communication occurs on verbal, nonverbal, and behavioral channels. You will probably be looking for behavioral changes as a measure of how things are going and to determine whether you are moving toward your goals. This should be considered part of the dialogue, especially if the problem gambler does not have a verbally expressive style and finds it easier to communicate by acting. In this case, you should still express your concerns and what you want as recommended. Tell him you will be listening for his answer by observing what he does, and remind him you still want to communicate verbally and that you will be asking for another chance to do that after you get his reply.

Are the behavioral messages consistent or inconsistent with what is expressed verbally? You'll need to identify the pattern of concordance and discordance between behavioral and verbal messages to completely understand another person's overall communication.

The Essentials of Realistic Listening

Appraise new data objectively. Active listening requires suspending judgment and criticism of the person. However, it does *not* imply suspending critical judgment of the data (the content of the problem gambler's comments). You may have learned from painful experience that gamblers tend to deny they have a problem. They may say things that are clearly at odds with factual data. Although you should not try to "catch" them in an inaccurate statement, you should be ready to compare what they say to objective (observable) facts.

The problem gambler may try to minimize or block your access to full information, or make false statements to explain facts. For example, your spouse may claim that your dwindling bank account is low ʙᴇᴄᴀᴜꜱᴇ ɪɴᴛᴇʀᴇꜱᴛ ʀᴀᴛᴇꜱ ʜᴀᴠᴇ ʙᴇᴇɴ lower for several months (explaining), although she may not allow you to see her income statements (blocking access). Or perhaps your daughter's bills from college have increased by $150 a month over previous semesters. She explains that her laboratory expenses and attendance at campus extracurricular activities (films, theater, sports) has grown as she has grown increasingly immersed in college life. However, she cannot produce receipts that document these expenses. How should you manage these situations?

You should thoughtfully and critically evaluate all available information. If information is missing that your family member has the power to supply, you should ask for it. If she doesn't grant your request, that refusal becomes a fact that you add to your data bank. This may, when combined with other signs (see chapter 2), lead to the conclusion that she is gambling excessively. (See the section "Responding" later in this chapter for more on this subject.)

Five Major Types of Objections

Your family member may raise constructive points or one of the following nonconstructive objections:

1. **Aggressive behavior.** This includes an element of attack (yelling, insulting, etc.) and must be distinguished from assertive behavior Not all behavior associated with anger is necessarily aggressive. Anger is a normal human emotion and if expressed appropriately, it has a proper place in a dialogue.

2. **Denial.** This is a complex response (see chapter 5). In some cases, the problem gambler may not realize he has a problem. In other cases, he may realize he has a problem but says he doesn't or may

even claim that he is not engaging in any significant gambling behavior.

3. **Manipulation.** This refers to behavior designed to achieve a goal through indirect and/or devious means. This goal can be accomplished either by pretending to pursue another goal, or sending messages on the emotional level primarily for the purpose of achieving that goal. The latter method is the one most commonly used in dialogues and the classic example is inducing guilt. For example, say you state your concerns about the financial impact of your family member's gambling. He replies, "I work two jobs but there's never enough money to meet your needs." If this maneuver were successful, the focus would shift to your excessive demands on an overworked person, which might induce guilt in you. Other emotions may also be induced in attempts to manipulate people. For example, many people are anxious when confronted with aggressive behavior. Although such behavior is not necessarily manipulative, it can be if its intended purpose is the induction of anxiety to inhibit you from pursuing your goals.

4. **Passive-aggressive behavior.** This is characterized by the expression of anger through the failure to do something that was agreed upon. For example, if your family member agrees to attend Gamblers Anonymous but consistently "forgets" to attend, then she is responding in a passive-aggressive way. Such behavior can not be deduced from any one situation; there must be a pattern.

5. **Insistence that additional gambling will solve financial hardships.** The problem gambler may honestly believe that the best solution to this problem is to regain financial well-being by winning money through gambling. This is the heart of chasing (see chapter 2). One major difference between problem gamblers and substance abusers is that gamblers see continued pursuit of their habit as a solution to the problem while substance abusers do not. Some problem gamblers who believe this is the most effective strategy will not spontaneously say so. You may have to ask the gambler directly if this is his or her preferred strategy.

Three Principles for Responses

There are three general principles for responding.

1. **Acknowledge your family member's point of view by restating and summarizing her points and checking to be sure you are accurate.** If you did not state the point sufficiently clearly, ask for more information and clarification. Depending on the situation, you may acknowledge the content and/or the emotion.

2. **Support and understand her point of view as much as you can. Search for areas of agreement.** If you can't find agreement, at least try to find an area that you can support in some way. If even that is impossible, try to express understanding of the basis of her ideas and/or feelings. By understanding what thoughts lead to specific emotions (see chapter 5), you should be able to delve beneath the surface of her emotions.

3. **Continue the dialogue remembering to incorporate any new information gained from listening.** You may be tempted or provoked into losing sight of your goals in the heat of a discussion so you'll need to stay focused. Maintaining control in the heat of the moment requires that you be aware of the thoughts, as well as emotions and behavior (see chapter 5), that characterize your response to each of the five different objections. If you know that your automatic tendency will not be a productive one to a particular objection, anticipating it will allow you to plan an alternate, more productive response. Managing your own emotional response allows you to convey an understanding of your family member and to keep the dialogue on track.

Here are some suggestions on how to respond to the five types of objections.

1. **Aggression.** If there are questions of physical safety, this is the *primary* concern. Turn to chapter 11 where we address this problem. In this discussion, we are assuming there are no threats to physical safety. Aggression provokes a variety of emotional responses, including anger, anxiety, and guilt. Are one or more of these responses characteristic of you? Follow the general guidelines by trying to anticipate and work on your response before being confronted with the behavior.

Anger is usually a response to perceived unfairness, injustice, or an attack. Aggression follows from poor anger management skills and/or a pursuit of a specific goal such as discouraging you from continuing the dialogue. Aggressive behavior may often be defused if you show that you understand the basis for the anger. Even in the face of a direct insult, you can understand the gambler's position and say, "You appear angry. I wonder if you think I am being unfair." You might add, "I can understand that my concerns about the finances may seem unfair to you. However, try to understand how not paying the rent affects our family. I am not trying to attack you but I am trying to work together to solve this problem. Therefore, I do want to return to the question of getting our finances straightened out."

2. **Denial.** In the face of denial, persistence is the key word. In the face of repeated denials, many people allow anger and impatience

to sidetrack the discussion. Although those feelings are common and reasonable responses to denial, your dialogue will be more productive if you manage them in accordance with the three general principles described in the section just prior to this one.

Many people feel powerless to persist in the face of repeated denials. Perhaps the problem gambler not only denies there are any financial problems but also denies he or she is gambling. Some people become extremely anxious if they continue to assert their concerns in the face of such direct denials. The size of the problem often forces these people to move past their discomfort, but frequently not before there are serious additional losses. Again, you may need professional help in assertiveness training to manage this difficult situation.

3. **Manipulation.** The keys to managing manipulation are these: awareness that it is occurring, awareness of your own reactions, and the ability to directly address the process that is taking place between the two of you. The gambler may use aggressive behavior to intimidate you or to make it unpleasant for you to develop a dialogue. (This is different from a situation where the aggressive behavior is primarily a matter of limited skills.) You might address this directly by saying, "When you yell at me like that, I get very anxious, even frightened. That makes it hard for me to continue with this discussion. However, I want to continue because I believe that working together offers us the best chance of solving our differences. I am open to your ideas about how to make this discussion work well. How can I present my point in a way that will be most acceptable to you?" Your family member may be responsive or may continue with aggressive behavior. Remember, you cannot control his behavior—your goal is to interact in a way that will maximize your chances of success.

4. **Passive-aggressive behavior.** This is tricky to identify because it requires discerning a pattern over time. The solution is to keep the focus on behavior rather than on promises or stated intentions, so that your family member is fully aware that your goal is behavioral change. This approach also minimizes the disappointment that can result if your hopes are raised by verbal assurances only to be dashed by a lack of follow-through.

5. **Insistence that additional gambling is the solution.** The problem gambler may leave this idea unspoken because he knows you do not agree. Because chasing is almost universal among problem gamblers, you should raise this issue and firmly state your view that this will aggravate the problem. The idea may be a tenacious one, however, and the problem gambler may require formal treatment to resolve it.

Exercise: How to Respond to Objections

Now, take out your journal and, after reading the objections, write down your responses to them by applying the three general principles of responding. Incorporate the specific strategy designed for each particular type of objection. (Example answers follow this exercise.)

1. **Aggressive.** "You're always putting me down. If it's not one thing it's another. You're a total nag and really awful."

2. **Denial.** "I just play a few scratch-off tickets and go to the track once in a great while with my friends. What's the big deal?"

3. **Manipulation.** "You know the kind of pressure I've been under with my eyesight failing and my best friends ill or gone. You know the doctor told me to find things that are enjoyable and relaxing. Gambling is the one thing that provides that for me and you begrudge me even that. You're undermining my health and you know my doctor would say the same thing."

4. **Passive-aggressive response.** "Yes, I can see that you are right to have these concerns. I am going to sharply cut back on my gambling activity at once."

5. **Further gambling as a solution.** "We are $65,000 in debt. I make only $30,000 per year. It would take twenty years to get out of debt by working. Winning it back is our only chance out of this mess."

Example Answers

1. **Aggression.** I understand that you might feel that way and perhaps you believe I am being unfairly critical of you (Principles 1 and 2). However, I do want to use this time for us to talk honestly and openly with each other, to express my concerns without being critical, and to understand your point of view. We did agree to use this time to do that and I would like to continue. If, as we proceed, you feel that I am putting you down, please point that out to me and I'll take a look at it. But I would like to continue now and express what I see and also I want to understand your point of view (Principle 3). Is that all right?

2. **Denial.** What I'm saying is that I have some concerns. Your comments suggest that you don't see the basis for my concerns (Principle 1). That's just why I asked for this time to talk together so that I could express my concerns and together we could figure out

whether those concerns have merit or, as you suggest, it's no big deal (Principle 2). So I'd like to get started on this so we can reach an understanding (Principle 3). Is that all right?

3. **Manipulation.** Recent years have been very hard for you and you absolutely deserve and need enjoyment and relaxation (Principles 1 and 2). When you suggest that I might hurt your health, my first reaction is to feel guilty. But if I stop to look at that, I know that there is nothing that I want more than for you and our family to be healthy. It's my judgment that gambling, which at first brought you relaxation, is now adding to your tension level. I want to use this time to express my concerns and to hear your point of view (Principle 3). I would like to stay focused today on the impact your gambling is having and I'd like to find another time for us to discuss various other ways that you might relax (Principle 3).

4. **Passive-Aggressive.** (If this is the first time your family member has said this, you might reply as follows.) I am very happy to hear you say that. That is a great beginning (Principles 1 and 2). Let's take a look at what exactly you mean when you say, "I am going to sharply cut back on my gambling at once." Perhaps it would be helpful to determine how much and how frequently you gamble now and how much and how frequently you would gamble over the next week. That way we can set some concrete and observable goals and review them together at the end of one month to see if you are meeting those goals (Principle 3).

5. **Further gambling as a solution.** I see how you can argue that gambling is the solution (Principles 1 and 2). However, it is my belief that gambling can and probably will make things worse. Other families have gotten out of this kind of debt with help and hard work and we can do it too. Let's work on ways to solve this financial mess without gambling (Principle 3).

Try to anticipate how the other person might respond. Keep the three general principles for responding in mind so you can manage the response no matter what it is. Objections can be complex, with more than one type combined into a single comment. Try to invent a few more possible objections the gambler might raise and figure out how you would handle them. If you have someone who can help you with this, you can role play it. Basically, role playing is practicing an interpersonal situation. Why not get some practice at it before you have to handle the real thing? That's how many people learn to handle difficult situations of all types—including interpersonal situations. If you have a trusted friend or family member whom you can role play with, doing so will add to your confidence and skill.

Chapter **8**

Repairing Relations Outside the Immediate Family

Problem gambling undermines trust and mutuality in relationships between the gambler and family relatives, in-laws, friends, neighbors, co-workers, and other members of the community. The problem gambler in desperation may have lied, manipulated others' emotions and goodwill, borrowed money without repayment, and even cheated and robbed. It is rare to find a problem gambler who has not seriously disrupted at least some of his or her family's important outside relationships.

As a spouse, partner, parent, or adult child of a problem gambler, you may have to endure the hardship of being targeted by the mistrust, suspicion, anger, and bitterness engendered by the problem gambler in those outside your family circle who were betrayed or harmed by the gambler's actions. In some cases, people may express their resentment directly to you as if you were somehow responsible for the gambler's behavior. In other cases, people may avoid you at school, church, or in your neighborhood. They may fail to return your phone calls. You may no longer be invited to social functions. Whatever form it takes, the damage to these relationships can be devastating because healthy external relationships are critical contributors to your well-being and that of your family.

Repairing these damaged relations with those people who are important to your family's life is an important healing step. Doing this will provide you, your gambling relative, and the rest of your family with needed support as you all recover from the corrosive effects of the problem gambler's behavior on life within the family. This process can be slow, difficult, and, at times, uncomfortable. It requires courage, persistence, and emotional fortitude. It is also important to distinguish between the responsibilities of the problem gambler to heal these relations and what you can do as an immediate family member. (See chapter 6 for a discussion of what you can and can't do to help the gambler.)

In this chapter, we provide you with a framework for assessing the nature of the damage caused by the problem gambler's behavior. We also provide a set of specific measures you, the problem gambler, and others in your family can take, both together and independently, to repair relations with those outside your immediate family. We urge you to begin this process as soon as possible because reestablishing relationships with people important to your family's life is the best way to get emotional and practical support during the challenging period of recovery.

Surveying the Damage

If you have lived a long time with a problem gambler, you have direct experience of the more obvious effects of the problem gambler's behavior on your immediate family and others outside the family. (See chapter 4 for some of the more subtle, destructive effects of problem gambling on family relationships.)

When surveying the damage to those outside the immediate family, it helps to distinguish between practical and emotional effects. Some people may have suffered significant practical consequences from relying on the gambler's word or attempting to help him or her. For example, they may have dipped into savings to lend the gambler money, or guaranteed the gambler's use of a rental car, or authorized the gambler to access cash deposits at a place of business. Until the gambler (preferably) or you or another family member acknowledges and at least apologizes for the practical consequences of the gambler's behavior, it is often difficult to move forward in the healing process and to reconnect with others.

Understanding the practical effects may make it easier to appreciate why some individuals react so strongly to the gambler's actions. People often react with strong emotions because they feel betrayed or taken advantage of *after* they have gone out of their way to be supportive or helpful to the gambler. When people trust us or extend a helping hand, they generally expect a reciprocal response on our part. The gambler has violated this expectation, which often results in anger and bitterness on the part of the betrayed person.

People outside the family may also have suffered emotional loss resulting from the distancing from relationships with you and other family members, including the gambler. Sometimes relatives, friends, neighbors, and co-workers may have chosen to withdraw out of anger. Other times, it may be you or other family members who have withdrawn from regular communication. As discussed in chapter 4, you may have cut off contact because you are preoccupied with difficulties inside the family. Alternatively, you may feel ashamed or guilty about the gambler's behavior and do not want to offer explanations and rationalizations for that behavior and the problems it is creating. Either way, both you and significant people outside the family experience loss and deprivation of important, nourishing contacts.

Reviewing Important Relationships

In chapter 5 you were asked to enlist the aid of other family members to prepare lists of all the important individuals with whom each family member has had supportive contact, on either a regular or infrequent basis. You may recall the contact could be face-to-face or by telephone, e-mail, or letter and could involve a variety of different kinds of support, including giving or lending money; helping with a project or task; advising, guiding, or sharing information; sharing thoughts and feelings in conversation; and engaging in leisure activities together. How often you have contact is less important than the quality of that contact. If you have not completed this exercise, we suggest you do so now.

Once you have finished this exercise, take the names you and family members have identified and transfer them to a master table with four columns as in the example in table 8.1. (Use table 8.2 at the end of this chapter as a model to prepare a comprehensive table of your family in your journal.) In the extreme left-hand column, write in the name of each individual family member. Then, in the second column list all individuals with whom each family member has had supportive contact. In the right-hand column you are going to write in some information about each of your family member's priority relationships.

Assessing Priority Relationships

The next step in the exercise involves prioritizing for each family member the relationships assembled under his or her name. The simplest way to do this is to ask each family member to go through his or her sub-list and pick out the three most important relationships. If others are participating, let each family member determine this in his or her own way. You can ask them something like this: "Among the people on this list under your name, who would you say are the three most important in your life right now?" Put a "1" next to these names in each person's sub-list. You can often learn a lot just by listening to other family members explain how they came up with their priority names. If you are doing this exercise alone, use your judgment in picking the most important relationships for each person in the family. Consider the importance of a relationship independently of any current problems caused by your relative's gambling.

Table 8.1: Master List of Important Relationships

Family Members	Important Relationships	P	Current State of Relationship
JACK	Brad Johnson (boss)		
	Pete Snow (fishing buddy)	1	No contact for 4 months-owe him $800
	Aunt Mary	1	Angry, but still talks to me
	Robert Drake		
	Reverend Wilson	1	Only nonfamily member who knows about our problem
	Dr. Hunter		
MARTHA	Holly (my best friend)	1	My closest support right now
	Carol and Sam next door	1	Since Jack lied to them and borrowed $400, won't speak to us
	Jane (organist at church)		
	Sylvia Roberts (co-worker)		
	Sam Fleming (my boss)		

	Holly (choir member)		
	Grace (choir member)		
	Sally (choir member)		
	Aunt Mary		
	Uncle Dave		
	Mother	1	Keeps telling me to divorce Jack—we get into arguments
TERRY	Wanda (my girlfriend)	1	Okay, but doesn't understand why I never bring her to meet Dad
	Forrest (best friend)	1	Talk to him two/three times a week
	Coach Lake	1	Upset I dropped out of varsity football to help Mom out at home
JOANNE	Sarah (friend from 6th grade)	1	Okay
	Joel (friend from 5th grade)	1	Okay
	Uncle Dave		
	Grandma	1	Love talking to her on the phone
	Ms. Hemingway (teacher)		

Often the same individual will show up on different family members' lists. For example, one woman who completed this exercise had a close friend living down the street who had known the children in the family since they were born and often took care of them after school. Her friend appeared as a priority relationship not only on her list, but also on the list of two of her three children. A name that appears as a priority relationship on several family members' lists is a "super-priority" relationship.

After you develop your master list of priority relationships, review each priority name and take the time to assess the current state of that relationship. For this part of the exercise, continue to include the gambling member of your family if at all possible. You should also ask other family members for their assessment of how things are going in a particular relationship. For example, you may know only superficially about the quality of the relationships that your children have with some of the people in their lives, particularly their friends and teachers at school. In some cases, other family members may have a very different assessment of the state of a particular relationship from what you assume it to be. Having a conversation with other family members can be an opportunity to learn more about each family member's experience of those relationships and any difficulties they are currently experiencing with the important people in their lives.

During your review, pay particular attention to identifying any previous interactions with the problem gambler that may have done damage to the relationship. Although you should rely on input from the problem gambler, you may consult other family members, as well, on this particular issue—if they are old enough or familiar enough with the situation to provide useful input. Their perspective may be somewhat different from yours or that of the gambler's.

Should Children Take Part?

Many parents wonder how old a child must be to include that child in this type of discussion. It's difficult to give hard-and-fast guidelines in this area because children mature at different rates, and families differ on the degree to which children are included in adult discussions. A conservative approach would be to include only children who are at least twelve years old in this discussion. A risk exists that younger children may be disturbed or threatened by a frank discussion of the impact of the gambler's behavior on family relationships. They may scapegoat the gambler as the cause of all the problems in the family, failing to understand fully the complexities of adult relationships.

Your own comfort level and the comfort level of your children are important guidelines. Generally speaking, children will let you know by their words and behavior if they feel uncomfortable in participating in such a discussion. So, pay close attention to your children's reactions when you invite them to participate and make sure they understand it's all right to say "no." Be sure they understand the purpose of the exercise. Keep them informed about follow-up efforts to restore important relationships in the family, and make it clear that it is not their responsibility to "fix" the relationship. Often, parents underestimate the degree of awareness their children have about family problems. If you know your older children are aware of damage to any of their relationships caused by the problem gambler's actions, it may make sense to include them in assessing the damage and understanding what you and others will be doing to heal the damage.

Reviewing Priority Relationships

As you review the various priority names on your master list, enter a few words describing the current state of the relationship in the right-hand column of the table opposite the name listed. For the "super-priority" names that appear more than once, write in the comments only the first time the name appears in the master list. Try to avoid vague descriptions like, "The relationship has some problems." Instead, focus on concrete particulars: "Jack borrowed $2,000 from Uncle Danny. No contact with the family for six months" or "The last contact with Sid was an angry confrontation in which he told Jack to 'get his act together' before coming back to work."

Be sure to enter brief comments about healthy priority relationships as well. Many of these will already have been identified in conducting the exercise outlined in chapter 5. Before you enter the comments, make sure you review your planned entries with each family member participating in the discussion to be quite sure your written comments accurately reflect various individuals' views of the relationship. If different family members have differing opinions of the state of a current relationship, consider it an opportunity to discuss your differing views. If there is still no consensus after this discussion, simply note the various perspectives in the right-hand column.

At least a few of the priority relationships in most families will have been negatively impacted *directly or indirectly* by the actions of the problem gambler. For some families, most of the priority relationships may have been affected. If at least some of your family members' top three identified priority relationships have been so affected, we suggest that you pause at this point. You now have plenty of information to begin planning a strategy for restoring the important relationships in your family's life.

You may complete this stage of the exercise, however, and find that none of the identified priority relationships has been negatively affected by your gambling relative's actions. If that is the case, we suggest you go back and repeat the prioritizing process for the next three most important relationships on each family member's list. Put a "2" in front of these names. Again, review these names and assess the current state of these relationships, focusing particularly on whether or not they have been damaged in any way by the problem gambler's activities. If none of these relationships appear to have been affected by problem gambling, then continue with a third round. Eventually, you will almost certainly encounter some relationships that have been negatively affected.

If many of the important priority relationships in your family members' lives have been damaged by problem gambling, doing this exercise may leave you feeling overwhelmed, depressed, or in despair. See chapter 5 to help you manage these feelings. Although it may be true that many of the relationships important to your family are currently in disrepair, there are many things you can do to change this situation. In addition, doing this exercise should give you and other family members a clearer understanding of who the important people in your family members' lives are and the ways in which they are important. You may also have a newfound appreciation for how many people are potentially available to provide you and your family with support while you address the effects of problem gambling on your family.

Don't be troubled if you have few people on your list, perhaps because you are new to town or because your family leads a relatively private life. The odds are that many of these people—and many more you might identify in the future—will be willing to offer friendship, support, and assistance, particularly if you take the first step in reaching out to them.

Restoring Important Relationships

Reaching out to others who have been negatively affected by the problem gambler's actions may seem intimidating. Still, it's important to remember three things. First, your willingness to take the initiative and your sincere desire to improve the situation are your best resources. Second, many people—particularly people who have made positive contributions to your family's life in the past—will respond positively to almost *any* initiative you take to restore your relationship. Third, persistence is golden. Even with those individuals who don't respond positively to your first attempt to break the ice, don't give up. If you continue to demonstrate in various ways your sincere desire to improve things, most people will be willing to forgive.

Before you, the gambler, or others in the family develop a plan of action, however, you should carefully distinguish between your goals and responsibility with regard to restoring relationships and the goals and responsibility of the gambler (see chapter 6). When sorting out the issue of responsibility, you may find it helpful to draw clear distinctions between the gambler's actions and the practical consequences of those actions. For example, suppose a problem gambler told a close family friend that she needed to borrow $1,000 to settle some outstanding family medical bills. She then lost the money playing blackjack at a nearby casino and is now unable to make repayment. Her lie to her friend and her failure to repay the loan were her actions. The practical consequences of her actions for the friend are the loss of $1,000.

Often family members have a tendency to assume blame, guilt, or responsibility for the gambler's actions. Yet, in most cases, nothing you or others in the family could have done would have prevented the gambler from gambling, lying, manipulating others, or cheating and stealing in order to continue the behavior. In this sense, almost everything the gambler may have done to damage a relationship can be thought of as the gambler's responsibility, not yours.

As was discussed in chapters 4 and 6, family members sometimes engage in co-dependent or enabling behaviors that unwittingly support or even reinforce the gambler's activities. If this was the case in your family, it's important for you or other family members to acknowledge your contribution to the situation. While acknowledging responsibility for your role in supporting the gambler's activities, you and other family members should also forgive yourselves. Similarly, if an outside relationship has been strained by your failure to put appropriate energy into maintaining that relationship or by your distancing yourself, acknowledge responsibility and apologize to the other person while reminding yourself that you and others in the family have done the best you could to cope with some very difficult circumstances.

Even though you may not be directly responsible for the gambler's actions, you may feel morally responsible as a member of the gambler's family when others have suffered financial or other practical harm as a result of those actions. Some of those who were harmed also may consider you morally responsible for the consequences. We cannot advise you whether you should take on the burden of settling any of your family member's debts out of moral considerations. However, we encourage you to reflect carefully on the reasons behind your sense of moral responsibility, your motivation, and the potential impact of your decision on both the gambler and the other party to the relationship.

Moral Responsibility

Many people may feel morally responsible for the consequences of the gambler's actions because they realize their failure to act, or to act effectively, contributed to the gambling relative's behavior and the ensuing consequences for others. Alternatively, they may subscribe to a cultural value that the misbehavior of one member of a family unit results in guilt and shame and collective responsibility for all family members. Shouldering the burden of repayment provides relief from this guilt or shame. In still other cases, family members may take on the burden to satisfy or placate an individual harmed by the gambler who believes that the family is somehow responsible. Repaying the debt frees up both the family member and the other party to resume normal relations.

If you do decide to assume responsibility for the gambler's debts, you may actually make it easier for the gambler to avoid acknowledging this responsibility to himself/herself as well as to those who suffered practical injury from the gambler's actions. Thus, you should emphasize to the gambler that you are freely choosing to make restitution, not to rescue the gambler, but to fulfill a moral obligation. You should also emphasize your expectation that the gambler eventually will acknowledge his or her responsibility to the individual who suffered the consequences.

Developing a Plan of Action

In developing a plan of action for restoring relationships, you should involve the gambler as well as other appropriate family members as much as possible in selecting which individuals to approach first and in making overtures to those individuals. This should be relatively easy if you have a history of good communication in your family and the gambler has acknowledged responsibility and is committed to recovery. If this is not your family's situation, you may need to begin the process on your own. Often through your example you can encourage the gambler and other family members to become involved in the process eventually.

In either case, it's important to be clear in your own mind that you are trying to improve a relationship primarily for the benefits it may bring to you and other family members and only secondarily for the benefits it may bring to the gambler. Review the ways this particular relationship has been beneficial to you (as well as to the other party to the relationship) and think about how you would like it to be in the future. By doing this, when you approach the individual, you will be prepared to discuss how important the relationship is to you and why you care so much about restoring it. This is more effective than acting solely as a spokesperson or intermediary for the gambler.

When reaching out to others, you should focus on only one or two of your priority relationships at a time. Other family members, including the gambler, should follow the same guideline. Relationship rebuilding takes time and emotional energy. Although some relationships will be restored easily, others may prove much more difficult. You may encounter temporary setbacks along the way.

Many people will have to work through negative feelings they harbor toward the gambler or toward you as a member of the gambler's family. If you try to spread yourself too thin—attempting to rebuild a large number of relationships all at once—you may leave yourself emotionally drained and frustrated. Restoring relationships is like building a brick wall. Proceed brick by brick to ensure that the wall's foundation is strong and secure. Otherwise, you risk putting the whole structure in jeopardy.

Try to get support from other members of your family as well as from at least one good friend not affected by the gambler's activities. That way, you'll have somebody to lean on for advice and reassurance if you run into difficulties. If you do not have close friends or relatives, or if the gambler's activities have created strains in all of your friendships, seek out a religious counselor or a therapist who can provide you with the support you need. As you begin to rebuild relationships with the important people in your life and the life of your family, each restored relationship can then serve as an additional source of support for you.

Making Contact

Many of the principles we outlined in chapter 7 for creating a dialogue with your gambling relative can be applied to making contact with individuals outside the family. Unlike your gambling relative, however, many individuals you approach outside the family will be interested from the start in achieving the same goal as you—reestablishing good relations—*if* their feelings and concerns are acknowledged and if a genuine apology is made for any negative consequences they have endured as a result of your gambling relative's behavior or your own inattention to the relationship.

Do not underestimate the power of an apology and the willingness of most people of goodwill to extend forgiveness if given the opportunity to do so. It is good to apologize even though you may not feel personally responsible for the gambler's actions or the consequences arising from those actions. A genuine apology communicates that you recognize the wrong done to the other person and you wish it had not occurred. It also prepares the ground for the other person to forgive the gambler, you, or anybody else they consider responsible in any way for the consequences they suffered. It is difficult for most aggrieved people to forgive a wrong until they believe their concerns and feelings have been acknowledged. A genuine apology accomplishes this. The subsequent act of forgiveness is a way of reciprocating the apology. Together, these two actions lay the groundwork for both parties to the relationship to move on from the current impasse.

Find the Right Time

When you are ready to reconnect with an individual, choose a time to make contact when both you and that person are likely to be less stressed, distracted, or fatigued. Calling at home in the evening after the dinner hour or on the weekend is often a good time. You may also approach the individual at social or community events if he or she is not likely to be otherwise preoccupied or engaged. Be honest and direct. Acknowledge that the relationship has been strained or damaged (or, if you have had no contact in a long time, that you suspect it has), and say that you would like to find some time when the two of you can talk at length without interruption about your relationship. Ask if now is a good time (if you don't already know). If the other person indicates it is, you may proceed. Otherwise, agree on a later time to continue the conversation. If the other person immediately starts talking about the issues between you or launches into a list of grievances, listen carefully, but at the first opportunity, check to make sure that now is really a good time for an extended discussion about your relationship.

Sample Opening Dialogue

Sue: Hi, Mary. I'm concerned about how things have been between us over the past few months and I'd like to find a convenient time when we could talk without any distractions. Is this a good time to have this kind of discussion?

Mary: (angrily) You know, Sue, Jack said he was going to pay back that $1,500 he owes us six months ago, and I haven't heard one word out of him. Both Fred and I are very upset about this. How come he never returns any of my calls?

Sue: I can certainly understand you and Fred being angry you haven't heard from Jack. I'd like to talk at some length about this. Do you have at least twenty minutes for us to talk without being interrupted?

Mary: Well, let me ask Fred to put the kids to bed and I'll call you back in about ten minutes.

Aim for a Win-Win Conversation

While it is reasonable to assume that both you and the other person want to put your relationship back on track, the other individual may have additional goals as well. For example, she may want you to acknowledge the injury she sustained, appreciate her feelings, and offer an explicit apology. Pay attention to the person's nonverbal behavior during the conversation, such as gestures, facial expressions, and tone of voice. Is the person's tone of voice relaxed? Is she animatedly engaged in the conversation or does she seem guarded and cautious? Often such cues can tell you whether the person is getting what she wants from a conversation. If you are not sure, a direct question may provide the answer: "Are you satisfied with our conversation?" or "Is there anything important we haven't covered?" are good questions to ask if you are not sure.

State Your Concerns

Begin by thanking the person for agreeing to take the time to talk with you. Indicate that you value the relationship highly and would like to reestablish good relations. You may disclose some of your own feelings about the disruption in the relationship. Acknowledge once again the recent damage your relationship has suffered. Give a brief, honest explanation for the damage, but do not go into detail to avoid becoming bogged down in a detailed discussion about the gambler's situation and your private life. You may make brief reference to any consequences suffered by the other individual if you are aware of these. You may also apologize at this point for those consequences, if you think it's appropriate to do so.

Sample Explanation

Sue: Thanks, Mary, for calling me back. Mary, we've been friends for over five years. I've felt very bad about the loss of regular contact with you over the past few months. I understand how upset you and Fred have been over Jack's behavior. Jack borrowed that money from you because until recently he has been unsuccessfully struggling with a gambling problem. He's currently receiving help for this problem and I know he will eventually want to work things out with you. I only found out about the loan two weeks ago when Jack sat down and told me everything. I'm just very sorry things have gone this way.

Listen to the Other Person's Concerns

At this point, you should stop talking and give the other person an opportunity to respond. Many people make the mistake of talking too much, trying to persuade the other person to let bygones be bygones. The most persuasive thing you can do is to actively listen without judgment to the other person's reactions and concerns (see chapter 7). Allow her to express her understanding of recent events and to vent any negative feelings she may have. Don't attempt to argue or dispute her version of events or the appropriateness of her reactions. Instead, pay attention to what she is saying, listening to both the content of the words and the person's feeling state. Acknowledge what she says, periodically asking for clarification and relaying your understanding of her communication.

Look to the Future

Reaffirm how important the relationship is to you and your desire to get the relationship back on track. Be as specific and concrete as possible in describing how you would like the relationship to be in the future. For example: "Until you lent the money to Rick, I felt I could drop by anytime to say hello and see how you were doing. I'd like to have that kind of relationship again."

Ask the other person what needs to be done (if anything) by you, the gambler, or other family members before she or he will be ready to put recent events behind them. Many people will be ready almost immediately to resume relations. Others may have specific requests. Some people may wish to speak with the gambler directly. Others may raise the issue of repayment of loans. You should listen without judgment to the person's requests. He or she will tell you what is needed to feel comfortable before resuming relations. If the person makes requests you consider unreasonable or outrageous, listening carefully does not mean you have to agree to any of them.

If you do agree to meet any of the person's requests, make sure you do so willingly. Don't agree to do things that you don't want to do in a misplaced desire to improve the relationship at any cost. Instead, see if you can't come up with alternative measures, which will satisfy the person's needs. Often this can be accomplished by listening for what lies behind the person's requests. For example, someone who is demanding full repayment of a loan may be satisfied by an apology directly from the gambler and a partial repayment, particularly if your family is currently facing difficult financial conditions.

In a few rare situations, it may be impossible to meet the person's prerequisites for resuming normal relations without sacrificing your own needs or principles. In such situations, you may need to accept that the relationship is unlikely to be restored at this time. Instead, let go of this situation for now and put your energies into strengthening relationships with people whose requests you can reasonably meet.

How Much to Tell

How much should you tell people about the gambler's situation and the situation that your family is facing? Don't be pressured by other people's questions or your own need to be viewed in a particular light into disclosing more than you feel comfortable revealing. Don't be led into thinking that by revealing more, you will necessarily satisfy others and thereby increase their willingness to reconnect with you.

Another guideline is to tell people only what they need to know in order to decide whether or not to resume normal relations with you. Making use of this guideline, you can begin by describing only the bare details of the situation. If they ask questions, or seem unsatisfied by this level of disclosure, you may choose to elaborate and then check to see if this seems to satisfy them. In most situations, a brief, honest, clear description of the facts will suffice. Once the other person appears satisfied, disclose more only if the other person seems receptive and you feel a need yourself to discuss the situation further and get advice or feedback.

Another way to view this issue involves thinking about the level of intimacy you have with different people. With one or two close friends or extended family members, you may choose to disclose a great deal about the situation. With other friends you may disclose correspondingly less. With many neighbors, co-workers, and others from the community, you may reveal only the barest of details, if that. With a professional or religious counselor, you may reveal much more than you would even with close friends or family.

Working Toward a Resolution

As we noted at the beginning of this chapter, relationship repair is a long-term project requiring much energy, patience, and devotion. With some individuals, it may require several meetings just to reach the point where they are comfortable talking about what they need in order to resume normal relations. For some people this may be due to the depths of their alienation or to their deep-seated sense of grievance. Others may simply never have thought about their personal relationships in terms of their needs, wants, and requirements. They may need to think about these issues before they can respond to you as you hope they will.

Repairing hurt feelings and damaged trust takes time and effort. Trust is based more on deeds than on words, and deeds take time. As you will see in chapter 12, trust is not an all-or-nothing phenomenon; neither is the restoration of a relationship. Viewing relationship rebuilding as a step-by-step process will help you to be patient and will provide you with the optimism and fortitude to continue in the face of temporary setbacks. Such a perspective enables you to be rewarded by the accomplishment of even small steps in the rebuilding process.

In relationship repair, persistence is a virtue. In today's busy world, very few people take the time to cultivate personal relationships. If you are dedicated to the restoration of important connections in your life, most of those people will be impressed and grateful for your attention and for making their relationship a priority. Nourishing the relationships with important people in your family's life in a purposeful way can yield benefits that go beyond simple relationship repair, because our relationships provide purpose and meaning in our lives.

Table 8.2:
Master List of Important Relationships

Family Members	Important Relationships	P	Current State of Relationship

Chapter 9

Dealing with the Financial Impact of Problem Gambling

Problem gambling can wreak havoc on family finances in addition to destroying the finances of the problem gambler. Family members may discover that the desperate problem gambler has gambled away income, looted savings, signed away assets, and run up enormous debts with credit card companies, banks, finance companies, friends and extended family, even loan sharks. Often, the first signs of this draining of the family's or the gambler's financial well-being may not be recognized until the situation is out of control. Creditors may begin calling the home leaving threatening messages. A spouse may discover unpaid bills squirreled away in a drawer or in the problem gambler's clothing. A seemingly pleasant encounter with a family friend or neighbor may lead to an uncomfortable conversation in which the gambling relative's unpaid debt is revealed.

The family's financial vulnerability is greatest when the problem gambler is the main breadwinner and loses his or her job, or the gambler has direct access to the family's principal assets and lines of credit. But even when the problem gambler plays a more peripheral role in your family's finances, the effects can be severe for both the family and the gambler. Parents of a young adult may feel compelled to pay off debts to save their child's reputation and to provide rescue from financial ruin or worse. They may be forced to allocate current income or savings for the upkeep of the problem gambler who would otherwise be living and working on his own. The same may be true for the adult children of a gambling senior who has gambled away savings and pension benefits and run up sizeable debts.

Dealing with these destructive financial consequences may seem overwhelming initially. While this is particularly so if your knowledge and experience in financial matters is limited, even those familiar with family finance can find the task daunting. These consequences can be dealt with successfully, however, and your family's financial well-being can be restored. The same holds true for the financial health of a gambling relative. The key is understanding that financially disruptive changes have both *practical* and *emotional* consequences. You should be able to manage the practical consequences if you are armed with some general knowledge of the basics of family finance and an understanding of the details of your family's current financial status or that of your gambling relative.

Addressing the emotional consequences can be a greater challenge. It is common to feel intense anxiety, anger, and loss in the face of a dramatic downturn in your family's financial situation. These reactions may exacerbate the feelings of disappointment, betrayal, and loss you may already be experiencing about your family member's past words and actions. You may be tempted to overreact impulsively, and try to shore up the financial health of your family or your relative immediately. Alternatively, you may feel completely powerless to deal with the situation. Try to avoid both these extremes. It may well be important for you to move quickly to avert any further financial losses. But you should take action to improve the situation only when you have your emotions under control and can plan the steps required to restore your family's financial well-being calmly and deliberately.

In this chapter we provide you with the outlines of a step-by-step guide for setting your family on the road to financial recovery. We will help you to take stock of your financial situation or that of your relative, gain control of the family finances, establish a financial recovery plan, deal with creditors and legal authorities, and, if necessary, build a financial firewall between you and the problem gambler. During this process, you may find yourself repeatedly experiencing strong and sometimes unexpected emotions. Much of this will be due to your financial vulnerability and the gambler's previous actions. However, dealing with money matters in general often evokes powerful and conflicted feelings, such as guilt, shame, and anxiety. It's important to recognize these feelings as they arise and to limit their influence on your financial decisions.

The steps to financial recovery are more or less the same whether the gambler is a spouse, an underage child, or an adult child or senior who is financially independent. Thus, throughout the rest of this chapter we refer to "your family's finances" even in those situations where you are assisting an adult relative to restore his or her financial well-being independent of the financial status of your immediate family.

Taking Over or Sharing Control of Finances

Before you can take practical steps to improve your family's financial status, we recommend you have adequate access to financial records and sufficient control to allow you to make informed financial decisions. When the problem gambler is your spouse, you may need to do little of a practical nature to ensure control if you are a primary breadwinner, actively manage your family's finances, and have your name on all major assets and accounts. However, if that role has been filled primarily by the problem gambler, usually you will need to take additional steps to ensure access to financial records and at least joint responsibility, if not sole responsibility, for family assets and income.

Any significant change in financial management roles in the family may arouse strong feelings on the part of the problem gambler and other family members. Couples consciously or unconsciously negotiate and determine their roles regarding money management early in their relationships. Often, those roles will be based on traditional cultural practices or the ways in which the couples' parents divided financial management responsibilities. Any break from this tradition may be experienced as disruptive and threatening. Additionally, if you propose a more active role for yourself in managing the family's finances, the problem gambler may view this as spotlighting his or her failure to do so effectively. If you have any concerns that your spouse might react to your proposal in a manner that threatens either his or her safety or the safety of other family members, we recommend that you first review the safety guidelines outlined in chapter 11 and consult a clinical professional for advice.

First Steps

Your first step should simply be to ask your spouse to agree to you taking a more active role in managing the family's financial affairs. Explain that your involvement should help restore financial well-being to both the family and the gambler. We recommend reviewing the steps for a productive dialogue outlined in chapter 7 to help you win your spouse's agreement. Initially, such a proposal may arouse resistance and feelings of anger, anxiety, shame, and guilt for the problem gambler. Acknowledge the gambler's feelings, but repeat the request, explaining again that your involvement should prove beneficial to the financial well-being of both the family and the gambler. You may choose to point out that a more active role on your part does not necessarily mean excluding the problem gambler from financial decisions. Explain that you would prefer to work together as a team in making financial decisions.

If you encounter continued resistance, encourage your spouse to discuss his or her concerns about your greater involvement in the family's financial affairs. This may open up the discussion so the two of you can create an arrangement that will allow you a more active role and allay your spouse's anxieties at the same time. Alternatively, you can propose a temporary "trial" arrangement where you take the lead in family finances for the next several months, after which you both agree to renegotiate roles.

You may be tempted to involve older children or extended family members in these discussions to support your position. *Try to avoid this tactic.* The problem gambler may feel "ganged up" on, and children should not be put in the awkward position of supporting one parent against the other. Extended family members often introduce their own agendas and ideas about appropriate arrangements for managing family finances, which actually may make it more difficult for you and your spouse to fashion an agreement for change.

Bypass the Problem Gambler

If you are unable to obtain agreement from your spouse after several attempts, you simply may need to bypass the problem gambler altogether for the time being. Access the family financial records, open your own checking and savings accounts, and develop your own family budget. If you are working, you can begin depositing your paycheck in that account. Revisit the issue with your spouse from time to time. When the problem gambler sees you taking a more active role, he or she may become more open to the new arrangement.

Gaining Control over Adolescents' and Seniors' Finances

When the problem gambler is an adolescent or young adult, the issues are slightly different. If your child is below the age of consent (age eighteen in most states), you may be legally obligated for any debts incurred by the child. You may also feel a strong ethical responsibility to protect your child's welfare. If you provide the primary financial support for the young person (for example, the child still lives at home or you are providing college tuition), you are in a powerful position to dictate the degree to which you become involved in managing his or her financial affairs.

Your child, however, is likely to resist your intervention, viewing it as an intrusion on his or her independence. You may also find it impractical to actively manage your child's finances if he is away at school or living on his own. In such situations, you may propose an advisory role for yourself, periodically sitting down with your child to review his or her financial situation and offering appropriate advice and suggestions. If you provide a significant share of financial support, you can make your continued support contingent on the child's willing participation in such an arrangement

With problem gambling senior relatives, any attempt to involve yourself in managing their finances is quite likely to trigger strong resistance and feelings, similar to the resistance encountered with a spouse or child who gambles, but for entirely different reasons. Such an intervention flies in the face of the traditional relationship between you and your relative, in which he or she was the adult who offered advice and made decisions and you were the dependent child. In addition, senior relatives are likely to interpret your efforts as signaling they are no longer capable of independently managing their affairs. Here again your best approach may be to propose an advisory role, working with the senior on a temporary basis until you are able to get his or her "financial house in order." Such a proposal may allow your senior relative to maintain dignity, while agreeing to needed assistance from you.

If you are unable to gain such agreement initially, we recommend you subtly persist in your efforts, asking questions and providing informal advice and support. Over time you may persuade your senior relative of the value of relying on you for financial assistance. Otherwise, unless a court of law judges your relative to be incompetent to handle his own financial affairs, you may have limited recourse despite your relative's dwindling resources. Problem gambling alone may not be considered sufficient evidence that someone is financially incompetent. If you think your relative may be incompetent, get expert advice to determine if this seems likely and how to proceed if such is the case.

Taking Stock of Your Financial Situation

Conducting a thorough inventory of your family's current financial situation or that of your gambling relative is important for two reasons. First, it will tell you where your family stands financially. Without this information, you cannot identify the areas where your family is most vulnerable financially nor can you plan intelligently to improve the situation. Second, taking action to survey the financial situation should leave you feeling more in charge and less at the mercy of out-of-control financial forces. Even if you are generally familiar with your family's finances or those of your relative, you will want to conduct a thorough review, since your family member's gambling activities may have reduced your family's assets or increased financial liabilities.

You may be tempted to postpone this step or avoid it altogether if you have little experience in managing your family's finances or if you consider your family so at risk that even thinking about finances leaves you anxious or depressed.

Do not give in to this temptation. If the task seems overwhelming, break it down into small steps and do a little each day. You may also want to enlist the help of a trusted friend, a family member, or a knowledgeable professional who is comfortable dealing with financial matters.

Preparing a Net Worth Statement

To prepare a net worth statement, the first thing to do is draw up a list of all financial assets and their location. This list should include the following items:

* money in checking, savings, and credit union accounts; * investments in stocks and bonds, mutual funds, and money market funds; * annuities, individual retirement accounts, and pension funds; * real estate holdings; * life insurance; and * valuable personal property, such as home furnishings, automobiles, and jewelry.

If your family or your relative has well-organized financial records, this task should be relatively simple. If financial records are out of date, disorganized, or nonexistent, completing this task will require more effort. You may need to contact financial authorities, retirement fund managers, your insurance agent, and others to obtain a comprehensive picture of financial assets.

Once you have a list of assets, develop a list of all financial liabilities. In this list include the following:

* current unpaid bills; * credit card debt; * personal bank loans; * credit union loans; * overdrawn checking accounts; * auto loans; * any amounts borrowed against life insurance or retirement funds; * mortgage and home improvement loans; and * unpaid taxes.

For each debt, list the name of the creditor and the outstanding amount still owed. Be sure to include personal loans made to the problem gambler by family members, friends, neighbors, and co-workers, as well as gambling debts to loan sharks, casinos, and bookies.

Having completed these tasks, you can prepare a statement of net financial worth (see Table 9.1) by taking your two lists, entering them on the same table, and comparing total assets against total liabilities. In the short run, you should be somewhat reassured by a positive net worth balance, particularly if that balance is significant. In such a case, you might be able to sell off some assets if your family is faced with sizeable gambling-related debts. The composition of assets and liabilities, however, may be more important than the size of your net worth or that of your relative.

It may be inadvisable to sell off any assets to eliminate a significant debt if major assets are vital to current security, relatively inaccessible, or relatively costly to liquidate (such as the value you own in your home or pension fund holdings). In such a scenario, even a positive net worth balance might not mean smooth sailing ahead. On the other hand, a negative net worth balance would be a definite cause for concern; it means you need to take active measures as soon as possible to improve your family's or your relative's financial health.

Table 9.1: Net Worth Statement

ASSETS	Value	LIABILITIES	Value
Cash on hand		Current unpaid bills	
Checking account		Credit card debt	
Savings account		Personal bank loans	
Credit union account		Credit union loans	

Individual stocks		Check overdrafts	
Individual bonds		Medical/dental bills	
Mutual funds		Auto loans	
Money market funds		Life insurance loans	
Pensions		IRA loans	
Profit-sharing plans		Mortgage	
401(k)		Home improvement loans	
IRA		Unpaid taxes	
Keogh/SEP		Personal loans	
Business interests		Gambling debts	
Real estate			
Life insurance			
Home furnishings			
Automobiles			
Jewelry			
Collections			
Total Assets		Total Liabilities	

Total Assets: _____

Total Liabilities: _____

Net Worth: _____

Evaluating Your Cash Flow

Before considering any moves to improve the situation, you need to review your family's or relative's income and expense patterns—your so-called "cash flow." Start by calculating your gross and net income for the previous year. In calculating gross income (income before taxes and other deductions), be sure to include the following:

* gross wages and salaries of each income-earning family member; * self-employment income; * interest and dividend income from bank accounts, stock and bond investments, and life insurance policies; * Social Security, pension, and disability or unemployment payments; * alimony, child support, and real estate income.

Enter your figures directly into a form similar to Table 9.2 and add them to obtain your total gross income. Then enter the amounts you paid in federal, state, and local income taxes, Social Security taxes, and any other deductions from your paycheck. Finally, subtract your total deductions from your total gross income to obtain your net income—the amount you had available to meet your expenses during the previous year. Dividing that figure by 12 will give you your average monthly income. You may also wish to estimate the average monthly amounts you received under different income categories.

Table. 9.2: Calculating Net Income

GROSS INCOME	Family Member 1	Family Member 2	Family Member 3	Annual Income	Monthly Average
Wages or Salary					
Bonus					
Self-employment Income					
Interest & Dividends					
Social Security					
Pension					
Unemployment or disability					

Alimony or child support					
Gifts					
Other					
Total Gross Income					
DEDUCTIONS					
Federal income taxes					
State income taxes					
Local taxes & fees					
Social security taxes					
Other					
Total Deductions					
Net Income					

(Gross Income - Deductions = Net Income)

On the expense side, divide family costs into two categories: fixed monthly and periodic expenses and flexible monthly expenses. Fixed expenses should include the following:

* any relatively stable expenses that you pay monthly or periodically throughout the year, such as rent or mortgage; * utility costs; * payments for homeowner's, medical, automobile, or life insurance; * real estate taxes; * federal and state income taxes; and * required payments on credit cards, car loans, personal loans, or other debt.

Under flexible expenses include the following:

* costs for groceries, take-out food, and dining out; * clothing purchases as well as laundry and dry cleaning; expenses; * pet care; * personal care; * gifts; * reading

material; * entertainment; * expenses for home repairs and furnishings; * car maintenance and repair; * transportation costs * education costs * out-of-pocket medical expenses; and * any charitable contributions.

Be sure to include any money lost gambling by the problem gambler in this flexible expense category.

Try to gather this information for at least the past six months, if not for the entire year. If this seems like an overwhelming task, at least try to account for the past three months. Much of this information can be obtained by reviewing pay stubs, bank statements, checkbook entries, and credit card bills. If many of your family's expenses are paid in cash, you may need to engage in some detective work, enlisting the aid of family members who contribute to the family's income or who spend it. Do not be too concerned if you need to make rough estimates for some expense categories. It's far better to complete this task than to postpone finishing until you are able to put your hands on all the necessary records. This will be particularly true for gambling expenditures. The problem gambler may be reluctant or unwilling to reveal the full extent of his or her gambling expenses. If a direct appeal on your part does not result in full disclosure, or if the gambler simply cannot recall accurately the amounts spent, you may be forced to rely on a rough estimate. You can obtain such an estimate based on the monthly flows of money in and out of the family budget and any major changes in known assets and liabilities.

Once you have gathered the information, enter it for each month on a form similar to Table 9.3. If you obtain figures for the entire year, modify your form accordingly to include the additional months. For many families, expenses will vary from month to month because of flexible expenses like taxes, automobile insurance payments, or holiday gift buying which may only be recorded during certain months of the year. For budget planning purposes, an average monthly expense figure is more useful. Calculate an average monthly expense total by adding together monthly expense totals and dividing that number by the number of months for which you have gathered data.

Comparing your average monthly expenses with your average monthly income (calculated during the previous task) should provide you with a clearer understanding of your family's or your relative's current income and expense patterns. If average expenses (including gambling expenses) have been exceeding recent income, it means your family or your relative has been either drawing down assets or incurring debt. Once again this is a signal to take action to remedy the problem.

Table 9.3: Fixed and Flexible Expenses

	Jan	Feb	Mar	Apr	May	June
FIXED EXPENSES						
Mortgage or rent						
Property taxes						
Gas/electricity/ fuel oil						
Water						
Telephone						
Property/ liability iInsurance						
Medical insurance						
Automobile insurance						
Life insurance						
Federal/state income taxes						
Automobile loan						
Other loan Repayments						
FLEXIBLE EXPENSES						
Groceries						
Take-out food/restaurant						
Clothing purchase/repair						
Dry cleaning/ laundry						
Personal care/cosmetics						
Pet care						
Gifts						

Books/ periodicals							
Vacations							
Movie/theater/ VCR rentals							
Cable TV							
Home furnishings/ repair							
Car maintenance/ repair							
Other transportation costs							
Education expenses							
Child care expenses							
Out-of-pocket medical							
Charitable expenses							
Savings							
Gambling expenses							
Total Expenses							

Monthly Average: Jan.–June total ÷ 6 = _____ (or expand to entire year)

Stabilizing Current Finances

Once you have a clear picture of your family's financial status, your first priority should be to ensure that expenses and income are brought into balance in the coming months. For the moment, set aside dealing with any debts incurred by the problem gambler, and concentrate on your form showing past expenses. Subtract out the gambling expenses (assuming your family member has stopped gambling) and recalculate the totals, month by month. This will give you a picture of how your expenses would have looked without any gambling by your family member during the time period covered by your calculations.

Next, project your income forward for the coming twelve months based on your current situation and any changes you anticipate in your income-earning potential. Make reasonable estimates of your deductions for taxes and other expenses to obtain an estimate of your annual net income. Again, divide this figure by 12 to obtain your anticipated average monthly income during the coming year. You can enter this information on another copy of the income form (see Table 9.2).

Also, project forward your total expenses based on any changes you anticipate compared with your expenses during the time period covered by your calculations (for example, you may know that your property is to be reassessed this year and your property tax is likely to increase by 10 percent). Enter this information on a copy of Table 9.3 expanded to include the next twelve months. This will give you a month-by-month picture of your projected expenses. Again, because your expenses may vary from month to month, you should calculate an average monthly expense figure for the next twelve months. Add together all your projected monthly expenses for the coming year and then divide by 12.

Now, you can compare your anticipated average monthly income with your anticipated average monthly expenses. Is your family's anticipated average monthly income greater than your anticipated average monthly expenses? If so, you may be able to maintain your current spending patterns and apply excess income to reducing any outstanding gambling debts. If you find that your family is likely to spend more than it is bringing in, even after gambling expenses have been eliminated, you must find a way to bring expenditures into line with income. You can accomplish this either by reducing expenses, increasing income, or both.

For many people, reducing expenses is the simplest option. Fixed expenditures are difficult to cut back without major changes in lifestyle (for example, moving to a less expensive house or apartment, or getting by without an automobile). You want to concentrate on flexible expenses, which you can either eliminate or postpone. Here you may want to ask other members of your family for suggestions on cutting back expenses. Because they are likely to be affected by expense reductions, it makes sense to get them involved. Together, you should be able to identify many areas where you can reduce or postpone expenses without major lifestyle changes. For example, you can buy food and household items in bulk; cut back on entertainment expenses; apply for discount utility programs, federal/state utility subsidy programs, or switch to a less expensive utility service plan; use public transportation instead of your car, and mothball or sell a vehicle you can do without.

Alternatively, you may choose to increase your family's income by moonlighting, taking a full- or part-time job if you are not currently working, or setting up a business at home. If you choose the latter option, we recommend you investigate any business opportunity thoroughly. Remember that many home businesses require an initial investment of capital and only a small number succeed. Be sure to explore too whether you or the problem gambler qualifies for any public sources of support, such as unemployment compensation or welfare payments.

Once you have developed a plan to bring expenses into line with income, recalculate your balance statement based on the changes you plan to put into effect. This revised balance statement is a budget you can use as a guide in the coming months to track your family's projected financial performance against actual expenses and income. By comparing this document periodically against actual performance, you will be able to see to some degree where your estimates are less than accurate. This will allow you to make corrective adjustments in expenses or income to maintain an actual balanced financial performance over the year.

Establishing a Debt Repayment Strategy

Once you are sure that you have spending and income in balance, you can turn your attention to creating a strategy to eliminate any debt confronting your family or relative. Having a strategy for debt repayment puts you in the driver's seat. Too many people with debts try to run away from the situation (at least in their minds), throwing bills in the wastebasket or not answering unpleasant calls from bill collectors. Then, they respond to the creditor or collection agency representative who sends the most intimidating letter or makes the most intimidating phone call on an ad hoc basis.

Your first step in developing a proactive strategy should be to determine a realistic amount you can devote each month to reducing debt. Choose a realistic amount given your family's current needs and income. You want to avoid making overly ambitious commitments to creditors, only to find you are unable to make promised payments a few months down the road.

Once you have identified a target amount you think you can allocate each month to debt reduction, consider debt payments a fixed monthly expense. If you can find a bank that will give you free checking, you may choose to set up a debt fund as a separate checking account in which you deposit a certain amount of money each month. The payments to creditors should be one of the first "must pay" checks you write each month, along with your mortgage or rent, utility bills, and other monthly payments like auto insurance.

If your family or relative is confronted by debts to multiple creditors, it's important to decide in advance how quickly you are going to repay creditors and in what order. First, make a separate list of all creditors and the amount owed to each from the information you gathered for your net worth statement. Next, prioritize creditors into three groups: (1) those who can affect your family's ability to meet essential short-term needs; (2) those for whom delayed repayment could cause you to lose other important assets; (3) all others. Include in the first category mortgage or rent bills; real estate taxes; utilities; auto loans, auto insurance, and auto excise taxes; child support; and federal and state taxes.

Failure to maintain timely payments to these creditors or authorities could lead to loss of your home, shutoff of basic utilities, loss of essential transportation, or legal measures against you for nonpayment of child support or taxes. In the second category include any additional secured debts, that is, debts for which your family or relative has pledged some important assets as collateral, such as a bank account, business property, or household goods. In the third category include credit card accounts; bills from doctors, dentists, and other professionals; accounts with local stores; and all other unsecured debts.

You should do all you can to maintain timely payments with creditors in the first category. Once you are confident you can do this, then you can begin making payments to creditors in the second category. Any residual monies in your debt repayment fund can then be applied to debts in the third category. When allocating funds among creditors in the second and third categories, first pay off accounts with the highest finance charges and then accounts with the smallest outstanding balances.

For each creditor, identify monthly, biannual, and annual goals for reducing the monies owed them. You can use these debt reduction targets in negotiating with creditors or collection agencies. Having such goals also will allow you to keep track over the coming months as to whether you are on target or not. You will be in a position to congratulate yourself, your gambling relative, and other family members involved in the budgetary process as you meet each of your debt reduction goals.

Resist the temptation to consolidate debts with one "super-creditor" or to refinance a debt at a higher rate of interest. Many people see debt consolidation or refinancing as a way to escape from the immediate pressure of a large number of unpaid debts and repeated calls and unpleasant letters from creditors. Consolidating debts into one account or pushing off deadlines for debt repayment to a later date may seem appealing, but in almost all cases, over the long run, it ends up costing you more money in finance charges.

You should also avoid consolidating your debts in a home equity loan unless you are confident of your ability to pay off the loan. Home equity loans can be attractive because they generally offer lower interest rates than many other loans, and loan repayments can be applied as deductions to your income taxes. If you are unable to keep up payments on the loan, however, you risk losing your home.

Dealing with Creditors and Collection Agencies

A proactive approach allows *you* to manage your financial situation rather than permitting creditors or collection agencies to manage it for you. Your first goal should be to work directly with creditors to avoid having them turn your account over to a collection agency or an in-house collection department. With creditors like small businesses, physicians, and other professionals, working directly with them may even prevent them from filing a report on the debt with one of the major national credit-reporting agencies such as Experian, Equifax, and Trans Union. (Many smaller creditors do not normally file such reports anyway.) Often large creditors, such as credit card companies or department stores, provide monthly updates to one or more of these national agencies on their customers' payment performances. If you or the gambler has failed to make on-time payments on your installment accounts with these large creditors, it's likely your credit rating has already been affected. While restoring the credit rating of your family or your relative should be your eventual goal, meeting this goal will first require settling outstanding debts, so keep your focus on debt reduction initially.

Once you are clear about your debt reduction strategy, call or write each of your creditors (or the collection agency to which they may have turned over the account). Do not allow yourself to become incapacitated by feelings of guilt or shame about your family's situation. Be honest and factual in explaining the situation. Indicate that you are now managing your family's or relative's financial affairs. Also explain that you have a specific plan for addressing the debt owed to each creditor.

With creditors in the first category who can affect your family's or your relative's ability to meet vital needs, such as the bank that holds your mortgage, you must agree to make current payments and provide some evidence that you will pay off any outstanding debts in a short period of time. Indicate, for example, that you have just been hired for a part-time job, which will provide enough income to bring the account into balance within two or three months.

For creditors in the second and third categories, indicate that you cannot begin making payments until a certain date or can only make partial payments during a specific time period. Explain that this is because you must first take care of your family's vital needs for food, shelter, utilities, and medical care. Emphasize that you are serious about making eventual restitution and explain that you have a financial recovery plan in place. Promise to recontact them by a specific date to arrange a regular repayment schedule. Many creditors will be satisfied with this approach. They know that waiting to be paid usually will prove less costly and be more effective than attempting to collect by other means. If you are able to make partial payments, some creditors may accept less than full payment to settle a debt and may even be willing to request deletion of a delinquent report previously filed with a national credit reporting agency or report the debt as paid in full. The key is to be polite, but stand firm in pressing for the best deal you can arrange. You may need to speak with a supervisor at the agency who has the authority to make such changes. If you are able to negotiate a settlement at less than full payment, be sure and obtain agreement from the creditor *in writing* before signing any new contract or making any additional payments.

For each account that has been turned over to a collection agency or an in-house collection bureau, take the same initial approach. Collection agency personnel may try to persuade you to pay off a bill entirely or to make higher payments. Be firm and stick with your original plan. Simply explain why you cannot make higher payments (e.g., "I have to make regular payments to my mother's nursing home to ensure that she receives proper care"). In reality, collection bureaus have little real leverage to force you to pay up, and most will eventually agree to your planned repayment schedule. Do not be swayed by threats to ruin your credit rating or that of your relative if you don't make payment immediately. Remember, creditors who can influence your ability to meet your vital needs or who can take ownership of your assets to pay off a debt will have no need to threaten you with damage to your credit rating.

Understanding Your Legal Rights

People recovering from financial difficulties have many legal rights, including protection from overzealous collectors, protection from certain consequences of creditor lawsuits, and the right to file for bankruptcy. It's important that you understand both your legal rights and responsibilities when making choices about appropriate actions to promote your family's financial recovery.

Curbing Overzealous Debt Collectors

Some collection agency personnel may go beyond reasonable measures in their attempts to persuade you to settle an account. It is illegal for collection agency staff to call repeatedly or continuously with the intent to annoy or harass you. They may not make contact before 8:00 A.M. or after 9:00 P.M. at night. Collection agencies may not call you or the problem gambler at friends' homes or at a work-site if they have been told it is inconvenient for you or personal phone calls are not allowed at work. They cannot threaten arrest, loss of children, or other actions for which there is no legal basis. They are prohibited from making insults, publishing your family name, or misrepresenting themselves. They cannot call friends or other family members and attempt to persuade them to settle the account.

If a collection agency engages in these kinds of unethical and illegal practices, you can file suit against the agency and collect up to $1,000 and your attorney's fees under the Federal Fair Debt Collection Practices Act (FDCPA). Also, you may be eligible for additional damages for emotional distress as well as punitive damages for particularly egregious c onduct. But even in situations where collection bureaus have not violated the law, federal law requires them to stop all contacts once a simple written letter of request, a so-called "cease" letter, is sent to the collection bureau.

If you prefer, you can ask an attorney to write such a letter for you. Another option to stop harassing conduct by collection agency personnel involves writing a letter of complaint to a government watchdog agency detailing the nature of the harassing communications.

You can write to the Federal Trade Commission, Bureau of Consumer Protection, Washington, DC 20580. Also write to the consumer protection division of your state Attorney General's office and any local office of consumer protection affairs. Send a copy of these letters to the collection bureau. This action alone is often enough to convince the collection agency staff to stop harassing contacts with you, other family members, or your gambling relative.

Creditor Lawsuits

If you follow all of the guidelines above, you will reduce the probability that a lawsuit will be filed by a creditor against you or other family members. Even if you do nothing, lawsuits usually are filed only as a last resort, and then only by certain creditors. Legal actions are expensive and time-consuming. Many creditors prefer to work out a settlement or write off an account as not collectable.

If, however, a lawsuit is filed, contact an attorney for advice. Certainly none of the information in this chapter should be taken as a substitute for legal advice. Be sure to monitor all certified mail and notices sent by a court. You or your family member may receive a summons in person or by mail describing the lawsuit and steps you must take to contest the suit. Make sure you understand these instructions and are clear about the type of court in which the suit is being filed. In most small claims courts it is possible to represent yourself without an attorney, although you may choose to have one. For other state courts we advise retaining legal counsel to represent you.

Be certain to respond to the court summons within the stipulated time limits. If you fail to respond, an automatic judgment will be entered against you or your family member. Since creditors count on most people ignoring court notices out of anxiety or a sense of humiliation, simply responding to the lawsuit may lead the creditor to drop or settle the suit. Similarly, if you have any legitimate defense against the lawsuit (e.g., the creditor agreed to accept partial payment to settle the account and is now reneging), be sure to raise that defense in your response to the court. Raising such a defense will put further pressure on the creditor to settle or drop the suit altogether to avoid the expense of a full trial.

Even if a court judgment is entered against you or your family member, certain kinds or amounts of property may be considered exempt from seizure under state laws. Only property that was put up as collateral on a loan will be definitely subject to seizure. Even after such a court judgment, you may be able to work out a repayment agreement with a creditor.

Filing for Bankruptcy

As a rule, you or your problem gambling relative should consider filing for bankruptcy only as a last resort. However, there may be certain circumstances where a bankruptcy filing has certain advantages. If you are overwhelmed by debt and have little likelihood of making restitution within a reasonable time period, a bankruptcy filing may allow you to protect certain key assets like your home or car from seizure by creditors. A Chapter 7 bankruptcy (liquidation) will automatically eliminate the legal obligation to repay most outstanding debts. A Chapter 13 bankruptcy (debt reorganization) will allow for the payment of debts in an orderly fashion over an extended period of time. Many people fear the effects of a bankruptcy filing on their credit rating. This should be less of a consideration if your credit rating or that of your family member is already seriously compromised. Although a bankruptcy filing will remain in your credit history for ten years (three years longer than information on other defaulted loans), paradoxically, it may be easier for you or your family member to receive credit again—once you have your financial house in order. Creditors will know you are not snowed under carrying other outstanding debts.

If you file under Chapter 7, creditors may also be reassured by the fact you are prevented from filing another Chapter 7 bankruptcy for six years. Currently, revisions to bankruptcy laws are being actively considered in the U.S. Congress. Although a bankruptcy filing is a relatively simple and inexpensive procedure, you should receive expert, up-to-date advice from an attorney or a nonprofit professional credit counselor about the pros and cons of bankruptcy for your family's particular financial situation before undertaking such a step.

Building or Restoring Creditworthiness

When dealing with the financial impact of problem gambling on your family or your relative, your goal should be to work closely with the problem gambler—if possible. If you are able to work together to pay off debt and stabilize the financial situation, eventually you will want to begin rebuilding the creditworthiness of the gambler and any other family members whose credit rating has been damaged.

In situations where the problem gambler continues to gamble or is unable to behave responsibly, you will need to take steps to build a "financial firewall" between yourself and the gambler. If the gambler is behaving irresponsibly, most likely he or she has already depleted existing assets and income. Therefore, you should focus on eliminating the gambler's access to *future* family assets and income by creating an independent financial identity separate from the gambler and limiting your liability for any future debts incurred by the gambler.

If the gambler is a child who has reached the age of consent or a senior relative, this should be relatively easy. Adult children and senior relatives are responsible for their own debts. Normally, they are not co-owners of family assets nor do they have direct access to family financial accounts. For a spouse with a problem gambling husband or wife, establishing and ensuring a separate financial identity can be somewhat more complicated.

Spouses are not considered legally responsible for each other's debts in the majority of states (with the exception, in some states, of debts incurred for family expenses such as child care or health care). In these states, a spouse's gambling debts would not serve as an impediment to the other partner developing a viable independent financial identity. In a small number of community property states, spouses *are* responsible for each other's debts. Community property states include Arizona, California, Idaho, Louisiana, Nevada, New Mexico, Texas, and Washington. If you reside in a community property state and are liable for your spouse's existing debts, developing an independent financial identity will be more difficult, but not impossible. The most important step will be to initiate debt reduction measures following the guidelines laid out in this chapter. If you are concerned about your liability for *future* gambling-related debts incurred by your spouse, we recommend that you consult an attorney for advice.

Some spouses may have no independent credit history, either because they have had only joint accounts with their spouses, or because their spouse has traditionally handled all financial matters for the family. Other spouses may have both joint accounts and accounts in their own names. If you share joint accounts and the problem gambling spouse is continuing to gamble, it is imperative that you work to establish your own separate credit identity for the future. In all cases, the route to developing creditworthiness is the same.

As a spouse, make sure you are jointly listed on all family assets. Request copies of your credit reports from the three major national credit reporting firms and correct any errors or out-of-date information. The details of how to do this are available in the references at the end of this chapter.

The next step is to set up your own checking or savings account. Then arrange for a small loan from the bank with a loan officer. Be straightforward about the purpose of the loan; you want to build a good credit history. Some banks may be reluctant to work with you, but many banks will be interested in developing your business, particularly if you can provide collateral in the form of deposits to your savings account. Once you have paid back that loan, obtain another copy of your credit report and check to ensure the bank has reported your payments. Now you should be able to obtain a credit card for a retail store or a card from one of the major gasoline companies. By making regular timely payments on those cards, you will shortly be in a position to apply for a major credit card, such as a MasterCard or VISA, and be on your way to establishing your own independent credit identity.

It may be easiest to apply for a bank credit card through the bank where you maintain your checking or savings account, particularly if you are known to your local bank officer. If you experience any difficulty in this step-wise building process, do not become discouraged but simply repeat one or more of the steps. For example, you may need to take out a second bank loan or establish a longer history of making regular payments on local retail cards before obtaining additional credit. This same process can be used for rebuilding damaged credit for a young adult or a senior relative recovering from problem gambling.

Finding Support and Expert Assistance

Many people will want to seek professional support and assistance from outside the family when navigating a financial crisis. We encourage you to do so, since many of the tasks involved in financial recovery are likely to be new to you, and laws and regulations in this area at both the federal and state levels are constantly being revised. Some individuals facing credit problems are tempted to use the services of for-profit credit repair agencies. These agencies advertise their services widely in the media and on the Internet, promising to assist you in financial recovery and to restore your credit rating. In most circumstances we encourage you to avoid these agencies. Although some are legitimate, many others may do little to justify the significant fees they charge. Some of these agencies are fly-by-night operations engaging in misrepresentation or outright fraud. If you do choose to obtain debt counseling through a for-profit agency, contact your local Better Business Bureau and state Attorney General's office or Office of Consumer Affairs to see if any complaints have been filed against the agency. Also be sure you understand all the fees and payments that will be charged by the agency and exactly what you will receive for those fees. Ask for agency references in the community and inquire about the training and experience of any credit counselor assigned to work with you.

A preferable alternative for seeking outside help can be found at nonprofit credit counseling centers in your local area operating under the auspices of the National Foundation for Consumer Credit (NFCC). These agencies generally offer reliable, low-cost advice on issues of financial management and working with creditors. Look in your local phone book under "Credit and Debt Counseling" for a nonprofit center that is a member of the NFCC in your area. You may also find a counseling center in your area by contacting the NFCC directly (1-800-388-2227 or on the Web at http://www.nfcc.org). The Credit Counseling Centers of America (CCC) is an NFCC member offering low-cost or free debt counseling at local offices nationwide (1-800-493-2222 or on the Web at http://www.ccc.america.com). Local CCC offices will work with you and your creditors to set up a debt-repayment plan.

You can also find low-cost courses on personal financial management at many local community colleges and adult education programs. In addition, there are many good books available on the subject, including those we recommend at the end of this chapter. For additional references, check with the reference librarian at your local public library.

Financial Life Beyond the Crisis

Dealing with the financial impact of problem gambling is an emotionally stressful experience. In addition, the tasks involved in financial recovery, i.e., budgeting for a reduced or limited income, planning a debt-repayment strategy, contacting and negotiating with creditors and legal authorities, and building a renewed financial foundation can all be challenging and time-consuming. Yet, coming to grips with the financial situation and mastering it can yield substantial benefits over the long run.

You are likely to develop new skills, knowledge, and self-confidence in managing family finances. Such a crisis can provide you and your family a valuable opportunity to reevaluate how you earn and spend money and your family's long-term financial priorities. It can also provide you with an opportunity to evaluate and possibly change deeply held attitudes, values, beliefs, and feelings you may have about the role and meaning of money in your life.

Many of us go through life without ever fully understanding our relationship to money and the powerful ways in which money influences our choices and decisions. You and your family can emerge from this crisis wiser and with greater confidence that the management of your finances is clearly aligned with your larger life goals and priorities.

Suggested Readings

Hammond, Bob. 2000. *Life After Debt: Free Yourself from the Burden of Money Worries Once and for All*. Third ed. Franklin Lakes, N.J.: Career Press.

Leonard, Robin. 1999. *Money Troubles: Legal Strategies to Cope with Your Debts*. Fifth ed. Berkeley, CA: Nolo Press.

National Consumer Law Center. 1999. *Surviving Debt: A Guide for Consumers in Financial Distress* Third ed. Boston: Author.

Ventura, John. 1998. *The Credit Repair Kit* (3rd ed.). Chicago: Dearborn Financial Publishing.

Chapter **10**

Treatment

This chapter explains how to navigate the world of clinical treatment. Since treatment requires the gambler's agreement (unless it was court-ordered), this chapter addresses the gambler directly. In this chapter, when we say "you", we are thinking of the gambler as the primary reader. At the same time, this chapter can be helpful to all family members.

Here's the bottom line: get the right treatment, complete it, and you are likely to do well. Doing so requires that you:

* recognize the need to change your gambling; * are motivated to do so; * believe treatment has a reasonable chance of helping you; * know how to get to the right treatment.

We will review treatments that have been successful and point you to resources to access those treatments. We will summarize the research showing that those who complete treatment are likely to do well. The findings of this research should encourage you to consult a professional about your gambling. Seeking such a consultation may then lead to progressively increasing your motivation to change. Recognizing the need to change and being motivated to do so often require a careful look at yourself, your behavior and the impact it is having on your life and those around you. Yet such recognition is generally not an all-or-nothing process. Starting down that path is a vital first step (see "The Stages of Change" section in chapter 6).

Getting Started

Only you can decide when it is time to change. People who care about you can encourage you, maybe even influence you. But the decision is yours. Perhaps you, like many people with gambling problems, will be the last to recognize that you have a problem. Perhaps you are familiar with this saying, which originally applied to substance abusers: "He'll get help only when he hits rock bottom." Perhaps you can convince yourself that now is not the time to try to change because you can imagine a rock bottom lower than where you are today.

For every person who has lost a substantial sum, there is someone who has lost his life savings and yet another who has lost his home or family. Some problem gamblers wind up on the streets; others succumb to the ravages of depression and, finally, suicide. The point at which you decide to change is *your* rock bottom; it does not have to be the lowest rock bottom that anyone can imagine. The time is up to you; we, like your family, can only encourage you to do it sooner rather than later.

Finding a Therapist

The skill, training, and experience of the clinician you choose are key factors to successful treatment. At present, few mental health practitioners are trained to treat problem gambling (Mello, Drebing, Federman, Krebs, et al. 1999). To help you find one who is, check with the National Council on Problem Gambling listed in Appendix A. They will point you to a state Council on Compulsive Gambling near you that can help guide you to experienced professionals in your area.

If you have not had mental health treatment before, it can be confusing to sort through your treatment options. These include the *setting* you will be seen in and the specific *discipline* in which your clinician is trained.

The clinician you ultimately choose may be in solo practice, group practice, or in a clinic. If the clinician has the proper training and can refer you easily to other resources as needed—to be evaluated for medication, for example—then any of these settings would be a good choice.

Mental health clinicians come from different disciplines with different training and include the following in their ranks:

* Psychologists have completed graduate school in psychology and direct clinical training. In most states they are required to have earned doctorates, Ph.D. or Psy.D., to be licensed.

* Psychiatrists are medical doctors who have completed medical school and a residency program in psychiatry.

* Social workers have completed a graduate degree in social work as well as direct training in clinical settings.

* Nurses with advanced degrees, generally at least a master's degree, and direct clinical training.

How can you choose among these different professions? First of all, select a practitioner who is licensed in his or her discipline in your state. Although you may have your own preferences for one discipline over another, give considerable weight to the individual's *overall* training and clinical experience as well as *specific* experience with problem gambling.

You should exercise your rights as a consumer of mental health services by asking questions as you decide which clinician is right for you. Questions to consider asking a potential clinician include the following:

1. How long have you been in practice?

2. How long have you been licensed?

3. How many individuals with problem gambling have you evaluated? How many have you treated?

4. What resources do you have to refer me to for other psychiatric or medical services?

5. What hours are appointments available?

6. What are your fees?

7. What are your policies regarding insurance? Are you an approved provider with my insurance company or HMO? If not, what fee arrangement can be worked out?

Assessment

All good clinical care begins with a thorough evaluation to assess whether you have any other psychological problems that require attention and to explore the reasons and motivations for your gambling. For example, *severe* problem gamblers in treatment have very high rates of depression (research shows a rate of 50 percent or higher) (McCormick, Russo, Ramirez, and Taber 1984). Since gambling can lead to depression and vice versa, it can be difficult to sort out which came first. Nevertheless, the depression must be treated, and in certain cases successful treatment of the depression will greatly help or even resolve the gambling problem. Similarly, substance abuse, attentional problems, and anxiety disorders are more commonly found in problem gamblers than in the general population (see chapter 3). Of course, any psychological disorder may be present along with gambling, not just those that are more commonly found. Getting a comprehensive assessment at the beginning of treatment is vital for proper planning.

Understanding what motivates you to gamble (see chapter 3) will enable you and your clinician to include treatment components specific to your particular needs along with those that are helpful to most problem gamblers. In the latter stages of problem gambling, it may seem as though you experience only distress and spend all your time chasing losses. Earlier on, however, you got some benefits from gambling. Your clinician should begin to explore these with you at the outset of treatment. Often, one's motivations for gambling are complex and outside of awareness. Determining these motivations may require ongoing work by you and your therapist.

Types of Treatment

Treatments available for problem gamblers include self-help groups, various forms of psychotherapy; inpatient treatment programs; and medication.

Self-Help Groups

Gamblers Anonymous (GA), the oldest and best-known self-help program for problem gamblers, is loosely modeled on Alcoholics Anonymous, the original twelve-step program. GA has chapters throughout the United States and Canada with representation in more than fifteen countries worldwide. Other twelve-step self-help groups have a local or regional presence. In addition, there is a program for families and friends of problem gamblers—Gam-Anon—again modeled after the program originally developed for families of problem drinkers, Al-Anon (see Appendix A).

Gamblers Anonymous considers pathological gambling a progressive disease that will grow increasingly severe unless the gambler quits gambling altogether. To accomplish this, GA members meet in weekly groups. Many members participate in more than one group and thus attend multiple meetings per week. The groups follow a consistent framework based on a twelve-step recovery model. (Gamblers Anonymous' twelve steps are listed on their Website which is provided in Appendix A). Within this framework, individual groups have their own style depending on the members' preferences. The groups offer mutual support, and members recount their stories of gambling at meetings to help themselves and others remain abstinent from gambling. Members also make telephone calls to other members between meetings to discuss problems such as urges to gamble, and older members act as "sponsors" to newer ones to help them refrain from gambling.

Evaluation

No studies have systematically followed up individuals who have attended GA. However, one major study did find that just 9 percent of those who had attended at least two meetings of GA were still abstinent and attending GA two years later (Stewart and Brown 1988). However, the researchers did not know whether the more than 80 percent who had dropped out of GA had returned to gambling. So, the 9 percent measures only those who both stayed with GA and remained abstinent.

Recommendation

Clearly, knowledge is limited about the effectiveness of GA alone. However, in practice, GA is often used as an adjunct and follow-up to other forms of treatment. For those who participate in GA in this way, clinical evidence suggests a much higher success rate than the 15 percent figure that Brown found. We recommend that gamblers who find the twelve-step model acceptable participate in GA as a part of a comprehensive treatment program and continue GA even after other treatments have been completed.

Psychotherapy

Several major types of psychotherapeutic treatments for problem gambling have been studied including psychodynamic therapy, behavior therapy, and cognitive-behavioral therapy.

Psychodynamic Therapy

Psychodynamic therapy is grounded in the work of Sigmund Freud who created psychoanalysis and laid the groundwork for psychotherapy in the twentieth century. Within the psychodynamic school, two major approaches stand out. The first perspective reviewed by Bergler in 1958 has limited support among modern researchers. Bergler (1958, 1970) asserts that the problem gambler is rebelling against the constraints and reality of everyday life and in so doing is unconsciously rebelling against parental figures. Since such rebellion is taboo, the gambler has an unconscious guilt that produces an unconscious wish to lose that outweighs any conscious wishes to win. Thus the problem gambler is destined to lose.

Treatment is directed at helping the gambler to discover this unconscious pattern and resolve the underlying conflict that leads to it,
thereby relieving the urge to gamble.

Rosenthal and Rugle (1994) advanced a comprehensive
approach to psychotherapy based on psychodynamic principles that
recognize multiple potential underlying motivational factors. To give
an idea of the thoroughness of their approach, they are not content
merely mentioning action or excitement as a rewarding state for the
gambler. Rather they look to the specific underlying motivation that
produces excitement in that particular gambler. Reasons might
include that successful gambling implies the gambler is loved, or
that he is aroused by living on the edge without losing, or that crises
provide meaning in his life. They advocate the integration of these
deeper psychological factors with an active and practical approach to
discontinuing gambling that includes full participation in Gamblers
Anonymous. They also indicate these principles are "entirely com-
patible with other therapies (supportive, cognitive-behavioral, phar-
macological, twelve-step)" (Rosenthal and Rugle 1994, p. 24).

Behavior Therapy

Behavior *change* is the prime target of behavior therapy, which
recognizes that most human behavior is learned in three fundamental ways. First, events that occur closely together are associated in the
mind. This phenomenon of classical conditioning was demonstrated
by Pavlov who trained his dog to associate a bell with the smell of
meat; the dog then learned to salivate at the sound of a bell. Second,
whatever follows a behavior can influence the frequency of that
behavior. This is the principle of operant (or Skinnerian) conditioning. Many people think of Skinner's pigeons pecking on a key to be
rewarded with food. The most well-known analogy to this in the
world of gambling is the slot machine; people pull a lever to be
rewarded with money. Third, humans, more than any other species,
learn by watching others. This highlights the importance of role
models and helps to explain behavioral similarities within families
and peer groups. For example, children of problem gamblers are
more likely to be problem gamblers.

When behavior therapy first tackled problem gambling, the primary intervention was aversive therapy. Here, the gambler in a mock
gambling situation (i.e., playing cards or situated in a mock casino),
receives a mild electric shock as he or she is about to bet. Betting
becomes associated with an unpleasant stimulus—the electric shock—
which, based on classical conditioning, leads the gambler to associate
gambling with negative or painful images. Although this treatment
had some success—about a 40 percent overall improvement rate

when a number of studies are combined (Walker 1992)—it has been largely abandoned in the last fifteen years in favor of treatments that are equally or more effective and less controversial.

More recently, an Australian team (McConaghy, Blaszczynski, and Allcock 1988) researched treatment based on the hypothesis that a "behavioral completion mechanism" originates when the idea of gambling is stimulated. By this, they mean that any stimuli that bring gambling to mind creates a state of arousal, or excitement, in the problem gambler that propels the person toward gambling to pacify the arousal. If the gambler can learn to respond without excitement to gambling stimuli (for example, when in a convenience store that also sells lottery tickets), there will be no pressure to gamble. In this treatment, the gambler may be taught to feel relaxed or even bored in response to such stimuli.

Cognitive-Behavioral Therapy (CBT)

As the name implies, cognitive-behavioral therapy or CBT builds on behavior therapy by focusing on cognitions, or thoughts, as well as behavior. The way one thinks, perceives, and interprets the world is a central aspect of this form of therapy. A comprehensive CBT approach considers thoughts, feelings, and behavior and recognizes that each has an impact on the others. The mechanisms of change are primarily through an examination of both thoughts and behavior with a consequent improvement in these as well as in emotional states.

A Canadian team (Sylvain, Ladouceur, and Boisvert 1997) has developed an exciting additional component to the treatment of problem gambling which focuses on the irrational thinking that most people exhibit about gambling, but that is generally more pronounced in problem gamblers. There are two essential components to this irrational thinking: the gambler's fallacy and the illusion of control.

The Gambler's Fallacy. This fallacy is the erroneous belief that past events will have an influence on future *random* events. For example, in a fair game of roulette, if red comes up five times in a row, then many people think this has an influence on the next spin of the wheel. Interestingly, some think that it means red is "hot" and is more likely to come up, others think red has run its course and is less likely to come up. In fact, the roulette wheel does not remember; what happened on the last five spins has no relation to the next spin. Every spin is independent and random. Because we learn from experience, it is natural for us to try to predict the future based on the past. However, when it comes to random events (which includes most gambling activities), past trends do not influence the future. A great deal of money is wagered and lost based on this fallacy.

The Illusion of Control. This is the idea that what we do influences events over which, in reality, we have no control. Once again, deeply programmed learning mechanisms help us to associate our behavior with events taking place around us. Most of the time, this serves us well. However, it also lies at the basis of many superstitious behaviors. For example, baseball players are notorious for developing superstitious rituals such as always stepping on a base on the way to the field. Gamblers often believe that what they do while gambling has an influence on the outcome. For example, they may pull the lever of the slot machine in a certain way or blow on the dice to increase their chance of winning. Once again, such thoughts are more prominent and intense in problem gamblers.

Although the gambler's fallacy and the illusion of control have a general form, they exist in specific ways in each gambler. Therefore, the Canadian team (Sylvain, Ladouceur, Boisvert 1997) has problem gamblers tape record their thoughts for six hours during mock, but realistic, gambling sessions. Thus, they discover the specific concrete ways that the problem gambler is thinking irrationally. With this information in hand, they develop a stepwise program to evaluate and confront each of these irrational ideas. Since the gambler has been called the "last optimist" (Bergler 1958, 1970), confronting these irrational ideas is an essential component of treatment that has not previously been so systematically developed. In addition, this team also teaches problem-solving skills, relapse prevention techniques, and social skills as part of their comprehensive treatment.

Evaluation

In 1958, Bergler published data on approximately 160 patients whom he evaluated or treated in psychodynamic psychotherapy. Research standards were far less demanding at that time than they are today and his work contains many technical deficiencies that make his results difficult to interpret with confidence. For example, we believe his treatment sample consisted of pre-selected highly motivated people who had gambling problems but who had not exhausted all their financial resources. Within this group of people, those who *completed* treatment had a good probability of success (57 percent). Unfortunately, Bergler's studies are the only data to report the outcome of a sizeable sample of problem gamblers who received long-term psychodynamic psychotherapy. Rosenthal and Rugle's (1994) psychodynamic model is more consistent with modern approaches to treating problem gambling; however, there are no well-controlled studies of its effectiveness.

Modern behavioral treatments for problem gambling show good results with individuals who *complete* treatment. About two out of three of these people discontinue gambling entirely or they learn to gamble in an acceptable and controlled manner over a two-year period following treatment.

The integrated cognitive-behavioral treatment pioneered by the Canadian team has shown very good results with those who *complete* treatment and can be located at one year follow-up. Among this select group, 88 percent successfully discontinued gambling.

Recommendations

It is impossible to compare these treatment methods to each other with full scientific rigor. Accurate comparison of treatment outcomes would require a clinical trial in which patients are randomly assigned to the different treatments. These studies have yet to be done. In the meantime, how can you decide which treatment to pursue?

Our review of the research and our experience suggest that a comprehensive cognitive-behavioral treatment is likely to be the most effective route for many problem gamblers. In addition, if you find twelve-step programs such as Gamblers Anonymous acceptable, keep in mind that many people enjoy additional support and protection against relapse from these groups.

However, there are factors that are more important than which school of psychotherapy you choose for treatment. In evaluating these treatments, we italicized the fact that we were reporting the results of those who *completed* treatment. In fact, it seems clear that entering and completing treatment is far more important to success than whether you choose psychodynamic, behavioral, or cognitive-behavioral therapy. It appears that completing treatment may double or triple your chance of doing well. By contrast, the benefits of different approaches appear to differ by a much smaller degree, perhaps by some 10 to 20 percent. Results like these have been found repeatedly in the psychotherapy literature. Different approaches to treatment are often (not always) comparably effective. However, entering and completing treatment has a huge effect on how well someone does.

In summary, although our view favors cognitive-behavioral therapy, starting and completing treatment with an experienced clinician is far more important than which theoretical approach you choose. With that in mind, you might responsibly choose psychodynamic therapy or behavioral therapy. Psychodynamic therapy has been clinically effective with a number of psychiatric disorders and problems in living particularly for those who are oriented toward psychological insight. If an insight-oriented approach (one that looks at your inner and sometimes unconscious motivations) appeals to you, you may want to see a psychodynamically oriented therapist with expertise in problem gambling.

Inpatient Treatment Programs

Historically, there have been very few inpatient treatment programs for problem gambling. Today, given the movement toward reduced inpatient care in general and reduced inpatient treatment for substance abuse in particular, it appears unlikely that many inpatient treatment programs specifically for problem gambling will be available anytime soon.

The oldest and longest running inpatient program in the United States was started in 1972 at the Veterans Affairs Medical Center in Brecksville, Ohio. Treatment includes psychoeducation, group therapy, attention to financial recovery, and Gamblers Anonymous. One follow-up study showed that about 55 percent of those who *completed* treatment and were able to be contacted at six months had remained free of gambling. Since it is likely that individuals admitted for inpatient care had severe problem gambling, this is a promising result.

Although there are very few inpatient programs for problem gambling, you can check with a state council on compulsive gambling in your area (see Appendix A) to explore whether one might be open to you. If inpatient treatment is indicated for other reasons (for example, depression or substance abuse), consider enrolling in a program specializing in these areas that will also attend to your problem gambling.

Medication

Studies of medication for the treatment of problem gambling are in the early stages. Naltrexone, a drug that has been used to decrease craving in the treatment of alcohol abuse, has been tried in several cases of problem gambling. Two reports suggest initial improvement with this medication and the need for further research (Crockford and el-Guebaly 1998; Kim 1998).

Fluvoxamine (trade name Luvox), which is in a class of drugs known as serotonin reuptake inhibitors (SRIs), has been tested in an uncontrolled trial with a small sample of ten patients with problem gambling. Seven of these patients showed significant improvement at the end of an eight-week period. This study is a preliminary one but in its authors' opinion is sufficient to call for a fuller study of the benefits of fluvoxamine and other SRI medications (Hollander, DeCaria, Mari, Wong, et al. 1998).

Evaluation

Studies of the benefits of medication for problem gambling are in the very early stages. Preliminary evidence suggests that Naltrexone as well as fluvoxamine and other SRIs merit further study.

Recommendations

Problem gambling is often associated with other disorders, e.g., depression, substance abuse, and attention deficit disorder. Some of these associated disorders are very responsive to medication. In addition, the fact that problem gambling runs in families (see chapter 3) suggests some individuals have a biological predisposition to gamble (though not necessarily an associated disorder). Thus, seek treatment with an experienced clinician who can refer you for psychiatric consultation, as necessary, to determine whether medication is appropriate to your situation.

Treatment Goals

The decision to change your gambling raises an important question: Should you discontinue gambling altogether or should you try to gamble in a controlled manner? We strongly recommend that you stop gambling completely since this will reduce your exposure to situations that promote relapse. We believe you should try to get the benefits that gambling provides you (for example, temporarily decreasing anxiety) in other, more constructive ways. Although at present there is insufficient research to prove that abstinence provides a better long-term outcome than controlled gambling, our clinical experience combined with a huge amount of research literature for other habit disorders suggest that abstinence is the wiser course. If you decide to pursue controlled gambling as your initial goal, we recommend that you write down precisely what your limits are. How often would you gamble during what time period? How much would your maximum wager be? How much would your maximum loss be on any one day, week, or month? If you try to stay within the limits you think you can handle and then exceed those limits, then controlled gambling is most likely not appropriate for you at this time.

Changing your gambling habit and its associated ills and disruptions will be a principal goal of treatment. To get there, you probably will have to accomplish some additional sub-goals along the way no matter which type of treatment you choose. Here is an overview of some of these sub-goals to help guide your thinking about treatment.

Treat Co-Occurring Disorders

Successful treatment of co-occurring disorders may bring dramatic changes in gambling behavior as, for example, is sometimes true for individuals with depression or attention deficit disorder. An exclusive focus on gambling while ignoring other disorders generally limits the probability of a successful change in gambling. Even in cases where gambling may be initially discontinued, the individual may be more vulnerable to relapse if other disorders like substance abuse are left untreated. Be open with your clinician; tell him or her about your other problems. Bear in mind that your clinician is there to help you, not to judge you. Disclosing what is weighing on your mind will help you and your clinician to best plan your treatment.

Get the "Benefits" of Gambling in Other Ways

Perhaps you gamble to forget your problems and limit your anxiety, if only temporarily. Treating your anxiety, and developing improved anxiety regulation and problem-solving skills will offer you more benefits than gambling. If gambling enables you to socialize, then treatment can help you to satisfy your social needs in more constructive ways. Perhaps you are a shy person who finds it hard to meet new people. You and your clinician can work together to overcome the hurdles that have limited your social contacts.

Take Responsibility

Growth at all stages of human development implies taking increasing responsibility for one's role in the world and the consequences of one's actions. As children grow into adults, they take increasing responsibility for themselves, including the effects their decisions and actions have on their own lives and others. Since the maturational process encompasses increasing responsibility, it follows that psychotherapy that promotes maturation and growth will have this as a goal. Therefore, taking responsibility for one's actions is a key treatment goal for problem gambling.

As you begin to exercise responsibility for your problem gambling, you may simultaneously develop an increased appreciation for how your behavior has affected your family. How profoundly and in how many areas your family has been affected will depend on the severity and the duration of your problem gambling. It may have damaged finances, trust, and communication. It may have increased distress and conflict in the family. It may even have contributed to a dramatic change in family structure, such as a separation or divorce.

We are *not* saying that problem gambling can be held solely responsible for difficulties within a family. We do say that it may have affected your family in some or all of these ways.

Taking responsibility for your role in these areas does not mean that you have to fix things right away. Indeed, many things are not amenable to a quick fix. Nevertheless, accepting responsibility for your role and dedicating yourself to working together to rebuild trust and better communication will not only be helpful to your family, it also will promote your own healing and growth. Engaging in a continuing dialogue with family members with goodwill and the intention to understand these issues may be helpful. Such discussions, even with the best intentions, can be thorny, so family therapy may be useful to guide you through these difficult issues.

Taking responsibility for the financial impact of your gambling requires special attention. Resolving your financial difficulties likely will present a challenge in its own right. In addition, financial issues may have impaired many relationships; taking responsibility for the financial aspect in the broader context of your relationships will promote healing.

Accepting responsibility does not obscure the fact that various forces such as predisposition, early learning, or current circumstances may have promoted your gambling. Such factors are helpful in understanding how and why your gambling developed but they should not be held responsible for your behavior (see "A Balanced Model of Responsibility" in chapter 6).

Correct Irrational Beliefs About Gambling

No one knows gambling as the gambler does. You know, in your gut, the highs and lows of the gambling life; you've felt the intensity, hit for some big ones, and been in the chase. You understand gambling lingo. You know the types of people who gamble and the social rules that govern the types of gambling you do. In these ways and others that have to do with direct experience, nobody knows gambling as well as you do. Because of your expertise in these areas, you may, like many problem gamblers, have difficulty recognizing those areas where your knowledge and ideas about gambling leave room for improvement.

Typically, problem gamblers hold inaccurate beliefs about gambling, including the gambler's fallacy and the illusion of control that were discussed above. A comprehensive treatment program will help you understand this. Your clinician may explore this area with you by considering questions such as the following:

1. On which activities do you gamble?

2. Which of these have an element of skill (meaning that it is not pure luck)?

3. For which of these activities do you have a system (or method) for betting? Do you use any special habits or rituals to increase your chances of winning?

4. Why do you use this system? Does it improve your chances of winning?

5. Do you sometimes hit a hot or cold streak? What evidence do you use to determine this? In which games might this occur? Does the sense that you are experiencing a hot or cold streak influence your play?

Questions like these will help you to determine if you, like most gamblers, hold beliefs about gambling that are not entirely logical. Remember, we are all designed to learn from experience and to make sense of the world. This is a deeply ingrained learning mechanism that allows us to prosper most of the time. However, when such deeply ingrained beliefs are applied to random events, as occur in gambling, this mechanism can lead us astray, causing significant difficulty. If you hold some beliefs about games of chance that are not entirely logical, recognizing such beliefs shows a readiness to confront challenging issues. Such recognition is the first vital step in correcting these ideas.

Determining which games you play are games of chance (see Appendix B) will help identify such ideas since any system, method, or habit that you apply to games of chance lack a logical basis. Even in games of partial skill, not all systems and methods are logically based. In the long run, you will have times when you win relatively more frequently and other times that you will lose relatively more frequently. Many people choose to call these hot streaks or cold streaks. But bear in mind, at any given point during those "streaks," they do not predict what will happen next in a game of chance.

Treatment that helps you understand the basics of probability (see Appendix B) will also help you to identify and correct irrational beliefs about gambling.

Increase Your Skills

Skills in the following four key areas greatly increase the problem gambler's chance of success at regulating and controlling his or her habitual behavior.

Emotional Regulation

Problem gamblers often gamble to escape negative feelings, including anxiety, sadness, and anger. Problem gambling, in turn, often leads to increased anxiety and depression. It follows that learning to regulate these emotional states is essential to minimize both the reasons for gambling and the painful aftermath of gambling.

Treatment can help you to manage emotional discomfort by:

> ✻ limiting or preventing its occurrence; ✻ calming or reducing its intensity and duration; and ✻ increasing your tolerance for the discomfort.

In chapter 5, we presented a cognitive-behavioral model to help your family member cope with the emotional distress that he or she may be experiencing. In that chapter, there is a brief introduction to techniques for both limiting and calming emotional discomfort. You may find it profitable to read chapter 5 yourself. Of course, this material is only introductory. Any good treatment program will target this area of your life in greater depth.

Problem Solving

It is likely that you are confronting multiple problems such as finding a job, coping with financial difficulties, finding the right treatment provider, or dealing with health problems. Although problem solving sounds like something that does not have to be taught, treatment can help you become more proficient in this area. One effective approach to problem solving consists of five steps (D'Zurilla and Goldfried 1971).

1. **Define the problem:** Be precise. Specific problems result in specific solutions. Identify what needs to change so that the situation is no longer a problem.

2. **Brainstorm:** Write down as many possible solutions that you or others can imagine. Don't discard any ideas at this point, even ones that seem unrealistic initially.

3. **Choose a solution:** Write down all the consequences—good and bad—of each possible solution. Pick the solution that yields the most favorable balance.

4. **Act:** Make a plan to put your chosen solution into action. You may have to acquire additional skills or obtain further help at this point. Consider possible obstacles and rehearse your plan with an eye to overcoming those obstacles. Put your plan into action.

5. **Evaluate outcome:** Did your actions solve or partially solve the problem? If your solution did not work, try to learn from the process. With this additional knowledge, you may be able to return to an earlier step (say, step two or three) and improve your solution.

Interpersonal Skills

Interpersonal problems may be among the most trying difficulties you face. You may have to mend fences with your immediate and extended family and friends as well as people on the job. Such tasks may require that you combine your emotional regulation and problem-solving skills with specific interpersonal skills to reach the most satisfactory outcome. "Interpersonal skills" is a broad term and covers a range of behaviors from the way you say hello to intimate encounters. You have undoubtedly acquired many interpersonal skills throughout your life, but often even the most accomplished people find room for improvement in this area. Two key areas in which treatment can be helpful are *communicating clearly* and *being assertive without being aggressive*.

In chapter 7, we provide information about clear communication to help you and your family member establish a dialogue. It introduces ways of stating your position clearly and also listening carefully. You might review this material as a starting point for further development in this area.

People often confuse being aggressive or overpowering with being assertive, believing that making a point in a nonpassive manner is necessarily assertive. They may be unaware that assertive behavior occupies a broad middle ground between passive and aggressive behavior. Assertive behavior expresses one's point of view, intentions, and, when necessary, one's feelings in a direct yet nonthreatening manner. Aggressive behavior is threatening to another's physical or psychological integrity and is often counterproductive. Although aggression may force others to submit, it leaves lingering resentment that in the long run can undermine the aggressor's goals. Therefore, very forceful people may need to learn assertive skills so that they can make their points clearly and, ultimately, have a better chance of achieving their goals.

On the other side of the continuum, many people easily make the distinction between being passive and being assertive. However, those who have learned that anger is taboo or that expressing one's own needs is unacceptably selfish may make unceasing efforts to be completely caring and understanding. Such people must first come to understand their underlying issues with anger or with reasonable demands for receiving and bestowing care before they can comfortably employ assertive skills.

Being assertive is helpful in a range of situations and is vital in being able to say "No" to those who suggest that you should gamble or enter situations where gambling is likely to be found.

Relapse Prevention Skills

Opportunities to gamble surround us. Many convenience stores sell lottery tickets, scratch tickets, and provide other gambling opportunities. Newspapers contain the point spread for football and other games. Even in Utah and Hawaii, where gambling is illegal, the Internet offers ready access to gambling, as do card games and many illegal gambling activities (for example, sports betting). No one can completely isolate himself or herself from gambling stimuli.

On the other hand, it is possible to put yourself in such high-risk situations that the probability of relapse is very high. Extreme examples of this would be vacationing near casinos or going to the track to "enjoy a day with the boys" and planning to refrain from betting. These would be set-ups for relapse.

Between total avoidance and extreme high-risk temptation lies a broad area. Learning to judiciously navigate this area is essential to preventing relapse. Treatment will help you to review your relationships with others, your range of leisure activities, and the places you spend your time. Do you have friends who are nongamblers? Are there ways for you to spend time with your friends who do gamble without entering high-risk situations? Are the places and ways you spend your leisure time conducive to nongambling activities? Exploring these and related questions in treatment will help you to decide which individuals and places present challenges that you can manage and which present overwhelming challenges that you should avoid.

Address Underlying Issues

Treatment that covers the key elements described above often provides substantial benefit. In some cases, however, underlying issues must be addressed to fully achieve a resolution. You should explore this with your clinician to determine whether this is true for you. Issues that originated early in life or during extremely stressful, traumatic, or intensely emotional times tend to require a more intense treatment focus. Some people have a double hurdle to confront if they endured chaotic or even traumatic periods early in their lives.

Some issues that may require lengthier treatment are more common in individuals with problem gambling. Although depression often may be well treated in a relatively short period, some cases require lengthier therapy. Some gamblers with parents who gambled may have to confront how their gambling interacts with their psychological relationship with their parents. In some cases, underlying issues about success and failure may need to be addressed. People with a history of trauma, even those who do not have post-traumatic stress disorder, may need to address this in the appropriate treatment context. Problem gamblers who have legal difficulties unrelated to gambling may have to address their gambling in the context of a broader pattern of behavior.

Do these or any other underlying issues fit your situation? Some people might have a tendency to overlook or minimize such issues. Others might see a component of their own situation in one of the possibilities just mentioned and become concerned that there are deeper issues when such is not the case. These matters are best explored with a trained clinician.

The Journey Toward Recovery

All therapies are partnerships between the treater and the treated. Even many straightforward medical procedures have better results when the patient is a fully cooperative participant and vigorously wants to get better. Imagine your journey toward recovery as traveling by rowboat toward a destination you have seen, but you don't know the way. Now imagine that you find a guide who knows the way and will help get you there by working one of the oars. If you pull together you can move the boat faster and easier than you could by yourself. If only one of you pulls an oar, the boat will move aimlessly in circles.

But there's a question that precedes finding the guide and doing your share: *Do you want to make the journey?* If this question gives you pause, that's understandable—it's a big question to confront at the outset. Rather, think of the journey as one that can be broken into many short trips; you decide how long each one should be. You can stop and rest at any point. If you don't like the journey, you can return quickly to the beginning or to a previous rest area. With this in mind, the proper question is: *Do you want to make the first short trip that begins the journey?* Now think of treatment as not only the guide and the shared effort but also as the rest places along the way. In these places you can replenish yourself and get ready for the next leg of your journey.

Chapter **11**

Maintaining Safety for the Gambler and the Family

Problem gamblers are at increased risk for both suicidal behavior and aggressive behavior toward others, each of which is also more probable for anyone who abuses alcohol or drugs. Since problem gamblers are also more likely to be substance abusers, this further elevates the risk of harmful behavior aimed at themselves or others.

Although the majority of problem gamblers will not engage in suicidal or violent behavior, the prevalence of these events is sufficiently high to make it wise for problem gamblers to be evaluated by a professional. Unfortunately, many gamblers refuse to go for evaluation or treatment of any kind. Therefore, you may be facing the decision about whether or not to take action on your own to help ensure your family's safety.

Get Personalized Expert Advice

Let's be clear. If you have *any* question about whether you or other family members will remain safe, you should consult a qualified professional *at once*. If the gambler will not go for an evaluation, get a consultation yourself to explore *your* family's situation. No book can adequately answer whether your unique family is at risk; neither can a book inform you sufficiently so that you can make that determination yourself. *When in doubt, consult a professional.*

That said, we can highlight some red flags that you can look for that emphasize the need for professional guidance. These red flags do not cover all possible warning signs; there may be other signs that will raise your level of concern. Only a professional who has evaluated your family's unique situation can make specific recommendations for you and your other family members. In the matter of safety, it is always better to err on the side of caution. In general, we recommend a professional consultation; do so without delay if you feel worried or see troubling signs. If the situation appears urgent, make an emergency call to 911.

Suicidal Behavior

Severe problem gamblers often consider suicide as a solution to their problems (Sullivan 1994). In one sample survey taken of Gamblers Anonymous members, 48 percent had contemplated suicide and 21 percent had attempted suicide (Frank, Lester, and Wexler 1991). The rate of suicidal behavior in a community sample of severe problem gamblers who were not seeking treatment was over 13 percent (Bland, Newman, Orn, and Stebelsky 1993), more than fifty times the rate of the general population.

The increased risk of suicidal behavior among problem gamblers is seen in regional data as well. The highest suicide rates in the nation are in the area around Las Vegas; Atlantic City is not far behind. The casinos in Atlantic City, built on promises of prosperity, ushered in elevated suicides rates not previously seen in the region (Phillips, Welty, and Smith 1997). In Louisiana, areas with higher per capita spending on lotteries have higher suicide rates (Campbell, Simmons, and Lester 1998–1999).

To *fully* understand why any individual attempts suicide requires understanding the very core of his or her being. However, we know that, in general, clinical depression raises the risk of suicide and that problem gambling and depression frequently co-occur. Among problem gamblers in treatment, about half have had clinical depressions; some studies yield estimates as high as 75 percent (McCormick, Russo, Ramirez, and Taber 1984).

(Note that because gamblers tend to seek treatment only when their situation is dire, it is likely that a lower rate of clinical depression would be found in problem gamblers who were not seeking treatment.)

Since suicidal individuals are often depressed, it is important to be able to recognize the signs and symptoms of depression.

Depressed mood or sadness is frequently evident, although in children and adolescents, an irritable mood may be more apparent. Also, look for a decrease in interest or pleasure in most activities, changes in appetite or weight (or lack of expected weight gain in children), difficulty sleeping or increased sleeping, movement that is more rapid or slower than usual, decreased energy, feelings of worthlessness or guilt, decreased concentration, indecisiveness, thoughts of death or thoughts of suicide (DSM-IV 1994). Be alert to any losses in the person's life including but not limited to gambling-related losses. These could include the loss of an important relationship, a job loss, or the loss of a hoped-for goal.

Suicidal individuals frequently convey some indication of their intentions. They actually may mention their suicidal thoughts or make statements to the effect that they would be better off dead or their death would improve the lives of others. They may put their affairs in order by making a will or giving things away. They may say good-bye in an unusual way.

Previous suicide attempts markedly increase the risk of another attempt. A family history of suicidal behavior also brings a statistically increased risk of such behavior. Each of these factors raises risk, but their absence does not preclude the need for vigilance—60 percent of completed suicides occur on the *first* attempt.

Asking your family member what he or she is thinking and feeling can be very helpful. If there is any cause for concern, it is okay to ask your family member directly if he or she has been thinking about death and self-harm. Sometimes, people are afraid that such questions will stimulate suicidal ideas in those who haven't thought about suicide. However, it is far more likely that such questions will help those who are frightened and isolated with their thoughts to talk about them.

In chapter 6, we talked about your responsibility for your family member as well as the limits of that responsibility. In the case of potentially harmful behavior, you should be ready to take more initiative. We are not implying that it would be your fault if something serious were to occur. Rather, we are saying the level of action and control to take should be based on your relative's abilities. In the case of a child or an impaired senior, your role is necessarily greater than it would be if the gambler were a cognitively intact adult (see chapter 6). Because depression impairs people's judgment, perhaps rendering them unable to act in their own best interests, others may need to assume a more active role to help them.

For example, if a person is suicidally depressed, the courts and mental health professionals can step in to protect him or her from self-harm even if it requires involuntary hospitalization. In the same way, you may also play a more active role under these circumstances. Of course, if your relative is both depressed and either a child or an impaired senior, then these factors would combine to further increase the role you may need to play to help your relative.

One important preventive measure to take would be to restrict access to firearms which account for some 60 percent of completed suicides in America. If there are firearms in your home, you may lower risk by safely disposing of them. Turn them over to the police or store them with a trusted relative until other risk factors (e.g., problem gambling, depression, substance abuse) are no longer present. If the gambler is depressed and is the owner of firearms, he or she may agree that your family would be safer without easy access to guns. If he or she does not agree, this provides another reason for you to seek professional guidance. Of course, children should never have independent access to firearms.

Violent and Abusive Behavior

Although violent behavior may appear out of the blue, in many cases it emerges in a relationship that is already abusive. Recognizing the signs of an abusive relationship may enable you to take steps to prevent the abuse from escalating to outright violence.

Abusive behavior is characterized by *unreasonable* control as well as threats and outright violence. Control can be psychological or economic. Psychological control may be manifested by abusive criticisms, *unreasonably* limiting your freedom to do what you want or associate with whom you want, or being *unreasonably* jealous. How reasonable is your relative's behavior? Since all relationships involve give-and-take, most people may ask their partners to limit activities at times or may get a little jealous. Therefore, not all behaviors that fall under these categories will be unreasonable. Some will be clearly so. Others may fall into a gray zone. You may want to review with a trusted friend, family member, or professional whether such behaviors fall outside an appropriate range.

Economic control may be evidenced by *unreasonably* limiting your access to family funds, or preventing you from developing your own income or developing personally in some other way. Once again, the key is how reasonable your relative's behavior is. All families must negotiate the allocation of their time and financial resources. So the guide for understanding if your relative's behavior is reasonable in the economic sphere follows the advice we've offered in the psychological realm.

Threats can be directed at you or another family member and may be spoken or implied by behavior. Behavioral threats may include a display of weapons or a loss of temper in which your family member's control appears tenuous. Outright violence may include any harm to property, pets, or people. Violence includes pushing, shoving, slapping, and any other direct physical assault. Violence also includes forced sexual behavior. Do not be under the misapprehension that violence has to rise to a certain level or include noticeable injuries before you take action. Any threats or violent behavior should be taken seriously and stimulate you to take steps to assure the safety of your family and yourself. Again, if there is an acute threat, call 911. If you have concerns, contact a qualified professional. Help is also available on the Internet and through toll-free hotlines. Resources are given at the end of this chapter.

Our purpose here is to alert you, not to alarm you. If you have concerns about your family's safety, contact a qualified professional.

Resources

Below you will find more detailed reading materials, as well as phone numbers and Websites, to help you find more information and get help in your area.

Additional Reading

Betancourt, Marian. 1997. *What to Do When Love Turns Violent : A Practical Resource for Women in Abusive Relationships.* New York: Harper Perennial Library.

Ellis, Thomas E., and Cory F. Newman. 1996. *Choosing to Live: How to Defeat Suicide Through Cognitive Therapy.* Oakland, CA: New Harbinger Publications.

Nelson, N. 1997. *Dangerous Relationships: How to Stop Domestic Violence Before It Stops You.* New York: Insight Books.

Quinnett, Paul G. 1997. *Suicide: The Forever Decision . . . for those Thinking About Suicide, and for those Who Know, Love, or Counsel Them.* New York: Continuum.

Shamoo, T. K., and P. G. Patros. 1997. *Helping Your Child to Cope with Depression and Suicidal Thoughts.* New York: Jossey-Bass.

Wilson, Karen 1997. *When Violence Begins at Home: A Comprehensive Guide to Understanding and Ending Domestic Abuse.* Alameda, CA: Hunter House.

Telephone Numbers and Websites

In an emergency, dial 911 or the emergency code in your area.

For concerns about domestic violence, call: 1 (800) 799-SAFE, or the National Resource Center on Domestic violence: 1 (800) 537-2238.

For concerns about suicidal behavior, contact the following:
The National Suicide hotline: 1-800-SUICIDE

The American Association of Suicidology:
4201 Connecticut Ave., NW
Suite 408
Washington, DC 20008
(202) 237-2280
Web address: http://www.suicidology.org/

Chapter 12

Looking to the Future

Although you are confronting a difficult period, keep in mind that noted thinkers have identified the potential for growth from such times. Ernest Hemingway (1996) wrote, "The world breaks every one and afterward many are strong at the broken places." Later Viktor Frankl (1998) stated, "There is nothing in the world . . . that would so effectively help one to survive even the worst conditions as the knowledge that there is a meaning in one's life." Frankl also noted that meaning can be achieved by "(1) creating a work or doing a deed; (2) experiencing something or encountering someone; and (3) the attitude we take toward unavoidable suffering."

By reading this book, you are addressing your family's problem. We hope you have gained new skills, ideas, and insights to help you through this process. We encourage you to do all you can to promote healing and enhanced meaning in your family's life while remembering that it is not within your power to control the future.

Keep a long-term perspective as you set goals and make decisions. Of course, the pressure and distress you feel propels you toward seeking immediate relief, perhaps without full regard for the big picture. Remember that change occurs over time and generally follows a predictable sequence (see chapter 6). Change is often slow, requiring periods of reflection, decision making, and trial and error, eventually leading to mastery of new behaviors. Balancing the urgency of the situation (see chapter 6) with your long-term goals will enable you to make the decisions that will give you and your family the best chance of a favorable outcome. You may be faced with the major problem of balancing the enduring value of your relationship to the gambler against the work required to heal it.

What If the Gambler Stops?

If the gambler stops gambling, he or she deserves a great deal of credit as do you and the rest of your family. First, allow your family to celebrate and appreciate these achievements before tackling the opportunities and challenges that such change will bring.

You now have the chance to both heal and rebuild your family and repair the damages caused by the loss of money, loss of time spent together, and loss of basic trust and mutual support.

Healing

Some healing may occur just with the simple passage of time. Unfortunately, it is not true that "time heals all wounds." Healing some parts of your family relationships will require accurate understanding and active pursuit of a solution. Combining these tools with goodwill can help you to restore the underlying resiliency in your relationships.

Trust

Trust, the bedrock of personal relationships, is often undermined in the relationship with a problem gambler. If you are able to restore trust, then you should have both the hope and the skills to heal other aspects of your relationship. Therefore, we will show you a way of thinking about trust that may help to repair this vital part of your relationship.

In chapter 4, we pointed out that trust is generally, incorrectly, thought of as an all-or-nothing phenomenon. There is an old saying, "Kick me once, shame on you; kick me twice, shame on me," suggesting that you should *always* be wary of someone who has violated your trust. However, in most relationships, trust is both earned and undermined in various *areas*. For example, we may trust someone to take a message, fix our car, provide child care, provide emotional support, handle our money, share our deepest secrets and dreams, and be sexually faithful. Within each of these areas, we may trust an individual to different *degrees*. Remember Chris and Linda from chapter 1? Let's return to them and look at a graph of Linda's trust of Chris as an example of how trust can be measured in various areas.

Although Linda retained virtually no trust in Chris regarding money, many areas in which she trusted him remained unchanged.

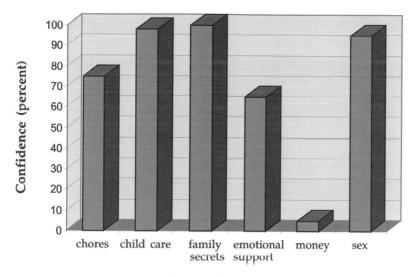

Areas of trust

She continued to have high trust in Chris's ability to care for the children, to keep family secrets confidential, to remain sexually faithful, and be caring and concerned about her sexual needs. Her trust in him to follow through on chores was only about 70 percent, but it had always been at about that level. Linda's confidence in Chris's ability to provide emotional support had fallen to 60 percent from the 98 percent where it had been average over the years. So her trust had been severely damaged in one area (money), compromised in another (emotional support), and unchanged in other areas.

As we observed in chapter 4, if someone violates our complete trust, it is easy to come to the conclusion that the absence of complete trust is no trust. However, Chris and Linda's example illustrates that trust is not an all-or-nothing phenomenon but one that varies by area and degree. With this in mind, we recommend the following steps to begin healing any breach of trust.

1. Acknowledge how profoundly important a breach of trust is in your relationship.

2. Access and honor the emotions you experience as a result (for example, sadness, anger).

3. Consider the various areas that trust has/did/should exist in your relationship.

4. Use your journal to write your ideas down and to figure out percentages for this exercise. Then, fill in Table 12.1 to assess the

status of your trust in the various areas. We have listed six areas and left room for you to fill in other areas that may apply. In each cell in the table, enter the percent of trust you have for the person in that area. The column "Historical trust" is the percent that you trusted that person during the course of your relationship prior to the development of the problem gambling.

Table 12.1: Evaluating the Level of Trust in Your Relationship

Area	Current trust	Historical trust	Minimum acceptable level of trust	Expected level of trust
Chores				
Child care				
Family secrets				
Money				
Emotional support				
Sex				

From this vantage point, you can accurately assess where your trust has been disrupted and where it remains strong. Most people will find that trust is preserved in some areas and can use this as a base for further development. In addition, your family has successfully weathered the gambling itself, providing a successful track record for working through a serious problem. Yet there is still substantial work to be done. You may be struggling with sadness and anger at all that has transpired, and resolution of these feelings (see chapter 5) must proceed to reestablish trust.

One common hurdle people face during this phase is they may have widely differing expectations about how long this process should take. At its extremes, the person who violated the trust may think several sincere apologies should suffice, and the victim of the violation may think that long-term penance across all areas of the relationship is required. Neither of these extreme expectations is likely to produce a successful outcome. The violator must recognize that he or she must provide the reassurance the other person needs, but may also reasonably look for some measurable increases in trust and decreases in the need for reassurance as *months* (not days, weeks, or years) pass. Achieving substantial resolution of this issue in about one year may be the amount of time upon which the two of you can reasonably compromise.

We suggest you use the skills you learned for building a dialogue in chapter 7 to work together to restore trust and to heal your relationship in other ways. You and the gambler have most likely been through some extremely painful experiences in your relationship. An honest and well-meaning dialogue that can take place in many sessions over time can lead to increased mutual understanding and healing.

In some cases, the hurts may be so **profound** that they will be very difficult to talk about without professional guidance. Even with the best intentions and excellent communication skills, some memories may stimulate such a barrage of emotions that the two people involved cannot have a profitable dialogue without outside help. In such a case, working with a professional counselor would be the wise choice.

Sharing

Vital relationships are built on sharing experiences, interests, and emotions, as well as sharing other resources. If these were disrupted, this sharing must be re-established for healing to proceed.

First, take stock of where you stand. Are you spending time together? Are you aware of what is going on in the other person's life and mind? Are you having your needs met and do you feel supported? Ask if his or her needs are being met.

Keep in mind that the answers to these questions must be measured against the backdrop of the way things were before the problem gambling emerged. In addition, normal developmental changes will alter relationships so consider these as well in your assessment. For example, the adolescent who was sixteen when he started gambling may now be a young man of twenty and like many twenty-year-olds may disclose less to his parents than he did four years earlier.

With this knowledge, you and your family member will be in a position to move ahead. Doing so can be as simple and as straightforward as making sure you share enjoyable activities as you used to do. It can be as intimate as sharing the thoughts that are really weighing on your minds. It can be as complex as understanding what you each want and need from the other and then working together to find a mutually satisfying solution.

Healthy Interactions

Negative patterns of interacting may have developed during the period of problem gambling. Since we tend to follow consistent patterns of behavior, from the way we shower to where we sit at the dining table, negative interactions may continue even after the problem gambling has been eliminated.

For example, one couple fought every Friday night, a pattern that was established when Friday night was the husband's primary gambling night. This pattern persisted despite the fact that he had been abstinent for six months. The mere fact that it was Friday night was sufficient to trigger the wife's anxiety and anger, although she remained unaware of the basis for her feelings and her consequent irritable behavior. Three sessions of counseling were sufficient for this couple to identify the cause of their quarrels and to convert the negative associations tied to Fridays to favorable ones by assigning Friday as their night out to have fun together.

To develop healthier interactions, begin by looking for any *patterns* of negative interactions in your relationship. These patterns may be linked to a common time, place, content area (such as money), or theme (for example, sensing that your needs are going unmet). The two of you working together may be able to establish a healthier pattern by developing behaviors that are incompatible with the negative patterns. A constructive dialogue (see chapter 7) may be a way for you to eliminate old, unnecessary, unhealthy patterns. You may find that professional counseling will be most helpful for identifying and changing these patterns.

Challenges

When gambling stops, some novel challenges may surface as your family adjusts to the new circumstances. Being prepared for these problems will reduce their potential for causing actual harm.

Problems Concealed by Gambling

Perhaps the focus on problem gambling has been so intense that other long-standing or newly emerging issues have been obscured. For example, a couple may have had poor communication skills throughout their marriage and, as a result, found it difficult to meet each other's needs. With gambling dominating the family landscape, this long-standing issue faded into the background as major financial and legal concerns emerged. Solving the gambling issue removes a major stressor but reveals some of the underlying communication and emotional issues.

Major developmental issues for the entire family may have been put on hold when a teenage child's problem gambling created emotional turmoil. With the resolution of the gambling issue, however, the child may be forced to confront issues of independence and loss while the parents must struggle with an empty nest and their own confrontation with a new phase of life. These issues, though arguably deeper than gambling, can be blocked by the acute pressures that gambling creates. As gambling recedes, their emergence may present significant new psychological and relationship pressures.

The old story about the fellow who seriously injured his pinkie and then had it surgically repaired is illustrative. After the repair, he asked the surgeon, "Doc, will I be able to play the violin now?" "I don't see why not," the surgeon replied. "That's funny," said the patient, "I never could before." Fixing a new problem doesn't fix old ones nor does it provide new skills.

Problems Developed During Gambling

Just as pressing financial and legal concerns can conceal old problems, they can push into the background important emotional and psychological issues that emerge during the gambling phase. For example, perhaps you were intensely angry and hurt by your partner's deceits while the problem gambling was going on. However, you ignored your feelings in order to maintain some financial stability for the children. Now that the financial situation has stabilized, you have the energy to focus on your own emotional state and you may be overwhelmed by how angry you are. Similarly, when adult children apply heavy-handed methods to prevent their elderly, but competent parent from gambling, the parent may feel tremendous anger when the gambling stops. The corrosive effects of the means the children applied—however well-meaning—may leave a lingering bitterness that must be worked through.

What Do You Do Now?

Concerned family members naturally focus on the gambler's welfare and the impact this has on the family. Over time, this concern may have become more pronounced and become a central focus of your life. Whether or not your behavior was "co-dependent" (see chapter 4), you no longer have to devote time and energy to the problem gambling. Of course, you will say, this is a plus. But it is also a big change and may require a major adjustment on your part as you establish new ways to focus your attention. Perhaps you will argue that now you will be able to attend to long neglected areas of your life. However, as true as this is, it is still a major life change for you that may require some adjustment on your part.

To the extent the problem gambling occupied center stage, you may have neglected your own needs and development. When the gambler stops, most likely you will have the time to confront some of your own aspirations that you have neglected. Some of these unfulfilled needs may have been an unavoidable result of the problem gambling. Others may be related to the problem gambling but, to some extent, may reflect your choice to focus intensely on the gambling. Finally, unfulfilled needs may be totally unrelated to the problem gambling. Try to sort these out carefully because there is often a tendency at this point to blame all re-emergent issues on the gambling.

Lapses and Relapses

Successfully stopping gambling does not necessarily imply that the problem will never reappear. In fact, it is important for both you and the gambler to be aware of the risks of gambling again, even if the gambler has participated in a good relapse prevention program (see chapter 10).

It is important to distinguish between a relapse and a lapse. A relapse is a reversion from abstinence to problem gambling whereas a lapse is *some* gambling behavior (when abstinence was the goal) such as betting at the track, buying scratch tickets, or betting on sports. A lapse may last for one day or considerably longer but doesn't result in the range and intensity of the problems associated with problem gambling.

Because lapses and relapses exist on a continuum, it is impossible to define a precise point that the former mergers into the latter. Understanding this distinction is important for both you and the gambler. Recognizing a lapse for what it is prevents you and the gambler from embracing ideas such as these: that the gambler has reverted to the worst stages of problem gambling again, that all is lost, and that there is no point in trying. Understanding the difference between a lapse and a relapse will help each of you keep the lapse in perspective, prevent all-or-nothing thinking (see chapter 5), and serve as a signal to rapidly deploy the efforts that were previously successful.

What If the Gambler Doesn't Stop?

In some cases, despite your best efforts and gambling's effects on the gambler, he or she continues to gamble—what do you do?

You are now confronted with an ongoing anxiety-provoking situation. In chapter 5, we pointed out that anxiety motivates avoidance behavior. Therefore, most people would at least have thoughts of avoiding or leaving the situation. If the gambler is your partner or spouse, avoiding the situation might include separation or divorce. If the gambler is your child or parent, avoiding the situation might include increasing your physical or emotional distance for a period of time. We are not necessarily recommending any of these actions. Rather, you should know that such thoughts are natural in your situation. Even if the gambler is a young adolescent and it is neither possible nor consistent with your values to avoid the situation, it is still natural to entertain such ideas.

We have previously emphasized the importance of attending to the urgency of the situation (see chapter 6), including but not limited to physical safety (see chapter 11). In this chapter, we assume that you have assessed and attended to any urgent matters and will maintain vigilance for any evolving emergencies.

If the gambler is your partner or spouse and you think separation may be the best option, we recommend that you review this decision carefully with professional counselors or clergy. The decision to leave, or for that matter to stay in an ongoing stressful situation, is a major life decision that will have repercussions on your life and those close to you for years. Major life decisions, by definition, require your best judgment. Chronic stress and accompanying emotional arousal (anxiety, sadness, anger) generally compromise judgment. Therefore, we recommend professional assistance, or at the very least, careful review with trusted family or friends. No book can assess your *unique* situation and advise you on such a major life decision.

As long as you remain involved, using the strategies you have learned in this book will help you to continue to care for yourself and your family.

Forgiveness and Personal Growth

At some point, you will confront the issue of whether to forgive the gambler. The concept of forgiveness is deeply embedded in religious thought. "Forbearing one another, and forgiving one another, if any man have a quarrel against any: even as Christ forgave you, so also do ye" (Colossians 3:13). And in the book of Genesis, we see a dramatic example of forgiveness when Joseph saves his brothers who had betrayed him.

The notion of whether forgiveness is beneficial, particularly in cases of *severe* wrongs such as child sexual abuse, has been controversial in the psychological community. Psychologist Suzanne Freedman observed that the controversy was due, to a great extent, to a failure to precisely understand forgiveness and to carefully distinguish it from pardoning, condoning, excusing, and reconciling (Freedman 1996).

Forgiving is letting go of one's anger and bitterness toward the offender. Many believe that full forgiveness includes understanding and compassion for the offender. This illustrates that forgiveness covers a broad range and is not an all-or-nothing phenomenon. It is clearly possible to let go of one's anger without extending compassion to the offender.

But forgiving does not imply that no offense was committed, nor that the offense is okay, nor that apologies, repentance, restitution, and justice are not warranted, nor that reconciliation in the sense of resuming a close personal relationship is necessary. According to Dr. Freedman, it is the confusion between these factors and forgiving that raises the question of whether forgiveness following severe offenses is healthy.

Forgiveness cannot be rushed. It is the culmination of a process. Remember, the necessity for forgiveness implies an offense that led to hurt and anger, which must be acknowledged, honored, and resolved.

If you choose to forgive, and you do so at the pace that's right for you, forgiving can be a transforming experience. The religious teachings of the past two millennia are now being joined by emergent psychological research. This research demonstrates that for many the act of forgiving decreases anger, anxiety, and depression while increasing hope and self-esteem. By freeing both psychological and physical energy for other pursuits, forgiveness can accelerate your personal development and growth.

If you are following the steps in this book and seek professional guidance as needed, you are doing what you can to address the gambling problem. This in itself is meaningful. Do you now have the time and focus to address your own growth as well? You can take heart from having confronted the crisis and done what you can to resolve it. This recognition should give you strength to review what other goals—interpersonal, academic, vocational, spiritual, or recreational—you have for yourself and your family. Which of these are your priorities? Which do you want to pursue? Confronting problem gambling probably revealed personal strengths that surprised you. Ride on the wave of these strengths toward your next goals.

Appendix **A**

Resources for the Gambler and Family Members

Councils on Problem Gambling

More than thirty states have a council on problem gambling that can help guide you to treatment and support services in your area. There is also a National Council on Problem Gambling. Calling the nationwide help line (1-800-522-4700) will connect you to your state council or one close to you if your state does not have one. If you have access to the Internet, you can also find information on state councils there. State councils are an excellent source for accessing resources, treatment, and support groups as well as written and taped materials. State councils provide outreach, prevention, and training programs as well.

1. **National Council on Problem Gambling, Inc.**
208 G Street, NE 2nd floor
Washington, DC 20002
Nationwide help-line: 1-800–522-4700
Phone: 202-547-9204
FAX: 202-547-9206

email: ncpg@erols.com
Website: www.ncpgambling.org/

2. Canadian Foundation on Compulsive Gambling (Ontario)
505 Consumers Road, Suite 801
Willowdale, Canada, Ont N2J 4V8
Phone: 1-416-499-8260, 1-888-391-1111
FAX: 1-416-499-8260
email: cfcg@interlog.com
Website: www.cfcg.on.ca/

3. **Programa Podemos of Puerto Rico**
P.O. Box 36952
San Juan, PR 00936-3952
Phone: 1-800-981-2002 (Puerto Rico only)

Treatment Programs

In addition to calling a council (state or national) to access treatment resources, consider the following resources.

1. **The Addiction Resource Guide** Website at www.hubplace.com/addictions/specpop/compulsiveg.html provides a listing of treatment programs across the United States and Canada that have either separate programs for problem gambling, separate tracks within a larger treatment program (for example, a problem gambling track within a substance abuse program), or simply groups for problem gamblers.

2. **Trimeridian, Inc.** has treatment programs in Indianapolis and Las Vegas for individuals and families affected by problem gambling. Contact information:
1701 North Senate Blvd.
Building C, Floor 2
P.O. Box 44757
Indianapolis, Indiana 46244
Phone: 317-929-1010
Fax: 317-929-1020

Self-Help Groups

1. **Gamblers Anonymous** provides support groups for problem gamblers.
International Service Office
P.O. Box 17173
Los Angeles, CA 90017

Phone: 213-386-8789
FAX 213-386-0030
email: isomain@gamblersanonymous.org
Website: www.gamblersanonymous.org/

Note: Local hotline numbers that identify location and time for GA groups are available at their Website.

2. **Gam-Anon** provides support groups for families of problem gamblers. Gam-Anon International Service Office Inc. can be accessed at www.gam-anon.org; email: info@gamanon.org; phone: 718-352-1671.

3. **Other Self-Help Groups**
Gamblers Anonymous and Gam-Anon both have groups nationwide. Other self-help groups for problem gamblers have a local or regional presence. For example, Bettors Anonymous has several chapters in Massachusetts. For help in finding such local self-help groups ask your state council or the state council closest to you.

Education and Training

1. *GamblingSolutions* provides consultation and training to colleges, high schools, businesses, and government. Contact information for *GamblingSolutions* is:
President: Edward J. Federman, Ph.D.
Address: P.O. Box 2058, Acton, MA 01720
Phone: 978-771-2319; email: service@gamblingsolutions.net
Website: www.gamblingsolutions.net

2. **The Centre for Addiction and Mental Health** in Toronto, Canada provides a bibliography of materials on problem gambling at http://www.arf.org/isd/bib/gamb.html.

3. **The Mayo Clinic** provides general information about problem gambling on the Internet at www.mayohealth.org/mayo/9712/htm/gambling.htm

4. **Wanna Bet** is an online magazine aimed at teenagers concerned about problem gambling. It has a youth-oriented format and offers tips and guidance on participating in constructive activities and eliminating gambling. Website: www.wannabet. org/

Other Groups

1. **The National Center for Responsible Gaming**, funded by the gaming (casino) industry, provides funds for research into problem and underage gambling. Contact information:

540 Pierce Avenue
Kansas City, MO 64110
Phone: 816-531-1878
FAX: 816-531-3459
email: contact@ncrg.org
Website: www.ncrg.org

2. The **National Indian Gaming Association (NIGA)** operates as a clearinghouse and educational, legislative, and public policy resource for tribes, policymakers, and the public on Indian gaming issues and tribal community development. This description is taken from their Website at http://www.indiangaming.org.

3. **The Institute for the Study of Gambling and Commercial Gaming** was established in 1989 by the University of Nevada, Reno. As the first academically oriented program of its kind, the Institute serves as a structure to broaden the understanding of gambling and the commercial gaming industries. Its aim is to encourage and promote research and learning so that the multifaceted issues surrounding gambling and commercial gaming, and the ways in which individuals and society at large are affected might be addressed. (Description quoted from their Website at http://www.unr.edu/gaming/frame.htm)
Contact information:
Institute for the Study of Gambling and Commercial Gaming
College of Business Administration
Reno, NV 89557-0208
Phone: 1-775-784-1442
Fax: 1-775-784-1057

A Primer on Probability

If numbers put you to sleep, all you need to remember about probability is this: If the odds are against you, the more you play, the more certain you are to lose.

In this appendix, we'll introduce three concepts that will help you understand why this is so: independent events, expected value, and the long run. We'll also talk about really big numbers.

Two events are *independent* if the outcome of each has no effect on the outcome of the other. To calculate the probability of two independent events occurring, we multiply the probabilities of each event occurring separately.

For example, a fair coin will turn up heads ½ the time in the long run. What is the chance that heads will turn up two times in a row if you toss a fair coin? There are four possible outcomes:

Table B.1

	First toss	Second toss
1	heads	heads
2	heads	tails
3	tails	heads
4	tails	tails

One of these four outcomes is two heads, so the chance of getting two heads on two tosses of a fair coin is one in four or ¼. To calculate the probability of two heads in a row more quickly, we apply the rule for independent events: we multiply together the probability of each separate event. The probability of a single coin toss coming up heads is ½, so we multiply ½ x ½, yielding ¼.

In fair betting, all bettors will break even in the *long run*. If we know the probability of an event, we can predict with virtual certainty what will happen in the long run.

What would be a fair bet on one toss of a coin? It would be an even bet—you get $1 if you call it right and pay $1 if you call it wrong. In the long run, you should break even. What would be a fair bet that heads would come up two times in a row? Since there is one chance in four this will occur (one that it will and three that it won't), a fair bet would pay you $3 for correctly betting on two heads in a row, while you would pay $1 for calling it incorrectly.

An unfair bet is one in which one side has an advantage. In the long run, the side with the advantage will win. Suppose someone would pay you $2 if heads came up two times in a row, and you would pay him $1 if it didn't. This doesn't sound like a good bet since we said that $3 would be a fair payment. In the long run, you will be certain to lose.

What is the expected outcome of this unfair bet? To calculate this, we multiply ¼ (the probability of heads coming up twice) by its payoff of $2, yielding $.50. We also multiply ¾ (the probability of coming up with any combination except two heads) by its payoff of -$1, yielding -$.75. We add $.50 and -$.75 to get the expected value of -$.25. Table B.2 summarizes these calculations.

Table B.2

Outcome	Probability	Payoff	Result
You win	¼	+$2	(¼ x $2) = $.50
You lose	¾	-$1	(¾ x -$1) = -$.75
Expected value			-$.25

Every two times you flip the coin, you can expect to lose $.25 on the average. Make 100 sets of two flips and you can expect to lose 100 times that, or $25.

This illustrates the important concept of *expected value*. The expected value of a bet is the sum of the probability of each possible outcome of the bet multiplied by the respective payoff for that outcome.

The expected value favors the house. In a nutshell, that's why the house always wins. All games of chance that are played against institutions that are in the business of gambling are unfair bets (blackjack is one often-discussed potential exception discussed below).

Suppose you are playing a game of roulette. Your expected payoff for every dollar you bet is 94.7 cents. If you bet $100, you can expect $94.70 back. If you bet $1 one hundred times, you can expect to be left with about $94.70 on the average.

Picture this. You are at a roulette table with many other people. You put in $100 and everybody else puts in what they wish. The compiler takes everybody's money and then gives each person back 94.7% of whatever he or she bet. For you that's $94.70. Next, he asks if you want to play again. If you do, he does the same thing to you. Look at the following table to see what the expected value of your $100 is periodically during the first twenty-five plays.

Roulette (beginning with $100)

Number of plays	Expected value
1	$94.70
5	$76.16
10	$58.01
15	$44.18
20	$33.65
25	$25.63

Can you win? Of course, anyone can win in the short run. The house doesn't care. Every day is the long run to them. Whether it's 1,000 players or 1,000 days, they don't care. They win. The frequent gambler who plays games with a negative expected value will lose over time with virtual certainty.

What about other games? On the average, the betting on slot machines is even worse. The average payoff for casino slots is only $.85 on every dollar. Your money will go even faster here than in roulette (percentage wise). See the following table for the expected value in a slot machine with an 85 percent return.

Slots, Video Poker, etc. (beginning with $100)

Number of plays	Expected value
1	$85.00
5	$44.37
10	$19.69
15	$8.74
20	$3.88
25	$1.72

Odds in Various Lottery Games

There are many variations on lottery games. The basic idea is that you pick a certain set of numbers (often six) from a larger set of numbers (usually at least thirty-six). Look at the following table to see what your chances are of picking six numbers correctly from a larger set (ranging from thirty-six to sixty-five). Sometimes there is an extra twist such as a powerball that stacks the odds against you even more.

Lottery Games		
Pick 6 from	Probability	
36	1:	1,947,792
40	1:	3,838,380
45	1:	8,145,060
50	1:	15,890,700
55	1:	28,989,675
60	1:	50,063,860
65	1:	82,598,880

Big Numbers

The odds against winning The Big Game are 76,000,000 to 1. How can we understand such a number?

Suppose the Big Game had started 2,000 years ago and one of your ancestors, let's call her Jane, had bet one dollar on the very first day the game was available. Now suppose that there had been a drawing every day since then and on each day one of your ancestors had wagered one dollar in an unbroken 2,000-year effort to bring fortune to your family. The odds against your family ever having won in these 2,000 years would still be greater than 100 to one.

Now, suppose that Jane had invested that same dollar 2,000 years ago at a meager two-percent annual interest and the money had been left to grow over the last two millennia. How much money would be in that account now? More than 158,000 trillion dollars. That's $158,614,732,760,369,000. How much is that? If you spent one billion dollars a day, your money would last nearly half a million years.

There are two major points here. First, to understand in a visceral way that odds in the range of many millions to one are so large that you can bet for thousands of years and still be unlikely to win. Second, we're illustrating the magic of compound interest. Of course, no one invests for thousands of years. However, even investing over decades brings enormous returns. Younger people can build wealth by investing early and allowing compound interest to work for them.

Perhaps you have noticed that lotteries are pure chance, yet if you win a big prize once, you probably will come out ahead over the course of a lifetime. This may lead you to wonder if the long run applies to lotteries. It does. However, when the odds against winning are very high (as in a lottery), then the long run required for big winners to lose more than they win becomes a very long time indeed, much longer than a single lifetime. Don't be misled by this technicality into thinking lotteries are good bets; they are particularly poor bets.

Games of Chance and Games of (at Least Partial) Skill

Chance	Skill (at least partial)
Lottery, Powerball, Big Game, etc.	Blackjack
Scratch tickets	Poker
Keno	Handicapping horses
Bingo	Sports betting
Roulette	Pool, bowling, golf, chess, etc.
Craps	
Slots	
Video poker	
Baccarat	

Blackjack and Other Games of Skill

Edward O. Thorp, a mathematician, calculated a strategy that would shift the odds in the favor of the player at blackjack. By following this strategy and by counting cards, a player can gain a minor advantage over the house. The house has minimized this advantage by playing with multiple decks (often six or eight) and shuffling the decks part way through. Even so, let's say that near-perfect play might put the odds in the favor of the player at one percent. There are many stories of people getting rich counting cards. How likely is this?

There are several major obstacles to making much money this way. First, the house is likely to exclude players who appear to be counting cards. Therefore, you need a team of players. Second, one percent is a lot to the house because they have a lot of people betting. But for a player or team of players to make a significant amount, they must make very large bets. Suppose the team is able to systematically bet $3,000 per hour. One percent of that is $30 and that has to be split two or three ways. It's no get-rich-quick scheme. Finally, only the house really has the benefit of the long run. At $3,000 per hour, the team could hit a bad stretch, or a series of bad stretches, lose substantially, and run out of money. They would need a huge bankroll (perhaps $100,000) to have a high probability of winning in the long run. Even then they're only making ten or fifteen dollars each per hour while risking many thousands. They'd do better with some conservative bond funds.

In the long run, players very rarely win games of (at least partial) skill in which the house takes a percentage off the top (as in betting on horses or sports betting with an institution or bookmaker). Although it is not a virtual certainty that any individual will lose at these games in the long run, the vast majority of players do. As a group, the players leave with less money than they started.

Conclusion

Organized gambling enterprises, whether the state, casino, or bookmaker, are running a business and turning a profit from their customers day in and day out. Review this appendix and your own experience to help you decide whether you want to be one of their customers.

References

Becona, E., M. Lorenzo, and M. J. Fuentes. 1996. Pathological gambling and depression. *Psychological Reports* 78:635-40.

Bergler, Edmund. 1958, 1970. *The Psychology of Gambling*. London: International Universities Press, Inc.

Bland, R. C., S. C. Newman, H. Orn, and G. Stebelsky. 1993. Epidemiology of pathological gambling in Edmonton. *Canadian Journal of Psychiatry* 38(2):108-112.

Blaszczynski, Alex. 1996. A History of Gambling. Paper read at National Conference on Gambling, at St. Edmund's Private Hospital, Australia.

Brenner, R., with G. Brenner. 1990. *Gambling and Speculation: A Theory, a History, and a Future of Some Human Decisions*. Cambridge: Cambridge University Press.

Campbell, F., C. Simmons, and D. Lester. 1998–1999. The impact of gambling on suicidal behavior in Louisiana. *Omega: Journal of Death & Dying* 38(3).

Crockford, D. N., and N. el-Guebaly. 1998. Naltrexone in the treatment of pathological gambling and alcohol dependence. *Canadian Journal of Psychiatry* 43(1):86.

Dickerson, M. G. 1984. *Compulsive Gamblers*. London: Longman.

DSM-IV. 1994. *Diagnostic and Statistical Manual of Mental Disorders, 4th edition*. Washington, DC: American Psychiatric Press.

D'Zurilla, T. J., and M. R. Goldfried. 1971. Problem solving and behavior modification. *Journal of Abnormal Psychology* 78(1):107-126.

Fabian, Ann. 1990. *Card Sharps, Dream Books and Bucket Shops: Gambling in 19th-Century America*. Ithaca and London: Cornell University Press.

Federman, E. J. 1998. Treatment of problem gambling. In E. J. Federman, chair, *Responding to Pathological Gambling: New Opportunities for Public Sector Clinicians*. Symposium presented at the American Psychological Association annual meeting. San Francisco.

Federman, E. J., C. Krebs, C. E. Drebing, N. Colburn, A. Beaman, J. Marshall, and W. E. Penk. 1998. *Gambling: An Under-Diagnosed and Costly Disorder*. Paper presented at the NIDA Town Meeting, Boston.

Frank, M. L., D. Lester, and A. Wexler. 1991. Suicidal behavior among members of Gamblers Anonymous. *Journal of Gambling Studies* 7(3):249-254.

Frankl, V. 1998. *Man's Search for Meaning*. New York: Washington Square Press.

Freedman, S. 1996. Forgiveness as an intervention goal with incest survivors. *Journal of Consulting and Clinical Psychology* 64(5): 983-992.

Hemingway, E. 1996. *A Farewell to Arms*. New York: Scribner

Hollander, E., C. M. DeCaria, E. Mari, C. M. Wong, S. Mosovich, R. Grossman, and T. Begaz. 1998. Short-term single-blind fluvoxamine treatment of pathological gambling. *American Journal of Psychiatry* 155(12):1781-1783. Dec.

James, W. 1918. *The Principles of Psychology*. New York: Dover Publications, Inc.

Keane, T., W. Scott, G. Chavoya, D. Lamparski, and J. Fairbank. 1985. Social support in Vietnam veterans with posttraumatic stress disorder: A comparative analysis. *Journal of Consulting and Clinical Psychology* 53(1):95-102.

Kim, S.W. 1998. Opioid antagonists in the treatment of impulse-control disorders. *Journal of Clinical Psychiatry* 59(4):159-64.

Ladouceur, R., and M. Walker 1996. A cognitive perspective on gambling. In *Trends in Cognitive and Behavioral Therapies*, edited by P. M. Salkoskvis. New York: John Wiley & Sons.

LeDoux, J. 1996. *The Emotional Brain: The Mysterious Underpinnings of Emotional Life*. New York: Simon and Schuster.

Lesieur, H. R., and S. B. Blume. 1987. The South Oaks Gambling Screen (SOGS): A new instrument for the identification of pathological gambling. *American Journal of Psychiatry* 144:1184-1188.

McConaghy, N. A., M. A. Blaszczynski, and C. C. Allcock. 1988. Behavior completion versus stimulus control in compulsive gambling: Implications for behavioral assessment. *Behavior Modification* 12(3):371-384.

McCormick, R. A., A. M. Russo, L. F. Ramirez, and J. I. Taber. 1984. Affective disorders among pathological gamblers seeking treatment. *Am J Psychiatry* 141:215-8.

Mello, A., C. E. Drebing, E. J. Federman, C. Krebs, R. Barnett, S. Brooks, P. Haley, et al. 1999. Pathological gambling and mental health professionals: Promoting early intervention. In E. J. Federman, chair, *Pathological Gambling: Natural history, Motivation and Early Intervention.* Paper presented at the American Psychological Association annual meeting. Boston.

National Council on Problem Gambling. 1999. Website Home Page. Retrieved Feb. 20, 2000 from the World Wide Web: http://www.ncpgambling.org

National Opinion Research Center at the University of Chicago. 1999. Gambling Impact and Behavior Study: Report to the National Gambling Impact Study Commission. Retrieved February 20, 2000 from the World Wide Web: http://www.norc.uchicago.edu/new/gamble.htm. See also National Gambling Impact Study Commission at http://www.ngisc.gov/.

New York Times. August 19, 1999. p. B6.

New York Times. September 25, 1999. p. A1.

Phillips, D. P., W. R. Welty, and M. M. Smith, 1997. Elevated suicide levels associated with legalized gambling. *Suicide and Life Threatening Behavior* 27(4):373-378.

Prochaska, J. O., J. C. Norcross, and C. C. DiClemente. 1994. *Changing For Good: The Revolutionary Program That Explains the Six Stages of Change and Teaches You How to Free Yourself From Bad Habits* New York: William Morrow.

Prochaska, J. O., J. C. Norcross, and C. C. DiClemente. 1995. *Changing for Good.* New York: Avon Books.

Rosenthal, R. J., and L. J. Rugle. 1994. A psychodynamic approach to the treatment of pathological gambling: Part I. Achieving abstinence. *Journal of Gambling Studies* 10(1):21-42.

Shaffer, H. J., M. N. Hall, and J. Vanderbilt. 1997. Estimating the prevalence of disordered gambling in the United States and Canada: A meta-analysis. Cambridge: Harvard Medical School.

Specker, S. M., G. A. Carlson, K. M. Edmondson, P. E. Johnson, and M. Marcotte. 1996. Psychopathology in pathological gamblers seeking treatment. *Journal of Gambling Studies* 12(1):67-81.

Stewart, R. M., and R. I. Brown. 1988. An outcome study of Gamblers Anonymous. *British Journal of Psychiatry* 152:284–288.

Sullivan, S. 1994. Why compulsive gamblers are a high suicide risk. *Community Mental Health in New Zealand* 8(2):40-47.

Sylvain, C., R. Ladouceur, and J. Boisvert. 1997. Cognitive and behavioral treatment of pathological gambling: A controlled study. *Journal of Consulting and Clinical Psychology* 65(6):727-732.

Thompson, W. N., R. Gazel, and D. Rickman. 1996. The social costs of pathological gambling. *Wisconsin Policy Research Institute Report*, 9(6):1–44.

The WAGER, The Weekly Addiction Gambling Education Report. 1996. 1(3). Seventh–twelfth grade students lottery activity exceeded only by alcohol prevalence., *Boston: Massachusetts Council on Compulsive Gambling and the Harvard Medical School Division on Addictions.*

Walker, Michael. 1992. *The Psychology of Gambling.* Oxford: Butterworth-Heinemann Ltd.

Winn, M. E. 1996. The strategic and systemic management of denial in the cognitive/behavioral treatment of sexual offenders. *Sexual Abuse: Journal of Research and Treatment* 8(1):25-36.

Edward J. Federman, Ph.D., is President of *GamblingSolutions*, an organization that consults for educational institutions, businesses, and government. He founded and served as first director of the Center for Problem Gambling at the ENRM VA Medical Center in Bedford, Massachusetts, where he also founded the Cognitive-Behavioral Therapy Center and served as Director of Psychology Training for fifteen years. Dr. Federman has published on a range of topics and has presented his original research on problem gambling and other matters at conferences internationally. He is on the faculty at the Boston University Medical School, and has also been on the faculty at the Simmons Graduate School of Social Work and Wilberforce University. Dr. Federman's Ph.D. is in clinical psychology, and he also holds an M.A. in mathematics.

Charles E. Drebing, Ph.D., is a research psychologist at the New England Mental Illness Research Education and Clinical Center (MIRECC) at the ENRM VA Medical Center in Bedford, Massachusetts, where he also serves as Senior Research Consultant to the Center for Problem Gambling. His research includes studies of the effect of gambling problems on veterans and their families. He is an assistant professor of psychiatry at the Boston University Medical School and has published books and articles on a range of topics. He received his Ph.D. in Clinical Psychology from Fuller Theological Seminary in 1990 and completed a research fellowship at the Neuropsychiatric Institute at UCLA.

Christopher Krebs, M.A., is a member of the clinical and research staff of the Center for Problem Gambling and the Mental Illness Research Education and Clinical Center (MIRECC) at the ENRM VA Medical Center. He has been active in both clinical treatment and research involving problem gamblers and has co-authored articles on problem gambling and on alcohol and substance abuse prevalence and treatment. He has also presented on these topics at national conferences. Mr. Krebs is currently a doctoral candidate in clinical psychology at the Fielding Institute. Prior to his career in psychology, Mr. Krebs worked for many years as a management consultant to industry and government.

More New Harbinger Titles for Personal Growth and Change

FROM SABOTAGE TO SUCCESS

Real-life examples, exercises, and action plans help you identify self-defeating behaviors and learn skills that can help you reach your life's true potential. *Item SBTG $14.95*

VIRTUAL ADDICTION

Explores the warning signs of Internet abuse and suggests a variety of steps that netheads can take, incluing help for those who can't seem to stop shopping or find themselves compulsively trading stock. *Item VRTL $12.95*

MAKING HOPE HAPPEN

A powerful program shows you how to break old self-defeating habits, overcome roadblocks, and find new routes to your goals. *Item HOPE $14.95*

YOU CAN FREE YOURSELF FROM ALCOHOL & DRUGS

A balanced, ten-goal recovery program helps readers make needed lifestyle changes without forcing them to embrace unwelcome religious concepts or beliefs. *Item YFDA Paperback, $13.95*

LIVING WITHOUT PROCRASTINATION

Provides effective techniques for unlearning counter-productive habits, changing paralyzing beliefs and attitudes, and attaining a new sense of purposefulness in your life. *Item LWP $12.95*

THE SELF-FORGIVENESS HANDBOOK

Guided exercises take you on an empowering journey from self-criticism to self-compassion and inner strength. *Item FORG $12.95*

Call toll-free 1-800-748-6273 to order. Have your Visa or Mastercard number ready. Or send a check for the titles you want to New Harbinger Publications, 5674 Shattuck Avenue, Oakland, CA 94609. Include $3.80 for the first book and 75¢ for each additional book to cover shipping and handling. (California residents please include appropriate sales tax.) Allow four to six weeks for delivery.

Prices subject to change without notice.

Some Other New Harbinger Self-Help Titles

Multiple Chemical Sensitivity: A Survival Guide, $16.95
Dancing Naked, $14.95
Why Are We Still Fighting, $15.95
From Sabotage to Success, $14.95
Parkinson's Disease and the Art of Moving, $15.95
A Survivor's Guide to Breast Cancer, $13.95
Men, Women, and Prostate Cancer, $15.95
Make Every Session Count: Getting the Most Out of Your Brief Therapy, $10.95
Virtual Addiction, $12.95
After the Breakup, $13.95
Why Can't I Be the Parent I Want to Be?, $12.95
The Secret Message of Shame, $13.95
The OCD Workbook, $18.95
Tapping Your Inner Strength, $13.95
Binge No More, $14.95
When to Forgive, $12.95
Practical Dreaming, $12.95
Healthy Baby, Toxic World, $15.95
Making Hope Happen, $14.95
I'll Take Care of You, $12.95
Survivor Guilt, $14.95
Children Changed by Trauma, $13.95
Understanding Your Child's Sexual Behavior, $12.95
The Self-Esteem Companion, $10.95
The Gay and Lesbian Self-Esteem Book, $13.95
Making the Big Move, $13.95
How to Survive and Thrive in an Empty Nest, $13.95
Living Well with a Hidden Disability, $15.95
Overcoming Repetitive Motion Injuries the Rossiter Way, $15.95
What to Tell the Kids About Your Divorce, $13.95
The Divorce Book, Second Edition, $15.95
Claiming Your Creative Self: True Stories from the Everyday Lives of Women, $15.95
Six Keys to Creating the Life You Desire, $19.95
Taking Control of TMJ, $13.95
What You Need to Know About Alzheimer's, $15.95
Winning Against Relapse: A Workbook of Action Plans for Recurring Health and Emotional Problems, $14.95
Facing 30: Women Talk About Constructing a Real Life and Other Scary Rites of Passage, $12.95
The Worry Control Workbook, $15.95
Wanting What You Have: A Self-Discovery Workbook, $18.95
When Perfect Isn't Good Enough: Strategies for Coping with Perfectionism, $13.95
Earning Your Own Respect: A Handbook of Personal Responsibility, $12.95
High on Stress: A Woman's Guide to Optimizing the Stress in Her Life, $13.95
Infidelity: A Survival Guide, $13.95
Stop Walking on Eggshells, $14.95
Consumer's Guide to Psychiatric Drugs, $16.95
The Fibromyalgia Advocate: Getting the Support You Need to Cope with Fibromyalgia and Myofascial Pain, $18.95
Healing Fear: New Approaches to Overcoming Anxiety, $16.95
Working Anger: Preventing and Resolving Conflict on the Job, $12.95
Sex Smart: How Your Childhood Shaped Your Sexual Life and What to Do About It, $14.95
You Can Free Yourself From Alcohol & Drugs, $13.95
Amongst Ourselves: A Self-Help Guide to Living with Dissociative Identity Disorder, $14.95
Healthy Living with Diabetes, $13.95
Dr. Carl Robinson's Basic Baby Care, $10.95
Better Boundries: Owning and Treasuring Your Life, $13.95
Goodbye Good Girl, $12.95
Fibromyalgia & Chronic Myofascial Pain Syndrome, $19.95
The Depression Workbook: Living With Depression and Manic Depression, $17.95
Self-Esteem, Second Edition, $13.95
Angry All the Time: An Emergency Guide to Anger Control, $12.95
When Anger Hurts, $13.95
Perimenopause, $16.95
The Relaxation & Stress Reduction Workbook, Fourth Edition, $17.95
The Anxiety & Phobia Workbook, Second Edition, $18.95
I Can't Get Over It, A Handbook for Trauma Survivors, Second Edition, $16.95
Messages: The Communication Skills Workbook, Second Edition, $15.95
Thoughts & Feelings, Second Edition, $18.95
Depression: How It Happens, How It's Healed, $14.95
The Deadly Diet, Second Edition, $14.95
The Power of Two, $15.95